W9-BJZ-955

The main objective of this book is to provide visitors to East Africa with a guide to the common wildlife most likely to be encountered during the course of a safari in and around the main National Parks and Game Reserves of Kenya, Tanzania and Uganda, although many of the species featured are also commonly found in adjacent countries. It was not our intention to produce complete coverage of the wildlife of East Africa. The species included in this edition were selected based on the personal experiences of the authors, gained during visits to the region over a period of twenty years. Anyone wishing to obtain greater and more detailed information on species should consult the bibliography.

An attempt has been made to provide as full a diagnostic description of each species featured, as space would permit. In most cases this information enables the species to be identified by size, plumage/pelage colour and shape. It should be remembered that in many bird species plumage variations could be quite marked as a result of age and the sex of the species. We have attempted wherever possible to bring this to the attention of the reader.

ACKNOWLEDGEMENTS

There are countless people to whom the authors owe a debt of gratitude for the production of this book. They would like to express special thanks to Myles Archibald, Katie Piper and their staff at HarperCollins. To the staff at United Touring International Ltd, London, United Touring Company, Arusha, Tanzania and United Touring Company, Nairobi, Kenya. We would like to make special mention of our drivers Joseph Nicholas Kwelukilwa, Suleiman Kiruwa and the late Moses Sengenge in Tanzania, and Dominic Gichinga, Eutychus Murage, Benson Muthama and Peter Mathara in Kenya, without whose driving skills and sharp eyesight, many of the illustrations featured in this book would not have been obtained. Thanks are also due to the management and staff of the Frank Lane Picture Agency, Graham Armitage Sigma UK Ltd, Chris Mattison FRPS and to all clients of Hosking Tours who have helped to make much of our time in East Africa such an enormous pleasure.

Lastly, we owe a huge debt of thanks to our wives Sally and Jean for their support and tolerance during the production of this book.

Martin B. Withers FRPS
David Hosking FRPS

A TRAVELLERS' GUIDE TO
SAFARI PHOTOGRAPHY

Before your Departure

It is always unwise to commence a holiday with new untested equipment. With digital cameras, take some pictures on each of your memory cards and check that they download correctly onto your computer. If you are taking a digital multimedia storage device, check that your memory cards copy successfully and that you can then transfer the files onto your home computer. Always put at least one roll of film through a new camera and carry out a full test on any newly purchased lenses. Before departure, make yourself familiar with all the commonly used camera and lens functions. Make sure you understand all the functions of any digital storage systems you will be using.

Time spent researching the areas you will be visiting can prove invaluable and, having established the flora and fauna you are likely to encounter, will aid you in selecting the most appropriate equipment to satisfy your own photographic needs.

It is also good practice to check that you have adequate insurance cover for all your equipment. Ensure that your policy fully covers equipment for loss or damage in all the countries you plan to visit and for the duration of your tour. Keep a checklist of camera and lens serial numbers. This will be useful if you have to make an insurance claim and as a record of the equipment you have taken with you. Should equipment be stolen, report it to the local police and obtain a statement confirming the report of the theft, as some insurance companies will be reluctant to settle any claim without such confirmation.

WHAT TO TAKE

Cameras

The choice of cameras available these days is vast. For really successful safari photographs a top brand Single Lens Reflex (SLR) camera, either digital or film, with an interchangeable lens facility is ideal. Many of today's top models have an auto focus facility which is a great asset to the wildlife photographer. This system can save valuable seconds and consequently secure pictures that may have been missed with manual focus equipment. Due to the rigours and stresses that any safari places on equipment, we strongly advise you to take at least two camera bodies – there will be little or no chance of getting any camera repairs undertaken outside major cities. It is obviously beneficial to have two identical camera bodies, but if this is not feasible you should ensure that your 'back up' camera accepts the same range of lenses and accessories as your principle camera body.

Compact cameras have either a fixed or zoom lens, are quick and easy to operate and prove ideal for those visitors wanting just a photographic record. If you are visiting coastal areas it is also possible to obtain underwater compacts. This is a relatively cheap way of getting started in underwater photography. As most of these underwater compacts are not pressurised they are only operational to depths of just over a metre.

Most compact digital cameras are similar to their film equivalent in size and operation but have the added advantage of instant replay, either through a small built in monitor or computer link. Images are recorded on a memory card, so pictures can be quickly sorted, saved or deleted, to make space for more photography. An increasing number of digital video records have a stills option, and these have the added advantage of being able to record hours of action. As most digital cameras are powered by rechargeable batteries, don't forget to pack chargers, leads and plug adaptors. A spare rechargeable battery and memory card are essential.

Lenses

If you choose the SLR option you will need to think about what interchangeable lenses to take with you. The wide variety of photographic opportunities that are presented to the nature photographer whilst on safari demand an equally wide range of lenses. The manufacturer of your camera system will have an excellent range of lenses to choose from. In addition, independent lens manufacturers will be able to offer competitive prices and maybe different focal lengths. A medium zoom lens of between 70 and 300mm and a short zoom lens of around 28 to 135mm will cover most photographic opportunities. For the more wary mammals and the vast majority of bird species, longer telephoto lenses are required. These lenses are usually 400mm, 500mm or 600mm and although often heavy and rather large, are essential for the more serious nature photographer. Some camera manufacturers even offer image stabilizer lenses. These use a vibration gyro which detects shaking and then counter balances the movement with a magnet and coil driven optical compensation system. These particular lenses are useful for handholding situations such as from a boat or vehicle. This technology really comes into its own when using longer telephoto lenses where camera shake is greatly magnified,

A medium zoom lens can be the most useful

Close-up and macro lenses open up a whole new world of African wildlife

it makes using 500mm and 600mm lenses with teleconvertors a far more successful option. Almost all new lenses will have auto-focus and this will offer three options. Firstly, by switching it off, you can manually focus, secondly, using single shot auto-focus the camera will lock on to whatever you are pointing at, but will need activating again should the subject move. Thirdly, servo-focus can be selected where the auto-focus will be constantly updating the focus point; this is ideal for moving subjects.

Macro Lenses
The inclusion of a macro lens in your equipment bag is essential if your photographic interests are in recording close-ups of insects and flowers. The most useful macro lenses have a focal length of between 90mm and 180mm; these allow a reasonable working distance from most subjects. In our experience macro lenses of around 50mm have too short a working distance, which can disturb some subjects. This short working distance can also often cause lighting difficulties, particularly when using flash. The macro facility offered by some zoom lenses can be useful, but it is rather restricted and in no way matches the quality of a true macro lens.

Cheaper alternatives to a macro lens include the use of extension tubes, placed between any lens and the camera body, thereby reducing the minimum focusing distance, the use of reversing rings and the use of close-up lenses attached to the front of an existing lens.

Lens Accessories
Tele-converters increase the lens magnification by a factor of either 1.4x or 2x and some zoom lenses are designed specifically to work with them. Extension tubes and close-up filter attachments are another way of increasing magnification for macro photography. A UV or skylight filter on each lens offers extra protection from accidental damage to the

A 2 x converter will double your image size

front lens element. A polarising filter is well worth taking, as it will help control reflections and increase colour saturation. Many enhancements that filters achieve on film can be added later to digital images through computer programs such as Photoshop.

Digital Storage

Almost all digital cameras use some form of removable storage memory card, such as XD, Smart Media (SD) or Compact Flash (CF). Storage capacity is measured in Megabits (mb) or Gigabits (GB). The higher the 'mb' or 'GB' the more images can be stored between downloads. It's a good idea to use a digital storage device to download your memory cards each night. These are palm size hard drives that vary in capacity from 20 to 100+ gigabits. Some have small colour screens for viewing. Travelling with a laptop is another alternative where images can be viewed, stored, or even burnt onto CD or DVD. Small battery power CD and DVD writers are also available and offer probably the most secure form of backup.

RAW or JPEG

Most digital cameras offer the option to shoot in Raw or Jpeg. This is the format that records your image, the digital equivalent of film. Jpeg is a file format that stores digital photographs in a very space efficient way. It uses compression to reduce file sizes at the expense of fine image detail to do this. The level of compression (and thus the loss of quality) can be varied. Raw files contain all the data collected by the sensor, not a sub-sample as is the case with Jpeg files. Raw gives the most flexibility for post correction of exposure and colour and is the preferred shooting format of most professional photographers.

Noise and ISO

As in film photography, the noise level increases with higher ISO settings and shows itself in the form of pixels of the wrong colour appearing at random in dark areas. At ISO settings up to 400 very little noise is noticeable, so keep the ISO below 400 and save the higher ISO setting for when there is no alternative.

Film

Whether you require negatives for prints or transparencies for projection, there is a vast array of films to choose from. Film speed or sensitivity to light is gauged by an ISO rating. The higher the ISO, the more sensitive to light the film will be. However, the results will look more grainy. As light levels in East Africa are general very good, it should be possible to take advantage of the finer quality of the lower ISO films. The quantity of film you require may be difficult to calculate. Try and work out a daily requirement and then double it!

CF and SD memory cards can be downloaded into a multimedia storage viewer

X-ray security checks at airports are standard procedure. However, those used for hand luggage checks should not cause any problems for film or digital. Hold luggage is often checked with more powerful X-rays, so always take your film as hand luggage.

Camera Bags

A good quality camera bag that will protect expensive camera equipment from damage, dust and rain is essential for the travelling photographer. There are many well-designed camera bags on the market today, with several more recent designs taking the form of rucksacks – these are excellent particularly if you expect to have to carry your equipment any great distance. In selecting a suitable bag, resist the temptation to purchase one that is too big – you will only feel obliged to fill it! With ever-tightening controls and restrictions being imposed by airlines on the size and weight of cabin baggage, the smaller the better. Waist-mounted camera and lens pouches can help to spread the load. Stuff bags, sold in most camping shops in varying sizes, offer an addional form of protection from dust and rain.

Camera Supports

The commonest cause of picture failure is undoubtedly lack of definition as a result of camera shake. Overcoming this problem will increase your success rate enormously. Most camera instruction manuals give details of 'How to hold your camera' and it is well worth developing a good technique in this area, with elbows locked tightly into the body.

Whenever possible we would recommend the use of a tripod. There are many light, yet sturdy models on the market which will fit comfortably into the average suitcase or roll bag. Monopods are also a good means of steadying the camera, but they do require a little practice. On most photographic safaris to East Africa the vast majority of filming will be undertaken from a vehicle during game drives, in most cases this precludes the use of a tripod or monopod. The best alternative for photographing from a vehicle is to employ the use of a beanbag, a very simple, but extremely effective method of camera support. Although beanbags are commercially available they are not difficult to make. All that is needed is a section of cloth or canvas sewn to form a zippered bag of around 300mm x 150mm. This can be packed in your luggage and, on arrival at your chosen destination, be filled with rice, peas or beans. When the beanbag is placed on the roof of your safari vehicle it quickly moulds around your camera and lens, forming a very efficient support.

Rifle stock and pistol grip supports allow freedom of movement when attempting to photograph moving subjects such as animals running or birds in flight.

If you have no option other than to hand hold your camera while shooting, you should always ensure that your shutter speed is as great or greater than the focal length of the lens in use, so for 50mm - 1/60th., 100mm - 1/125th., 200mm - 1/250th., 500mm - 1/500th. and so forth.

Flash

An electronic flashgun is well worth it's place in your camera bag, not only to record any nocturnal creatures that you may encounter, but also as a 'fill in' to soften harsh shadows during the daytime and to light any close-up macro photography. Most modern day flashguns feature TTL (Through the Lens) exposure control which will guarantee correct exposure automatically. Many of these flashguns also feature an infrared auto focus system, which overcomes the problem of focusing in the dark. In the absence of this facility, a head-mounted torch can prove invaluable, allowing you to illuminate your chosen subject while at the same time leaving both hands free to focus manually.

A Tripod makes a solid camera/lens support

Camera Accessories

A cable release is an excellent way of reducing camera shake, and your camera should accept either an electronic or mechanical type. A wide camera strap with some degree of elasticity will help to distribute the weight of your camera and lens. A small hot shoe spirit level for checking straight horizons can be a great aid to landscape workers.

Batteries

The drain on battery power by auto focus systems is far greater than that

of manual focus systems. As a result you should ensure that you carry a good supply of camera and flash batteries with you. The diversity of batteries employed by differing manufacturers is enormous, and it may be difficult to obtain the batteries for your particular model even in

A beanbag is a very effective camera/lens support

major cities in East Africa. Please remember to dispose of used batteries without damage to the environment, even if it means bringing them home with you.

As most digital cameras use rechargeable batteries, don't forget there chargers, leads and international plug adaptors and where available a car charger. Remember to have enough spare rechargeable batteries to allow for those days where main electricity may not be available.

CARE AND MAINTENANCE

As a general rule it is advisable to thoroughly check and clean all your camera bodies and lenses at the end of each day's shooting. All equipment used on safari is subject to the potentially damaging effects of sunlight, damp, rain and dust. Do remember to keep camera bags and film stock out of direct sunlight whenever possible. Remember that a single piece of dust or sand grain on the image sensor will show as a dark speck on every image, or can badly scratch a complete roll of film. A rubber blower brush or mini vac sucking device is ideal for keeping the inside of your camera clean, while lens elements and filters are best cleaned with specially purchased cleaning fluid and tissues. Alcohol or even fresh water could be used as a last resort. The outer casings of both cameras and lenses can be cleaned using an ordinary paintbrush. It is always worth having a supply of large plastic bags with you, into which you can seal your entire camera bag on the days when you are travelling from one location to another. This will greatly reduce the risks of dust entering the most sensitive parts of your cameras.

PHOTOGRAPHIC TECHNIQUES

For the most part, the secret to successful photography lies in the photographer's ability to master and control several major factors – those of exposure, lighting, depth of field, definition and composition. If all these factors are successfully mastered you will be producing many pleasing pictures.

Exposure

The vast majority of modern cameras have built-in metering systems, which work to a high standard and greatly reduce the possibility of picture failure as a result of incorrect exposure. However, there are many occasions when an automatic metering system may let you down, for example when photographing white birds, or light coloured animals, against a dark background or, alternatively, dark birds or animals against a light sky or background. Under such lighting conditions knowledge in the use of +/- compensation is required. In the case of white/light subjects against dark backgrounds, the metering system may well be influenced to a great extent by the dark areas, thereby over exposing your main subject. This will require you to under expose to retain detail in the important white/light subject areas. Conversely in the case of dark subjects against light skies or backgrounds, the light areas may well over influence the metering, resulting in a silhouette of the main subject. This problem will require you to over expose in order to obtain detail in the shadow or dark areas of your subject. Many present day cameras have a +/- compensation facility to aid the photographer with these awkward exposure situations. Alternatively the same result can be obtained by changing the ISO rating of the film being used, although with the advent of DX coding this may not always be possible. Whichever way you choose to compensate, do remember to cancel any over or under exposure settings before moving on to the next situation.

In cases where determining the correct exposure is in doubt, it is advisable to 'bracket' your exposures. If your metering system indicates an exposure of 1/60th at f8, for example, take one picture at this setting, then two further exposures either side of it, so 1/60th at f5.6 and 1/60th at f11. One of the resulting exposures should produce what you require, but experience with your own equipment under these difficult conditions is the only real answer.

It should also be remembered that the exposure tolerance of transparency film is far lower than that of negative film. The LCD monitor on digital cameras will give an instant indication of what your pictures look like and badly exposed results can be deleted and retaken.

Lighting

During the course of a single day in East Africa, the lighting conditions experienced can vary tremendously. The conditions experienced in the early morning are often the most pleasing, the low angle of the sun producing wonderful soft lighting, with excellent modelling of the subject. These lighting conditions are often repeated in late afternoon with the addition of a warm glow towards sunset. From late morning to mid afternoon lighting conditions can be very challenging, with the sunlight often directly overhead, resulting in rather flat lighting effects.

In most cases, standard portraits of East Africa's birds and mammals are taken with the sunlight behind the photographer, thereby fully lighting the subject. It is always worth experimenting with other lighting arrangements, particularly side or back lighting. These lighting conditions often produce spectacular and unusual pictures of even the most common bird and mammal species.

Depth of Field

The range of 'f' stops available on each individual lens determines depth of field. In most landscape pictures, taken with wide-angle or standard lens, there is a necessity for maximum depth of field, to render as much of the foreground, middle and far distance as sharp as possible. To achieve this result, it is necessary to select a small aperture ('f' stop) of f16 or f22. This will consequently result in a slow shutter speed, so ensure you use a tripod or some other means of support to reduce the risk of picture failure as a result of camera shake.

For individual images of birds or mammals, using longer lenses, it is often better to select a large aperture of f5.6 or f4. This will result in the background being thrown well out of focus, which in turn will help to isolate your main centre of interest be it bird or mammal. The use of a large aperture in these circumstances will also help to eliminate background distractions by rendering them out of focus.

Don't forget that you can check the depth of field created by any given

Early morning and late afternoon light is the most pleasing

'f' stop, by using the depth of field button on your camera body. This button allows you to preview the finished image and to adjust it to your own satisfaction prior to making any exposure.

Definition

The success or failure of any photograph is dependent to a great extent on definition. On the whole, modern lenses are produced to a high standard and give excellent definition; any unsharp results are usually attributable to other causes. The most frequent cause is, undoubtedly, due to camera shake during exposure (See Camera Supports). Another cause can be movement of the subject during exposure; this can be lessened to a great extent by the use of a fast shutter speed.

It is, however, worth remembering that in some instances movement of the subject during exposure can often result in a pleasing pictorial image, such as animals running or flocks of birds flying.

Composition

Unlike many elements of a photograph which are automatically undertaken by the camera itself, composition demands an active input from the photographer. It is therefore in your own interest to be fully conversant with the factors relating to good composition.

Many newcomers to photography tend to produce all of their images in a horizontal format. Cameras work equally well when turned through 90 degrees! Do remember to fully utilise the possibilities of a vertical format.

Also remember to consider changing your viewpoint on occasions. Don't always photograph from a standing position, and explore the possibilities of photographing a subject by kneeling or even lying on the ground. Don't always photograph from the open roof of the vehicle on game drives. Use the windows occasionally, as it can often add impact and provide better scale to the resulting pictures.

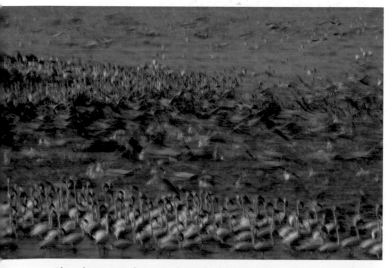

Slow shutter speeds can produce pleasing results

13

A crouching approach creates less disturbance

In the case of bird or mammal portraits, having decided on your format and viewpoint, you need to concentrate on the size and placement of your subject within the picture area. Generally speaking most subjects need room to move or look into the picture space, so avoid cropping your image too tightly, unless of course it is your intention to show a close-up of the subject's head.

Try to avoid placing your subject in the centre of the picture space, instead consciously divide the space into 'thirds', both vertically and horizontally and place your main point of interest where the lines cross. Do pay attention to the line of the horizon, particularly in landscapes. Keep it along the 'thirds' and, at all costs, keep it level.

When it comes to precise framing, zoom lenses are very useful, allowing control over subject size and perspective. In some cases the size of the main subject can be quite small within the picture space, provided that the inclusion of more surroundings adds information or pictorial interest to the finished image.

By utilising a range of lenses it is often possible to secure an interesting sequence of images of a bird or mammal, i.e. 50mm showing the creature in it's habitat, 200mm or 300mm producing portraits and 500mm or 600mm depicting the head only. Sequences like these can often add variety to subsequent slide shows or print albums.

The Moment of Exposure
Having located your subject and decided on the elements of exposure, lighting and composition, when do you press the shutter? This, of

The auto focus servo mode is best for flying birds and running animals

course, is very subjective, but any animal or bird portrait will be greatly improved and have a 'sparkle of life' if you can make your exposure when a 'highlight' is visible in the eye of your chosen subject. This is particularly important if the eye of the subject being photographed is dark and surrounded by black fur or feather.

You should always attempt to maintain concentration when photographing any subject, remaining alert to the possibility of a yawn, scratch or wing-stretch, which may provide you with only a fleeting moment in which to capture the action.

Moving Subjects

Animals or birds 'on the move' present the photographer with some interesting problems. Supporting the camera is a major concern as the use of a tripod of monopod is usually too restricting for this type of work. Other than hand-holding the camera, a rifle stock or shoulder pod is probably the only option available. Either way you should endeavour to use the fastest shutter speed available, to minimise the risk of camera shake. Capturing any moving bird or mammal is best accomplished by 'panning'. This technique involves moving the camera in the same direction and at the same speed as the subject and taking the picture while the camera is still moving. Any resulting pictures will have a feeling of movement, showing the subject in sharp focus with the background blurred due to the motion of the panning camera.

Use the fastest shutter speed available

Getting Close to Birds and Mammals

Whilst on safari the vast majority of your photography will be undertaken from a vehicle during game drives. Many opportunities also exist for wildlife photography on foot, within the grounds of safari lodges and at specially designated areas within the National Parks and Reserves.

At many of the lodges getting close to birds is often quite easy, due to the tame nature of many species. Others, however, require some knowledge of basic 'stalking' procedures to gain a close enough approach for a worthwhile image size in the finished pictures. Avoid walking straight towards your intended subject, as this is likely to cause it to fly away, whereas a slow angled approach is more likely to succeed. Watch your subject during your approach and should it appear concerned 'freeze' for a while until it again looks relaxed. A crouched approach during a 'stalk' can also be beneficial. The smaller you appear, the less likely you are to frighten your intended subject. It is also a good idea to make use of any natural cover that the terrain may offer.

Many of the safari lodges in East Africa provide food and water for the local bird population and these feeding areas can offer good photographic opportunities. Even if the bird tables themselves are non-photogenic you can attempt to photograph birds on natural perches as they make their way to and from the feeding areas.

You should exercise considerable caution when 'stalking' mammal species, always keeping in mind that they are wild animals and can be extremely dangerous. Never try to tempt monkeys or baboons to come closer with food items – this is a sure way to get badly bitten.

Notes

Sometimes the identification of the vast number of animals and other subjects you are able to photograph on safari can be a nightmare. Keeping detailed notes on each series of photographs can be a great help later. Either date or number each film you expose so that the images can be matched to your notes when captioning pictures upon your return home.

CODE OF CONDUCT

The National Parks and Reserves of East Africa operate a strict Code of Conduct for both drivers and visitors. A short, simple list of do's and don'ts have been implemented to minimise disturbance to the birds and mammals, to lessen the impact of tourism on the environment and to ensure that all visitors experience safe and enjoyable safaris.

- Please do not pressurise your driver into breaking Park regulations, you will be jeopardising his job and run the risk of expulsion from the Park.

- Please keep noise to a minimum, particularly when close to animals and never leave the vehicle, sit or stand on the roof, or hang precariously from the windows.

- Never discard any form of litter, apart from being unsightly it can cause serious injury or even kill animals if ingested.

- Cigarettes are best avoided during game drives, the careless or accidental discarding of a match or cigarette stub can lead to uncontrollable fires, resulting in the deaths of many living creatures.

GENERAL NOTES

Many people visiting East Africa express a wish to photograph the local people. Before doing so please obtain permission and be prepared for the possibility of paying for the privilege. On no account attempt to photograph military installations or personnel.

BIBLIOGRAPHY

The following books are recommended for further reference.

Brown, L.H., Urban, E.L., Newman, K., Fry, C. H. & Keith, S. *The Birds of Africa,* (6 vols to date). Academic Press.

Brown, L. H. & Amadon, D., *Eagles, Hawks & Falcons of the World.* Country Life Books.

Cramp, S. *et al.* (Eds). *Handbook of the Birds of Europe, the Middle East & North Africa (The Birds of the Western Palearctic),* (9 vols) Oxford University Press.

Dorst, J. & Dandelot, P. A., *A Fieldguide to the Larger Mammals of Africa.* HarperCollins*Publishers.*

Eley, R. M., *Know your Monkeys – A Guide to the Primates of Kenya.* National Museums of Kenya.

Estes, R. D., *The Safari Companion – A Guide to Watching African Mammals.* Tutorial Press.

Guggisberg, C. A. W., *Birds of East Africa* (2 vols). Mount Kenya Sundries Ltd., Nairobi.

Haltenorth, T. & Diller, H., *A Fieldguide to the Mammals of Africa including Madagascar.* HarperCollins*Publishers.*

Kingdon, J., *East African Mammals* (7 vols). The University of Chicago Press.

Kruuk, H. *The Spotted Hyena.* The University of Chicago Press.

Mackworth-Praed, C. W. & Grant, C. H. B., *Birds of Eastern & North-Eastern Africa* (2 vols). Longmans.

Norton, B., *The Mountain Gorilla.* Swan Hill Press.

Passmore N. I. & Curruthers V. C., *South African Frogs.* Southern Book Publishers

Roberts, A., *The Birds of South Africa* (revised edition by Mclachan, G. R. & Liversidge, R.). The Trustees of the John Voelcker Bird Book Fund, 1977.

Schiotz A., *Treefrogs of Africa.*

Serle, W., Morel, G. J. & Hartwig, W. A., Collins *Field Guide Birds of West Africa.* HarperCollins*Publishers.*

Spawls S. & Branch B., *The Dangerous Snakes of Africa.*

Spinage, C. A., *The Natural History of Antelopes.* Croom Helm.

Van Perlo, B., Illustrated Checklist Birds of Eastern Africa. Collins

Zimmerman, D. A., Turner, D. A. & Pearson, D. J., *Birds of Kenya & Northern Tanzania.* Christopher Helm.

PICTURE CREDITS

The authors would like to thank the Frank Lane Picture Agency for their assistance in the compilation of the photographs used in this book . All the photographs are by the authors with the exception of those listed below:

Termite Fritz Polking
Wahlberg's Eagle P. Steyn
Pallid Harrier W S Clark
Little Sparrowhawk Wendy Dennis
Red-chested Cuckoo A & K Riley
Alpine Swift Silvestris
Red-backed Scrub Robin J Karmali
Grey-backed Camaroptera M Gore
Variable Sunbird M Gore
Beautiful Sunbird M Gore

Black-headed Oriole P Steyn
Squire-tailed Drongo J Karmali
Giant Forest Hog G Davis
Common Duiker J & C Sohns
Bongo F Lane
Lesser Kudu L Batten
Tree Hyrax Mark Newman
Aardwolf Wendy Dennis
Patas Monkey F Lane
African Civet F Lane

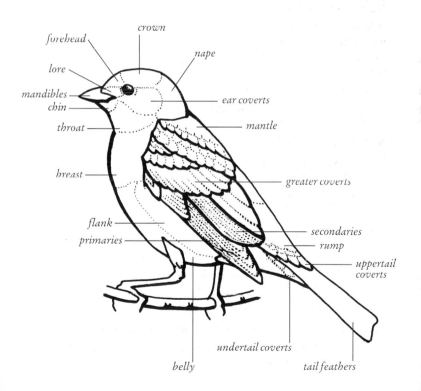

Parts of a bird

BIRDS

Common Ostrich *(Struthio camelus)*

The largest bird in the world standing 2-2.5m in height, and weighing up to 130kg, which makes this flightless species almost impossible to misidentify. The adult male (A) has black and white plumage, the white being restricted to the tail and the tips of the stunted wings. The head, neck and thighs are pink. The plumage of the female (B) is a mixture of greys and browns with the head, neck and legs dull grey-brown. The Somali Ostrich (*Struthio camelus molybdophanes*) (C), a sub-species, also occurs and is found in parts of Ethiopia, Somalia and Kenya. The male differs in appearance in having blue-grey neck and thighs and a red stripe on the front of the lower leg. They prefer areas of short grass plains and dry semi-desert bush and scrub. During the breeding season several females may lay in the same nest and 70+ eggs have been recorded. It is only possible for the incubating bird, usually the 'major hen', to cover around 20 eggs so in circumstances of larger clutches many go to waste. The incubation period is 45 days and after hatching chicks from many different broods may join together in a crèche. A 'major pair' often undertakes the raising and protection of the chicks, which continues for around 9 months, with other adults in loose association. Resident. Size: 2-2.5m.

Great Crested Grebe *(Podiceps cristatus)*

The largest grebe in Africa, found on large open areas of both fresh and alkaline water, where they feed almost exclusively on small fish. The forehead, crown and hind neck are blackish. The sides of the face, throat, fore neck and underparts are white. In breeding plumage the ear coverts become chestnut edged with black and the feathering on the crown lengthens and forms into a crest. The back is blackish streaked with brown. The bill is black with a reddish tinge. The eyes are red. The sexes are similar. Resident. Size: 52cm.

Black-necked Grebe *(Podiceps nigricollis)*

A small grebe of both freshwater and alkaline lakes and ponds. In breeding plumage the head, neck and back are black contrasting with striking golden-yellow ear coverts. The flanks are chestnut and the underside almost pure white. They are often encountered in flocks during non-breeding periods, when the plumage on the forehead, crown, nape, hind neck, back and wings is greyish-black, the throat, fore neck and underparts are off-white. The bill is dark grey-black and curves slightly upwards. The eyes are orange-red. The sexes are alike. Resident. Size: 30cm.

Little Grebe *(Tachybaptus ruficollis)*

The commonest grebe on the freshwater and alkaline lakes of the rift valley. They are also found on small ponds and sluggish rivers. A small, squat grebe with the forehead, crown and hind neck black. The cheeks, throat and fore neck are rich chestnut, and the back and wings are brown. The flanks are rufous and the breast and underparts white. The short bill is dark with a patch of cream at the base. The eyes are dark red. The plumage becomes duller and greyer during non-breeding periods. The sexes are alike. Resident. Size: 25cm.

Great White Pelican

(Pelecanus onocrotalus)

Recognisable when at rest or on water by their almost completely white plumage which often has a flush of pink during the breeding season. In flight the black primary and secondary wing feathers are prominent. The large bill is greyish-yellow and the pouch yellow to pinkish-white. Immature birds are greyish-brown, becoming whiter with age. The legs and feet are orange-pink. The eyes are dark brown and surrounded by a patch of unfeathered pink skin. A very gregarious bird normally fishing in groups on freshwater and alkaline lakes. Resident. Size: 165cm.

Pink-backed Pelican

(Pelecanus rufescens)

Found on large lakes throughout the region, usually fishing singly. Smaller and greyer in appearance than the White Pelican (*Pelecanus onocrotalus*) they have loosely arranged mottled grey feathering on the back, wings and breast, which often gives a shaggy appearance. In flight the back and rump show a flush of pink. The primary and secondary wing feathers are blackish-brown. The bill is grey-pink and the pouch pink with streaks of yellow. The eyes are dark brown surrounded by areas of bare grey-pink skin. The feet are yellow. In breeding plumage they develop an eye patch of black, yellow and pink, and a crest of grey feathers on the crown. Immature birds have pale grey-brown plumage. Resident. Size: 132cm.

Great Cormorant

(Phalacrocorax carbo)

A common water bird of freshwater and alkaline lakes as well as rivers and, to a lesser extent, coastal regions. A large blackish-brown bird with white throat and fore-neck and, in breeding plumage, a white patch to the sides of the rump and a crest of black feathers on the crown. Immature birds are duller and browner than adults with the throat, neck, breast and belly white, streaked and flecked with greyish-brown. The bill is dark with a red-orange mark on the lores. The eyes are emerald green. They are normally found in large flocks, feeding by pursuing fish underwater and are often seen following a feeding session, perched with wings spread to dry. Resident. Size: 90cm.

Long-tailed Cormorant

(Phalacrocorax africanus)

Usually found singly or in small groups. A common and widespread bird of freshwater lakes, rivers and coastal areas. A much smaller cormorant than the White-necked with almost entirely black plumage and a small crest of erectile feathers on the forehead. The wing coverts are distinctly marked with silver-grey. In breeding plumage white plume feathers appear to the rear of the eyes. The tail is long. The bill is yellow and the eyes a rich red, the legs and feet are black. Immature birds have upper-parts brown-black while the underparts are white flecked and streaked with brown. Resident. Size: 58cm.

African Darter

(Anhinga rufa)

A bird of freshwater lakes, rivers and marshes widely distributed throughout the region. Distinguished from the cormorants by the thin, pointed bill, small slender head and long thin neck. The forehead, crown, hind-neck, back and tail are black. The front and sides of the neck are chestnut edged with white. The wings are black streaked with white and the underparts are all black. The rich colours of the head and neck are less pronounced in the female. Immatures resemble females but have underparts of brown. They are solitary feeders pursuing fish underwater which they spear with their dagger-like bills. Like the cormorants they will often perch with wings out-stretched to dry following a feeding session. Resident. Size: 95cm.

Black-crowned Night Heron
(Nycticorax nycticorax)

Primarily nocturnal this distinctive heron hides away in thick waterside vegetation during much of the day. The crown, hind-neck, mantle and scapulars of adult birds (A) are a glossy black, often showing a green-blue sheen. The forehead, throat, front and sides of the neck, breast and underparts are white. The wings and tail are grey. The legs and feet are bright yellow and the eyes a rich crimson. During the breeding season 2 or 3 long white plumes flow from the crown. The bill is dark almost black. The sexes are alike. Immature birds (B) have dark brown upper-parts flecked and spotted with white, and buff-grey underparts streaked with dark-brown. Resident, numbers increase with the arrival of palearctic winter visitors. Size: 60cm.

Squacco Heron
(Ardeola ralloides)

Common and widely distributed throughout East Africa, frequenting lakes, rivers, streams, marshes and ponds. A small brownish-buff heron with a rich cinnamon crown, nape and hind neck. During the breeding season long black and white feathers appear on the crown and plumes of cinnamon feathers flow from the mantle. The throat, neck and underparts are white. In flight the white wings, rump and tail contrast strongly with the darker areas of plumage. The bill legs and feet are yellowish-green. The sexes are alike. Immature birds have the crown and breast streaked with dark brown. Resident and winter visitor from the palearctic region. Size: 45cm.

Cattle Egret
(Bubulcus ibis)

A very common and widely distributed bird of open plains, lakes, rivers and marshes. Often in association with plains game animals, feeding on insects disturbed from the grasses by the grazing herds. The plumage is almost entirely white during periods of non-breeding. At breeding times golden-buff elongated plumes appear on the crown the breast and the mantle. The bill is yellow-orange, the legs and feet yellow or pale orange-pink. The sexes are alike. Immatures resemble non-breeding adults but with the bill, legs and feet black. Resident. Size: 50cm.

Green-backed Heron
(Butorides striatus)

Widely distributed throughout East Africa frequenting lakes, rivers, marshes, estuaries and coastal areas. A small heron with a dark green crown and nape. The mantle and the sides of the neck and hind neck are grey. The upper breast is rufous and the underparts are light grey. The wings are dark green above and grey below. The legs and feet are yellowish-green and the bill is black with a yellowish base. The sexes are similar, females tending to be slightly duller in appearance. Immatures are browner, streaked and spotted with white above and dark brown below. Resident. Size: 40cm.

Great Egret
(Casmerodius albus)

The largest egret to be found in East Africa. Widely distributed and quite common on lakes and other expanses of open water both inland and coastal. The plumage is completely white, the legs and feet are black and the bill, during the breeding season, is black with a variable amount of yellow towards the base. During periods of non-breeding the bill is yellow. The eyes are red during the breeding period and yellow at other times. The sexes are alike. Immature birds resemble non-breeding adults. Resident. Size: 90cm.

Yellow-billed Egret
(Mesophoyx intermedia)

Widespread and reasonably common on freshwater lakes as well as in coastal areas. Like a smaller version of the Great Egret (*Casmerodius alba*), the Yellow-billed Egret has all white plumage. The legs and feet are black and the bill is yellow-orange. The eyes are yellow during periods of non-breeding and, like the bill, turn redder during the breeding season. The sexes are alike. Immature birds are similar to non-breeding adults. Resident. Size: 65cm.

Little Egret *(Egretta garzetta)*

A widely distributed species on lakes, swamps, marshes, ponds and in coastal regions. A small egret with entirely white plumage, easily identified by the black legs and bright yellow feet. The bill is grey-black and the eyes are yellow. During the breeding season they develop long thin plume feathers which flow from the rear of the crown and from the mantle and lower fore neck. The sexes are alike. The immatures resemble non-breeding adults. Resident and palearctic winter visitor. Size: 58cm.

Black Heron *(Egretta ardesiaca)*

Although widely distributed in East Africa it is not an easy bird to locate. They frequent marshes, lakes, rivers and coastal mudflats. The plumage is slate grey-black with plumes on the nape, mantle and lower fore neck. The legs are black and the feet yellow. The bill is grey-black and the eyes are yellow. Normally found in flocks, feeding by forming a canopy with the wings thereby shading the water surface from reflections and attracting potential prey into the shade. The sexes are alike. Resident. Size: 56cm.

Grey Heron *(Ardea cinerea)*

A common and widespread species on lakes, swamps and marshes. A large heron with body and wing plumage grey-blue. The forehead, crown, chin, face and neck are white. A black stripe extends from above and behind the eyes to the back of the crown from which flow several long black plumes. A line of black streaks extends down the centre of the fore neck terminating at the white breast. The belly, wing tips and shoulders are black, the bill, legs and feet are greyish-yellow. The eyes are bright yellow. The sexes are alike. Immature birds are generally paler and duller than adults, with underparts streaked with brown. Resident and palearctic winter visitor. Size: 100cm.

Black-headed Heron *(Ardea melanocephala)*

An inhabitant of areas of permanent open water, marshes, swamps and rivers throughout East Africa. The plumage of the upper and lower body, the tail and the wings is dark slaty blue-grey. The chin and throat are white. The upper portion of the head, from just below the eyes, is black extending over the nape and hind neck merging with the slate-grey of the mantle. The lower neck is white heavily marked and streaked with black. The legs and feet are black. The bill is grey-black and the eyes bright yellow. The sexes are alike. Immature birds are browner with off-white underparts. Resident. Size: 96cm.

Goliath Heron *(Ardea goliath)*

The largest heron in Africa, with mainly slate-grey upper body and wing plumage. The head, the sides and hind neck are chestnut brown. The chin, throat and fore neck are white with the lower part of the neck heavily streaked with black. The underparts and thighs are deep chestnut, the legs and feet are black. The bill is grey-black and the eyes are yellow. The sexes are alike. Immatures are duller and paler than adults, showing more brown in the body and wing plumage. The underparts are lighter and streaked with browns. Resident. Size: 150cm.

Purple Heron *(Ardea purpurea)*

An inhabitant of lakes, swamps and marshes throughout East Africa. A slim heron readily distinguished from the Grey Heron (*Ardea cinerea*) by the bright rufous feathering of the neck and head. The plumage of the upper body and wings is slate-grey washed with rufous. The forehead and crown are black, two black stripes extend from the gape, one following a line to the nape and down the hind neck, whilst the other extends down the sides of the neck to the breast. The throat and fore neck are white heavily streaked with black. The breast, belly and shoulders are chestnut. The bill is deep yellow, the legs and feet yellow-black and the eyes yellow. The sexes are alike. Immatures are paler and mottled in appearance. Resident and palearctic winter visitor. Size: 85cm.

Hamerkop
(Scopus umbretta)

Occurs throughout the region in suitable areas usually in the vicinity of water. A bird with a dull russet brown plumage paler on the cheeks, neck and breast. A large crest on the crown and nape gives the bird a distinctive hammerhead appearance. The substantial bill is black as are the legs and feet. The eyes are dark brown. The sexes are alike. Immature birds are similar to adults. Resident. Size: 60cm.

Abdim's Stork
(Ciconia abdimii)

A gregarious stork with head, neck, upperparts and wings metallic purple-black. The breast, belly, underparts and rump are white. The bill is yellow-green. There are patches of unfeathered skin on the face, red in front of the eyes and blue on the chin. The legs and feet are greenish with a flush of red around the joints. The eyes are dark brown. The sexes are similar. Immatures have a browner appearance with facial patches, bill and legs duller. Small numbers do breed in East Africa but the vast majority are migrants. Size: 80cm.

Black Stork
(Ciconia nigra)

This species can be confused with Abdim's Stork (*Ciconia abdimii*) but differs in being larger and having the bill, legs and feet red. The upperparts, tail, breast and wings are glossy black with a green-purple metallic sheen. The lower breast, belly and underparts are white. The eyes are dark brown surrounded by a red area of unfeathered skin. The sexes are alike. Immatures lack the red facial patch which appears grey and have the bill, legs and feet greyish-green. A migrant visitor to East Africa. Size: 96cm.

White Stork
(Ciconia ciconia)

Often found in large flocks feeding on grasshoppers and other insects on the open savannahs. The head, neck, back, breast, wing coverts and underparts are white, the primary wing feathers black. The large bill, long, thin legs and feet are red. The eyes are dark brown. The sexes are alike. Immatures have primary feathers tinged with brown and a brown-red bill, legs and feet. A palearctic winter migrant. Size: 102cm.

Woolly-necked Stork
(Ciconia episcopus)

An inhabitant of lakes, rivers and coastal areas over much of East Africa, usually found singly. The upperparts, wings and breast are glossy blue-black. The head is white with a black crown, the neck is white and has a woolly appearance. The belly and underparts are white. The bill is blackish, red towards the tip, the legs and feet are blackish and the eyes are blood red. The sexes are alike. Immature birds lack the white forehead and have browner upperparts and wings. Resident. Size: 85cm.

Saddle-billed Stork
(Ephippiorhynchus senegalensis)

East Africa's largest stork. The head, neck, tail and wing coverts are black. The back, breast, belly and underparts are white as are the primary and secondary wing feathers. The bill is large and has a slightly upturned appearance, the base and tip are bright red and a broad centre section is black. On top of the bill in front of the forehead, sits a bright yellow saddle. The extremely long legs are black with the feet and joints red. The sexes are similar, the female is smaller and has a bright yellow eye, and the eye is dark brown in the male. Immatures are dull, rather grey birds lacking the bright features of the adults. Resident. Size: 168cm.

African Open-billed Stork
(Anastomus lamelligerus)

A gregarious stork of lakes, rivers, swamps and marshes over much of East Africa. The plumage is entirely glossy black-brown often showing an iridescent sheen of bronze-green. The bill is yellow-brown becoming whitish towards the base, the shape is unique among storks in that the upper and lower mandibles meet only at the base and tip, having a prominent gap towards the centre. This specialised bill allows the bird to feed on freshwater mussels and snails, prising open the hard exterior shells with ease. The legs and feet are blackish. The sexes are alike. Immatures are duller and browner, particularly the underparts, and have white flecking on the hind neck. The bill is also less well developed, the gap gradually widening with age. Resident. Size: 90cm.

Marabou Stork
(Leptoptilus crumeniferus)

An extremely large and widely distributed stork with a rather grotesque appearance. The upperparts, wings and tail are blue-black. The breast, belly and underparts are white. The head is unfeathered, pink to red in colour and mottled with black at the base of the bill, the forehead and around the eyes. The neck is white and sparsely feathered but has a ruff of whitish feathers at the base. The bill is pale yellow-cream. The legs and feet are grey-black, but quite often 'whitened' with droppings. A large pendulous pink throat pouch is often present. The sexes are alike. Resident. Size: 150cm.

Yellow-billed Stork
(Mycteria ibis)

Widespread and very common in suitable habitats, lakes, marshes and swamps being favoured. The head, neck, upper and underparts, back, breast and belly are white, often with a flush of pink. The tail and primary wing feathers are black. The face and forehead are bright red and the long bill is bright yellow. The legs and feet are bright red. The eyes are dark brown. The sexes are alike. Immature birds are duller with the white body feathering light to mid-grey. Resident. Size: 105cm.

Sacred Ibis
(Threskiornis aethiopicus)

Widely distributed throughout East Africa, usually in wet habitats but often in areas of cultivated land. The body plumage is white, the wings have black tips to the primary feathers. Long black plumes flow from the lower back over the tail. The head and neck are black and unfeathered. The black bill is long and decurved. The legs and feet are black. Patches of bare skin on the underwing show bright red in flight. The eyes are dark brown. The sexes are alike. Resident. Size: 75cm.

Hadada Ibis
(Bostrychia hagedash)

An inhabitant of wooded riversides and open forests. The upperparts and wings are bronze-grey with an iridescent sheen of green particularly on the wings. The head, neck, breast and belly are grey-brown and a white stripe extends from the gape across the lower cheek. The long decurved bill is black with a red stripe along the top of the upper mandible. The legs and feet are grey-black with the tops of the toes striped red. The eyes are pale yellow. The sexes are alike. Immatures are a dull version of the adults. Resident. Size: 75cm.

Glossy Ibis
(Plegadis falcinellus)

Under certain lighting conditions the Glossy Ibis appears entirely black, although in actual fact the plumage is brown with an array of iridescent greens and purples. The head and neck are lightly flecked with white. The long decurved bill is a dull dark flesh pink. The legs and feet are greenish-brown often darkening at the joints. The eyes are dark brown. The sexes are alike. Immature birds are generally browner than adults. Resident and palearctic winter visitor. Size: 60cm.

African Spoonbill
(Platalea alba)

Occurs over much of East Africa favouring both fresh and alkaline lakes, rivers, marshes and swamps. A bird with pure white plumage. The forehead, front of face and chin are bright red and unfeathered. The most obvious identification feature is the large spoon-like pink and grey bill which is used in a sweeping motion when feeding. The legs and feet are pink-red. The sexes are alike. Immatures have the plumage streaked with brown and lack strong colour in the face, bill and legs. The feet are black. Resident. Size: 90cm.

Greater Flamingo
(Phoenicopterus ruber)

The larger of East Africa's flamingos they occur in large numbers throughout the rift valley, frequenting alkaline and freshwater lakes. The head, long slender neck, back, underparts and tail are white with a flush of pink. The wing coverts are bright scarlet and the primary and secondary wing feathers are black. The bill is broad and curved, bright pink with a black tip. It is specially adapted for filtering small prey items from shallow water. The long thin legs and feet are vivid pink. The sexes are similar, the female being smaller. Immatures are brown-grey in plumage with grey-black bill and legs. Resident. Size: 140cm.

Lesser Flamingo
(Phoeniconaias minor)

Found in enormous flocks on the alkaline lakes of the rift valley. The plumage varies from almost pure white, in young and non-breeding birds, to pale rose pink during breeding periods. The primary wing feathers are black and the wing coverts deep crimson. The bill is broad and curved, black at the base and the tip with a varying amount of deep red in the centre portion. The eyes are bright yellow-orange and the long, thin legs and feet are bright red. The female is smaller and paler in colour than the male. Immature birds have a grey-brown plumage. Resident. Size: 100cm.

Fulvous Whistling Duck
(Dendrocygna bicolor)

A duck of freshwater lakes, rivers and flood plains throughout East Africa. An upstanding, erect duck with rufous plumage, generally darker brown on the hind neck, back and scapulars. The rump and tail are black. The upper tail coverts are white and prominent in flight. Some white flecking on the upper flanks. The fore neck and throat are buff darkening to rufous-brown on the lower breast and belly. The undertail coverts are white. The bill and long legs are blue-grey. The sexes are alike. Immature birds resemble adults but have paler plumage. Resident. Size: 50cm.

White-faced Whistling Duck
(Dendrocygna viduata)

A very gregarious and distinctive duck inhabiting inland lakes, swamps and marshes. An upright, long-necked duck with the frontal portion of the head, face and throat white, the rear of the head and upper neck are black and the remainder of the neck and breast is chestnut. The belly and underparts are black and the flanks and sides of the breast are white, boldly barred with black. The mantle and wing coverts are olive-brown and the rump and tail black. The bill is black with a blue band towards the tip. The legs and feet are bluish and the eyes dark brown. The sexes are alike. Resident. Size: 46cm.

Egyptian Goose
(Alopochen aegyptiacus)

A common and widely distributed goose, favouring inland waters, swamps and rivers. Predominantly grey-buff on the head, fore-neck, breast, belly, back, underparts and flanks. A dark brown patch encircles the orange eyes. The nape and wing coverts are chestnut and an irregular blotch of chestnut feathers can be seen on the lower breast. The rump, tail and primary wing feathers are black. The secondary wing feathers have an iridescent sheen of metallic green. The bill is dark pink and the legs and feet a rich red. The sexes are similar, the females being slightly smaller. Resident. Size: 60cm.

Spur-winged Goose

(Plectropterus gambensis)

The largest goose in Africa, found in aquatic habitats, grasslands and areas of cultivated crops. The upperbody, neck, back of the head and wings are bronze-black with the latter often showing a sheen of iridescent green. The underparts from the lower breast to the tail coverts are white. The head and face are white to the rear of the eyes and unfeathered pink-red to the fore. The bill, which often has a knob at the base of the upper mandible, is deep red with a pale tip. The legs and feet are pinkish-red. The female is duller and smaller than the male. Immatures are browner and lack the bright bare facial patch. Resident. Size: 84cm.

Knob-billed Duck

(Sarkidiornis melanotos)

A substantial black and white duck of lakes and rivers throughout the region. The upperparts and wings are blackish with washes of iridescent greens and purples. The rump is brown. The head and neck are white speckled with black. The breast, belly and undertail coverts are white and the flanks grey. The bill is black, the males having a large swelling at the base of the upper mandible during the breeding season. The legs and feet are grey-black. Females are smaller less well marked and lack the knob on the bill. Resident. Size: 60cm.

Cape Teal

(Anas capensis)

A small duck encountered mainly on alkaline lakes and shallow pools over much of the region. The back and scapulars are dark brown edged with buff. The breast and underparts are grey-white as are the flanks which are blotched with brown. The head and neck are grey finely speckled with brown. The bill is pink with a black base, the legs and feet are grey-yellow. The eyes are orange-brown. The sexes are alike. Immature birds resemble adults but lack strong bill and eye colour. Resident. Size: 35cm.

Eurasian Wigeon

(Anas penelope)

A palearctic winter visitor which can be found on freshwater lakes and coastal mudflats, often in large flocks. The males have a cinnamon red head and neck, with a patch of light buff on the forehead and crown. The breast, belly, flanks and mantle are greyish-white. The tail coverts are black and the primary wing feathers brown-black. The bill is slate-grey with a black tip. The legs and feet are grey. The female has a mottled plumage of buff, grey and reddish-browns. Some non-breeding individuals remain year round but the vast majority are migratory. Size: 45cm.

Yellow-billed Duck

(Anas undulata)

Distributed over much of the region being very abundant in some areas. Found on freshwater lakes and marshes. Most of the body feathering is dark brown with buff-white edging. The underparts and tail are dark brown. The head and neck are brown with fine buff streaking. The wings, in certain lights, show a flash of iridescent green. The eyes are brown and the bill bright yellow with a patch of black around the base and the tip. The legs and feet are brown-black. The female is smaller and generally less bright than the male. Resident. Size: 50cm.

Red-billed Teal

(Anas erythrorhyncha)

A common and widely distributed species in suitable habitats. Present on freshwater lakes, marshes and flood plains. The feathers on the upperparts and scapulars are dark brown edged with buff. The breast, belly and flanks are buff-white with brown crescent speckling darkest on the flanks. The top of the head, from the base of the bill to the nape and the hind neck, is dark brown-black, the rest of the head and face being buff-white. The bill is bright red, the eyes dark brown and the legs and feet blue-grey. The sexes are alike. Resident. Size: 38cm.

Garganey
(Anas querquedula)

A palearctic winter migrant to freshwater lakes and flood plains. The most distinctive field marking of the male garganey is the broad white stripe extending from the side of the forehead through the eye to the nape and hind neck, contrasting with the dark brown head. The breast is brown marked with black crescent barring. The belly and underparts are white finely barred with black. The wing coverts and scapulars are dark bluish-green the latter edged with white. The primary wing feathers are brown. The bill is dark and the legs and feet dark blue-grey. Females have browner underparts with much blotching and streaking. The head is dark brown with buff eyebrow and cheek stripes above and below a dark eye stripe. The underparts are white. A palearctic winter visitor. Size: 38cm.

Northern Shoveler
(Anas clypeata)

Easily recognised by the large dark grey-black spatulate bill, with which it dabbles for food in its favoured habitat of shallow freshwater lakes and marshes. The head is glossy bottle green, the breast white and the belly and flanks chestnut. The back and rump are grey-black. The scapulars are dull green, black and white. The eyes are bright yellow, the legs and feet orange-red. The female is generally brown with buff featheredges and has the bill and eye colour much reduced. A palearctic winter visitor. Size: 50cm.

Hottentot Teal
(Anas hottentota)

The smallest duck in East Africa, favouring shallow lakes, ponds and marshes fringed with reeds. Males have the forehead, crown and nape dark brown-black contrasting with the buff-white face. A blackish patch is present to the rear of the head adjacent to the nape. The breast and underparts are tawny-white spotted and barred with dark brown and black. The back, rump and tail are brown-black. The wing feathering is mostly dark brown edged with buff, the secondaries showing a greenish iridescent gloss. The bill, legs and feet are slate blue-grey. The eyes are dark brown. Females are generally duller than males and lack barring on the underparts. Resident. Size: 28cm.

Maccoa Duck
(Oxyura maccoa)

A stiff-tailed diving duck of shallow open waters fringed with tall, dense emergent vegetation. The males have the head and upper neck black with the breast, mantle, flanks and tail coverts a bright chestnut. The underparts are grey-brown and the tail feathers are black and held stiffly at an angle of about 45 degrees. The bill is bright blue, the eyes dark brown and the legs and feet dull grey. The females and non-breeding males have grey-brown upperparts flecked with buff, light brown flanks with fine buff-white flecking. The head has a grey-brown cap below which is a whitish stripe extending from the base of the upper mandible towards the nape. The chin, throat and lower neck are whitish. Resident. Size: 44cm.

Secretary Bird
(Sagittarius serpentarius)

Almost unmistakable. A large long-legged bird of prey usually encountered in pairs walking across the open short grass savannahs in search of snakes, lizards, small rodents and large invertebrates on which they feed. The forehead, crown, nape, mantle and wing coverts are light grey and the chin, neck and throat are off-white. Long flowing, black tipped crest feathers emerge from the nape. A patch of unfeathered skin surrounds the eyes and varies in colour from yellow-orange to bright red. The belly, thighs and wing feathers are black. The grey tail is very long with the central feathers banded black at the tip. The eyes are brown and the legs and feet pale pink. The bill is grey with a flush of yellow at the base. Resident. Size: 100cm.

Ruppell's Griffon Vulture *(Gyps rueppellii)*

A large common vulture of savannah and hill regions in the vicinity of gorges and cliffs which are required for roosting and nesting. The head and neck are covered with sparse downy grey-white feathers, often becoming dirty, matted and soiled when feeding. They have a fluffy white ruff at the base of the neck. The back, wing coverts and speculars are dark brown edged with white, the primary wing feathers are dark brown-black. The feathering of the underparts is brown with buff-cream edges and tips. The bill is cream, the legs and feet are dull grey-brown. The sexes are alike. Immature birds lack white feathering on the head and neck and the pale featheredges are less well defined. With young birds taking at least seven years to attain full adult plumage the variation is extreme and varied. Resident. Size: 86cm.

African White-backed Vulture *(Gyps africanus)*

The commonest and most widespread of East Africa's vultures. The head and neck are black, sparsely covered with downy grey-white feathers. The off-white neck ruff is rather thinly feathered. The mantle is dark brown. The wing coverts are sandy brown and the primary wing feathers and tail are brown-black. The back and rump are white, very pronounced in flight. The bill, legs and feet are black. The sexes are alike. Immature birds are darker than the adults, taking six to seven years to attain full adult plumage. This results in many plumage variations. Resident. Size: 80cm.

Lappet-faced Vulture *(Torgos tracheliotus)*

The largest vulture in Africa, inhabiting open grassland savannahs. The unfeathered head and neck are pink to red, with flaps and folds of skin on the sides of the head and crown. At the base of the neck is a short, spiky ruff of dark brown feathers. The upperparts and wings are dark brown-black. The flanks, thighs and underparts are covered with white, downy feathers. The breast has long brown feathers edged with white. The eyes are dark brown. The massive bill is dark grey-blue tipped with dull yellow. The legs and feet are grey-blue. The sexes are similar, the female being slightly larger than the male. Immature birds are browner in plumage with the head and neck paler. Resident. Size: 100cm.

White-headed Vulture *(Trigonoceps occipitalis)*

Distinct among East Africa's vultures in having a pronounced white-pink head. A collar of dark brown-black feathers sits around the neck. The back, tail and wing coverts are brown-black, the secondaries are white and the primary wing feathers are black. The belly, thighs and undertail coverts are white. The bill is red towards the tip and pale blue at the base. The legs and feet are pink. The sexes are alike. Generally seen less often than other vulture species. Resident. Size: 80cm.

Hooded Vulture *(Necrosyrtes monachus)*

A widespread and common species in savannah and grassland areas. A small vulture with head and neck pinkish-red. The body plumage is almost entirely mid-brown with darker brown-black tail and wing feathers. A 'hood' of tight pale grey feathering covers the hind neck, nape and crown. The thin bill is light grey-pink at the base darkening towards the tip. The legs and feet are light grey-blue. The sexes are alike. Immature birds have the face and neck white and the 'hood' brown. Resident. Size: 70cm.

Egyptian Vulture *(Neophron percnopterus)*

A widespread but sparsely scattered species frequenting savannah and open plains. A small vulture with plumage almost entirely white, the exceptions being the black secondary and primary wing feathers. The unfeathered area of the face is bright yellow-orange. The feathering on the crown, nape and throat has a shaggy appearance. The legs and feet are pale yellow-pink. The dark brown bill is long and thin. The sexes are alike with the female slightly larger. Immature birds are generally browner and quite easily confused with the hooded vulture which has a rounded tail unlike the longer wedge-shaped tail of the Egyptian. Resident. Size: 68cm.

Palm Nut Vulture *(Gypohierax angolensis)*

A bird of coastal forests and savannah woodlands, feeding on oil palms and assorted fruits as well as fish and amphibians. Will feed on meat occasionally, comes regularly to the leopard bait put out at Samburu Lodge in northern Kenya. The head, neck, breast, belly and wing coverts are white. The scapulars and secondaries are black and the primary wing feathers white tipped with black. The tail is black and has a white tip. The orange-yellow eyes are surrounded by patches of bright orange-red unfeathered skin, a similar patch is present on the chin. The legs and feet are flesh pink. The sexes are alike. Resident. Size: 70cm.

African Marsh Harrier *(Circus ranivorus)*

Inhabits a wide range of habitats from open grasslands, lake edges, swamps and marshes to cultivated fields of wheat. The plumage is mainly dark brown streaked and blotched with rufous. The throat, breast and belly are white streaked with browns. The upper tail is brown banded with brown-black, lighter below barred with grey. The plumage variation is considerable. The eyes are yellow. The sexes are similar. They usually hunt by slowly flying at ten to fifty feet above the ground, from where they pursue small birds or pounce on small mammals, reptile, amphibians and insects. Resident. Size: 50cm.

Montagu's Harrier *(Circus pygargus)*

A palearctic winter visitor during which times they become the commonest harrier of open grassland areas. Feeding on small birds and mammals, reptiles, amphibians and large insects. The males have upperbody plumage of pale blue-grey. The throat and breast are grey and the undertail coverts white. The underwings and flanks are white, heavily barred with chestnut, the upperwing has a distinctive black wing bar along the secondaries, the primaries are black. The eyes, legs and feet are bright yellow. The female is dark brown on the upper wing surfaces, the under wings are buff streaked and barred with browns. The tail is dark brown heavily banded with blackish-brown. The rump is white. The throat, breast and belly are buff streaked and flecked with rufous. Winter visitor. Size: 45cm.

Pallid Harrier *(Circus macrourus)*

A palearctic winter visitor inhabiting open grasslands where they hunt small birds and mammals, grasshoppers, locusts and other large insects. At a distance the male may be confused with Montagu's Harrier (*Circus pygargus*) but is generally paler and lacks the black wing bar and the rufous barring on the flanks and underwings. The female is very similar to the female Montagu's Harrier but lacks the chestnut underwing barring, this is however very difficult to observe unless very close views are obtained. The eyes, legs and feet are yellow. Winter visitor. Size: 48cm.

African Harrier Hawk *(Polyboroides typus)*

An inhabitant of forests and woodlands. The face is unfeathered and bright yellow-pink. The head, neck, mantle and breast are slate blue-grey. The lower breast, flanks, thighs and underparts are white with heavy black barring. The wing coverts and scapulars are grey with black blotches. The primary wing feathers are black. The tail is long and broad, black with white bands across the centre, the base and the tip. The legs are yellow and very long aiding the bird to extract young from the nests of other birds, particularly tree hole and tunnel nesters. They also feed on fruits, small mammals, reptiles and insects. The sexes are similar, the female being larger and more heavily barred. Resident. Size: 68cm.

Bateleur
(Terathopius ecaudatus)

One of the easiest eagles to identify in flight, having an extremely short tail and long broad wings. The adult male (A) has the head, neck, breast and belly black. The back, tail and feathers of the mantle are chestnut, although a light phase does occur in which the mantle is grey-cream. The wing coverts are pale brown-white. The upper surface of the primary and secondary wing feathers are black, the underside white with black tips to the primaries. On the face there is a patch of bright red unfeathered skin at the base of the bill, the cere is bright red and the bill orange-red with a dark tip. The eyes are brown and the legs and feet red with dark talons. The female is slightly larger than the male and has secondary wing feathers grey-brown. In flight, only a narrow band of black is visible along the trailing edge of the wings, this is much broader in the male. Immature birds (B) are pale brown with variable amounts of streaking and flecking. The unfeathered facial patch and the cere are pale blue-green, the bill, legs and feet are pale grey. It takes up to seven years for immatures to attain full adult plumage. Resident. Size: 60cm.

Black-chested Snake Eagle
(Circaetus pectoralis)

Sparsely distributed over much of the region, favouring areas of lightly wooded savannah and thin woodlands. The head, neck, throat, breast and back are dark brown-black. The wings are dark brown with some feathers edged with pale buff-white. The belly and thighs are pure white. The eyes are a very bright yellow contrasting strongly with the dark plumage of the face and head. The bill is dull blue-grey and the legs and feet flesh pink-grey. The sexes are similar, the female being slightly larger than the male. There is much variation in the plumage of immature birds which are dark brown above and pale rufous brown below. They are often to be seen perched in the high branches of trees from where they scan the ground below for snakes, lizards and amphibians, occasionally also taking birds and small mammals. Resident. Size: 70cm.

Shikra
(Accipiter badius)

Found throughout lowland areas of East Africa in woodlands and lightly wooded savannahs with tall rank grass undergrowth. They feed on small birds and mammals, lizards, amphibians and insects. The adult male has the head, back, wings and tail plain slate grey. The face, throat, breast, belly and underparts are whitish with a flush of pink. The lower breast, belly, flanks and thighs are barred with rufous brown. The eyes are yellow-orange. The legs and feet are yellow-pink, the cere is yellow and the bill blue-grey. The female is larger than the male, darker grey above and with bolder barring below and on the flanks. Resident. Size: 30cm.

Little Sparrowhawk
(Accipiter minullus)

Found over much of the region but seldom seen as a result of spending much of their time in dense woodlands and thickets, where they hunt small birds and insects. The adult male has the head, neck, back and wings dark slate-grey. The upper tail is black with two ragged white stripes across the centre, below the tail is grey-white with bold banding. The breast, belly flanks and underparts are white barred with rufous brown. The throat and rump are pure white, the latter being very pronounced in flight. The eyes, cere, legs and feet are yellow. The bill is dark. The female is browner above and more heavily barred below. Immature birds are dark brown above, streaked with buff while the underside is white boldly marked with irregular blotches of dark brown. Resident. Size: 28cm.

Eastern Pale Chanting Goshawk *(Melierax poliopterus)*

A long-legged bird of prey with an upright posture. Found over much of the region where it favours areas of dry bush and sparse woodlands. Adult birds (B) have the head, neck, mantle, back and wing coverts pale slaty grey. The primary wing feathers are black edged with grey. The chin, throat and upper breast are pale grey. The lower breast, belly, thighs and flanks are white finely barred with dark grey. The rump is pure white and very prominent when seen in flight. The tail is white below while above the centre feathers are black with the outer feathers barred grey and white. The cere is orange-yellow and the tip of the bill is dark. The long legs and feet are red. The eyes are dark brown. The sexes are similar. Immature birds (A) are dull grey-brown on the head, nape, back and wing coverts. The primaries are black, the secondaries grey-brown edged with black. The belly, thighs and flanks are grey-white barred with brown. The throat and breast are grey-white heavily streaked with brown. The cere and bill are grey-blue. The eyes, legs and feet are pale yellow. Often seen in the early morning hunting from favoured perches. They feed on lizards, insects, small mammals and birds ranging from small passerines to francolins. They often spend time walking in areas of open ground in search of reptiles and insects. Resident. Size: 48cm.

Dark Chanting Goshawk *(Melierax metabates)*

Inhabits open acacia woodland and thorn bush country, usually in the west of the region. The head, neck, mantle, back and wing coverts are dark slate grey. The primary wing feathers are black edged with grey. The throat and upper breast are grey, the lower breast, belly, flanks and underparts are grey-white finely barred with dark grey. Very similar in posture and appearance to pale chanting goshawk but the upperparts are a darker grey, the rump is white barred with grey and the cere is bright red. Immature birds are dark brown above, paler brown-grey below with broad streaking on the breast. Usually feeds from elevated perches swooping on lizards, small snakes and rodents. They will also take insects and birds up to the size of guineafowl. Resident. Size: 48cm.

Gabar Goshawk *(Micronisus gabar)*

Widespread throughout East Africa in areas of woodland, particularly light thorn bush. Feeds on other bird species by pursuing them in flight and by robbing nests containing young chicks. They will also take insects and lizards. Adult birds have the head, neck, back, upper breast and wing coverts slate-grey. The rump is white, the tail grey-brown above, off-white below with four cross-bands of dark grey-black. The lower breast, belly, flanks, thighs and underwings are white barred with grey-brown. The cere is yellow and the bill dull blue-grey. The eyes are dark red, the legs and feet orange-red. A melanistic phase occurs in which the entire plumage on the upper body is black with the tail barred grey-brown and black. The sexes are similar, the female is larger than the male. Immature birds are brown above heavily streaked on the crown. The underside is white with the throat and upper breast heavily streaked with brown. The lower breast, belly and the thighs are barred with brown. The tail is banded grey and brown. The eyes, legs and feet are yellow. Resident. Size: 38cm.

Augur Buzzard *(Buteo augur)*

Well distributed over much of the region. Found on moorlands, in mountainous areas and hill country. The head, neck, mantle, back and wing coverts are black irregularly flecked with white. The throat, breast and underparts are white, the throat often spotted with black. The primary and secondary wing feathers are black barred with white. The tail is a bright chestnut offering an easy guide to identification, particularly in flight. The cere is yellow and the bill dark. The legs and feet are yellow with black talons. The sexes are similar. A melanistic phase occurs, the yellow legs contrasting strongly with the all black plumage, it does however retain the chestnut tail. They feed on a wide variety of birds, mammals, insects and reptile including many venomous snakes. They often perch along roadside verges where they scavenge on creatures killed by passing traffic. Resident. Size: 56cm.

Long-crested Eagle
(Lophaetus occipitalis)

A bird of forest edges and woodlands of all types throughout East Africa. Easily recognised by the long loosely feathered crest and dark brown-black plumage which covers the entire bird with the exception of whitish feathering on the thighs, on the underwing coverts and the wing edges at the shoulders. The tail is brown-black with three broad grey bands. The eyes are golden yellow, the cere, legs and feet are yellow. They feed mainly on rodents, lizards and large insects. The sexes are similar, the female being slightly larger than the male. Resident. Size: 55cm.

African Crowned Eagle
(Stephanoaetus coronatus)

The largest of Africa's eagles, frequenting areas of highland forest and woodlands throughout the region. The male has the forehead and crown dark brown with crest feathers tipped with black. The remainder of the head and neck is pale to mid-brown. The chin and throat are dark brown. The breast, belly, thighs, legs and underparts are buff-white heavily barred and blotched with dark brown and black. The back and wing coverts are charcoal grey/black, the primary and secondary flight feathers are brown, barred and tipped with black. The long tail is charcoal black broadly barred with grey. The eyes are yellow. The bill is blackish with the gape and cere yellow. The large powerful feet are dull yellow. The female is larger than the male, has a shorter crest, a longer tail and is usually more heavily barred on the underside. Immature birds have the head and underparts white, with a hint of brown on the breast and black spotting on the lower flanks, thighs and legs. Resident. Size: 92cm.

Martial Eagle
(Polemaetus bellicosus)

A very large eagle, widespread throughout East Africa frequenting riverine forests, dry bush and lightly wooded savannahs. The head, neck, back, wings and upper breast are dark brownish grey-black. The lower breast, belly, thighs and underparts are white conspicuously spotted dark brown-black. The tail is brown-black barred with grey-black. The eyes are bright golden yellow. The cere and feet dull yellow-green. The sexes are similar, the female being slightly larger and with bolder spotting on the breast. Immature birds are generally paler, have a white throat and lack the spotting on the underside. Resident. Size: 86cm.

Tawny Eagle
(Aquila rapax)

The commonest eagle of the region. The plumage is subject to tremendous variation and can be anything from light buff to dark brown. The primary wing feathers are usually dark brown. The eyes are pale tawny-yellow and the feet are yellow. The bill is grey tipped with black and the cere is yellow. The sexes are similar, the females being larger and often darker than the males. Resident. Size: 75cm.

Verreaux's Eagle
(Aquila verreauxii)

Found in small numbers throughout the region in the vicinity of rocky outcrops and inland cliffs. The only eagle in the region almost entirely black both above and below. A white 'V' shaped line extends from shoulder to shoulder across the upper back and the base of the primary wing feathers on the underside are greyish. The eyes are dark brown with a yellow eyebrow. The cere and feet are yellow. The sexes are similar. They feed almost exclusively on rock hyrax in areas where hyrax densities are high, but will also take dik dik and young klipspringer as well as the occasional bird. Resident. Size: 80cm.

Wahlberg's Eagle
(Aquila wahlbergi)

A small, slender eagle of woodlands, riverine forests, wooded savannahs and bush over much of the region. A bird of uniform brown plumage with a variable amount of streaking and flecking. Usually paler on the head, wing coverts and underparts. The long tail is dark brown with sporadic banding. The eyes are mid brown, the cere and feet are pale yellow-grey. The sexes are similar, the female being slightly larger than the male. At a distance it could well be mistaken for a tawny eagle, but the narrow wings, long tail and smaller size aid identification. Feeds on a variety of birds, mammals, reptiles and amphibians. Resident. Size: 56cm.

African Fish Eagle
(Haliaeetus vocifer)

Widely distributed in the vicinity of both alkaline and freshwater lakes, swamps, marshes and rivers. Adult birds (A) are unmistakeable having pure white head, neck, mantle and breast contrasting with rufous brown underparts and dark brown back and wings. The primary wing feathers are blackish. The tail is pure white. A patch of unfeathered skin in front of the eye along with the cere is bright yellow. The bill is grey-blue tipped with black. The eyes are dark brown and the legs and feet are yellow. The female is larger than the male. Immature birds have the crown and upperparts brown, cheeks and neck white, breast and underparts buff to brown heavily streaked with black. The tail is off-white with a brown terminal band. The immature (B) plumage stages are subject to extreme variation. The cere, legs and feet lack the intense colour of the adults, being dull grey-yellow. Feeds mainly on fish but will also take some waterbirds including flamingos. Resident. Size: 75cm.

Black Kite
(Milvus migrans)

A very widely distributed species throughout East Africa, found in a wide variety of habitats from woodlands to open plains as well as towns and cities where they scavenge on human refuse. The head, neck, mantle, back, wing coverts, and underparts are mid-brown streaked and flecked with dark brown. The tail is dark brown at the base and paler towards the deeply forked tip. The underside of the wings are rufous brown streaked and flecked with dark browns. The eyes are dark brown, the cere and gape, like the legs and feet are bright yellow. The bill is yellow darkening towards the tip. The sexes are similar, the female being slightly larger than the male. Immature birds are generally paler above, browner below with white streaking and flecking. Resident. Size: 58cm.

Black-shouldered Kite
(Elanus caeruleus)

A small grey kite common over the whole region, ranging over a variety of habitats including open plains, woodlands, forests and farmland. The head, face, neck, breast, belly and underparts are white, the head, nape and breast having a blue-grey wash. The back and upper wing coverts are slate blue-grey. The median wing coverts are black and very prominent in flight. The primary and secondary wing feathers are blackish. The underwing coverts are white. The tail is white with some grey on the central feathers. The eyes are a piercing bright red contrasting strongly with the white face and dark eyebrow. The cere, legs and feet are bright yellow. The sexes are similar. They hunt from perches and by hovering, dropping onto prey which consists almost entirely of rodents. Resident. Size: 33cm.

Osprey
(Pandion haliaetus)

A winter visitor to much of the region, frequenting large lakes, rivers and estuaries. The crown and nape are white streaked with brown. A dark brown eye stripe extends from the eye down the sides of the neck to the mantle. The mantle, back and upper wing surfaces are dark brown. The throat and breast are white, the latter flecked with a variable amount of brown. The belly, thighs and underparts are white. The underwings are white with brown flecking. The upper tail is dark brown the underside is whitish with dark barring. The eyes are pale golden yellow. The cere, legs and feet are pale slate grey. The sexes are similar. Feeds entirely on fish which are plucked from close to the surface of the water but on occasions will splash dive feet first, snatching fish from up to a metre below the surface. Winter visitor. Size: 58cm.

Pygmy Falcon
(Polihierax semitorquatus)

A very small falcon of dry thorn bush regions. Can be easily overlooked, resembling a shrike from a distance. The crown, back and wing coverts are grey-blue. The rump, face and underparts are white. The primary wing feathers and the tail are black, the latter with grey banding. The eyes are dark brown. The cere is red and the bill pale blue-grey at the base darkening towards the tip. The legs and feet are orange-red. The sexes differ in plumage, the mantle and back of the male being grey-blue while in the female they are rich chestnut brown. They feed mainly on large insects, small birds, rodents and lizards. Resident. Size: 20cm.

Lanner Falcon
(Falco biarmicus)

Found in a wide range of habitats from dry semi-deserts to woodland and forest edges and open country. The crown is rufous brown, the cheeks and throat white. A black moustachial stripe is present, as is a black stripe from the eye to the lower nape. The upperparts are grey-brown with darker barring and streaking. The primary and secondary wing feathers are dark brown. The breast and underparts are white washed with pink, some brown blotching is visible on the flanks and thighs. The tail is brown with grey banding. The dark brown eyes have a yellow orbital ring. The cere, legs and feet are yellow. The female is larger than the male and has more pronounced blotching and barring on the underside. Resident. Size: 46cm.

Peregrine Falcon
(Falco peregrinus)

A strong powerfully built falcon. The crown, nape, cheeks and moustachial stripes are blackish, the back is blue-grey. The chin, throat, breast and underparts are white washed with buff and boldly spotted and barred with black. The eyes are dark brown, the cere, legs and feet are yellow. The female is larger than the male, browner above and with heavier spotting and barring on the underside. Occurs in a variety of habitats from bush country to lakes and farmland. Resident and palearctic winter visitor. Size: 46cm.

Grey Kestrel
(Falco ardosiacus)

Often found in lightly wooded areas, along side watercourses and marshes, perched in a tree from where they hunt mainly lizards, small rodents and some birds. The plumage is almost entirely soft slate grey. The primary wing feathers are blackish. The cere, the orbital ring and the legs and feet are bright yellow. The eyes are dark brown. The sexes are similar, the female being slightly larger than the male. Resident. Size: 36cm.

Common Kestrel
(Falco tinnunculus)

Found over much of the region in a variety of habitats with light woodlands, as well as towns and cities. The male has the crown, nape, moustachial stripe and tail slate blue-grey. The mantle, back and wing coverts are pale chestnut spotted with black, the primary wing feathers are blackish-grey. The throat and belly are white-buff, the breast and flanks are buff heavily streaked and spotted with dark brown. The eyes are dark brown. The orbital ring, cere, legs and feet are yellow. The female, who is larger than the male, has the crown and nape light chestnut streaked with black and the tail pale chestnut banded with black. Resident and palearctic winter visitor. Size: 35cm.

Lesser Kestrel
(Falco naumanni)

A very abundant palearctic winter visitor throughout the region. Often encountered in sizeable flocks, the male has the head, nape and the tail light blue-grey, the end of the tail is black with a fine white tip. The mantle, back and wing coverts are plain light chestnut. The primary wing feathers are blackish. The chin, throat, breast, flanks and underparts are creamy-white with loose black spotting on the breast and flanks. The eyes are dark brown. The orbital ring, cere, legs and feet are yellow. The female has the crown and nape pale chestnut streaked with black. The tail is pale chestnut with numerous black bands. The chestnut back and wing coverts are streaked and flecked with dark brown. Palearctic winter visitor. Size: 30cm.

Greater Kestrel
(Falco rupicoloides)

Distribution restricted to western Kenya, northern Tanzania and eastern Uganda. Can be easily mistaken for a female kestrel (*Falcon tinnunculus*) but has plumage more straw colour than chestnut, blackish barring on the rump, tail, mantle and flanks and eyes of creamy-white. The sexes are alike. Immatures have barred rump and a rufous not grey tail, dark brown eyes, and cere and orbital ring blue-green. Resident. Size: 36cm.

Coqui Francolin

(Francolinus coqui)

Found in Tanzania, central Kenya and southern Uganda, an inhabitant of open grasslands and lightly wooded savannahs. The male has the crown and nape rich rufous brown blotched with grey-black. The face and neck are ochre yellow, the mantle and breast are white with distinctive black barring. The back and wings are a mosaic of chestnut, grey, black and buff-white. The underparts are white with black barring. The eyes are dark brown, the legs and feet are yellow. The female has thin black stripes above and below the eye and from the corners of the gape in a downward loop across the throat. The breast is light ochre and lacks any barring. Immature birds are similar to adult females but are paler and have more rufous and buff-brown feathering. Usually encountered in pairs or small parties searching areas of short grass for seeds, beetles, ants and other small invertebrates. Resident. Size: 25cm.

Crested Francolin

(Francolinus sephaena)

An inhabitant of thick bush and woodlands with sparse ground cover, usually in the vicinity of water. The crown is dark brown-black, the eye and moustachial stripes are black. The neck is white-buff heavily blotched with dark brown. The back and wing feathers are brown-grey edged with buff-white. The tail is black with much brown and grey flecking. The breast, belly and underparts are buff-rufous brown streaked with white. The eyes are dark brown and the legs and feet are pink-red. The bill is black. The sexes are similar, the female having more cryptic plumage and being slightly smaller. Immatures are like females but usually paler. They are usually encountered in pairs or small parties scratching around in the leaf litter for insects and larvae, seeds, berries and other plant material. They soon become very tolerant of man, if left unmolested, and often scavenge around bush camps. Resident. Size: 27cm.

Jackson's Francolin

(Francolinus jacksoni)

An endemic resident of the mountain forests of Kenya between 2,200 and 3,700m where they are quite abundant. A large francolin with a grey-brown head. The breast and belly feathers are rich chestnut edged with off-white. The mantle is grey-brown, the wing coverts and primary feathers are rufous brown. The tail is chestnut. The eyes are dark brown, the bill rich red and the legs and feet are bright red, the backs of the legs are darker. The sexes are similar, the female being slightly smaller than the male. Immature birds are generally darker in appearance and have dark brown barring on the wings and tail. In some areas within the Aberdare's National Park they have become very tame and often frequent picnic sites and lodge grounds on the look out for food scraps. Resident. Size: 38cm.

Red-necked Spurfowl

(Francolinus afer)

A bird of wooded grasslands, having a distinctive bright red throat patch. The crown is dark grey-brown, the neck, breast and belly are grey-brown heavily and boldly blotched with black. The mantle and wings are olive brown streaked with black. The tail is brown with fine black barring. The eyes are dark brown surrounded by bright red areas of bare skin. The bill, legs and feet are bright red. The sexes are similar, the female being slightly smaller than the male. Immature birds have dull brown plumage, brown bill and the wing feathers streaked and barred with grey. They roost in trees, descending to the ground at dawn to forage for food among the leaf litter, taking mainly grass shoots, seeds, roots, berries and a variety of insects and larvae. Often located as a result of hearing the loud raucous call. Resident. Size: 36cm.

Hildebrandt's Francolin

(Francolinus hildebrandti)

A francolin of dense thickets, scrub and grassy areas on rocky hillsides. The male has the forehead dark brown flecked with white, while the crown is uniform buff-brown. There is a rufous flush to the ear coverts, while the sides of the head, neck and throat are white streaked with dark brown. The feathers of the back are grey-brown with creamy-buff edging, the tail is plain grey-brown. The chin and throat are white with fine black mottling. The remainder of the underparts are white more heavily streaked with black, particularly on the breast. The undertail coverts are barred with buff. The bill is black with some red at the base, the eyes are dark brown and the legs and feet are dull red. The female has upperparts rufous-buff with faint barring, while the sides of the head and throat are buff. The underparts are buff with some pale edging to the feathers. Resident. Size: 35cm.

Grey-breasted Spurfowl *(Francolinus rufopictus)*

Restricted in distribution to north-west Tanzania where they inhabit woodlands and thickets along river edges, venturing into surrounding grasslands only in the early morning and late afternoon. The crown and nape are dark brown-black with some light flecking, the neck is blackish with streaks of grey. The back and wing coverts are chestnut with grey and black streaking. The primary and secondary wing feathers are grey-brown with buff edging. The tail is grey with black barring and flecking. The breast is grey with black streaking, the belly and underparts are light grey streaked with black and buff. The eyes are dark brown surrounded by an area of bright orange-pink unfeathered skin. The moustachial stripes and eyebrows are white. The bill and throat patch are orange. The legs and feet are dark, almost black. At a distance they may be confused with Red-necked Spurfowl but the throat patch of orange and legs of black ease identification. The sexes are similar, the females being slightly smaller. They can be found singly, in pairs or in small parties foraging among grass and leaf litter for seeds and insects. Resident. Size: 38cm.

Yellow-necked Spurfowl *(Francolinus leucoscepus)*

A very common species throughout much of the region, an inhabitant of open country, dry bush and woodland and forest edges. The crown and nape are brown-black with some fine flecking. The hind neck is brown-black with bold white streaks. The throat patch of bare unfeathered skin is bright pale yellow. The upperparts, breast and belly are dark brown heavily blotched and streaked with chestnut and buff-white. The primary and secondary wing feathers are grey-brown with fine black speckling, in flight a pale patch on the wings is conspicuous. The tail is brown with fine grey flecking. The eyes are dark brown surrounded by patches of pink-red unfeathered skin. The bill is blue-grey to black and the legs and feet brownish-black. The sexes are similar, the female being slightly smaller than the male. They roost off the ground in trees and bushes descending at daybreak to forage singly, in pairs or small parties for seeds and insects. Resident. Size: 36cm.

Helmeted Guineafowl *(Numida meleagris)*

Common throughout the region in open grasslands with scattered bush, along woodland edges and on cultivated farmland. The head and neck are unfeathered and boldly marked with bright red on the forehead, around the base of the bill and on the lower cheeks. The sides of the face and neck are bright powder blue. On the crown is a reddish-orange casque of variable size. The hind neck has a line of short, spiky black feathers and the throat and fore neck are black. The plumage of both upper and underparts is dark brown-black with white spots, the spots being smaller and more concentrated on the lower neck, breast and back becoming larger towards the rear. The primary and secondary wing feathers are dark brown-black with white bars rather than spots. The eyes are dark brown. The bill is dull yellow-orange, the legs and feet brownish black. The sexes are similar, the female being slightly smaller than the male. They roost above the ground in trees and spend the daytime foraging in large flocks feeding on seeds, roots and a variety of insects including grasshoppers and termites. Resident. Size: 56cm.

Vulturine Guineafowl *(Acryllium vulturinum)*

The most handsome of East Africa's guineafowl species found in arid areas of Kenya, Somalia, south-eastern Ethiopia and north-west Tanzania. The head and neck are blue-grey and unfeathered with the exception of a collar of dull chestnut feathers around the nape. The breast and mantle feathers are long and loose, striped black, white and rich cobalt blue. The back and wings are black evenly spotted with white. The primary wing feathers are brown-black edged with white and the secondaries are brown-black edged with violet. The black and white spotted tail is long, with the central feathers often trailing along the ground. The eyes are bright red, the bill pale grey and the legs and feet grey-black. The sexes are alike. They feed usually in large flocks on seeds, berries, fruits and a variety of insects. Resident. Size: 60cm.

Grey-crowned Crane *(Balearica regulorum)*

A large long legged bird of open grasslands, lakes, swamps and farmland. The forehead and fore-crown are black, the hind-crown and nape have a stiff crest of golden yellow feathers. The neck is light grey with loose feathers at the base trailing onto the breast and mantle. The upperparts are black. The wing coverts are buff-white to golden yellow, the secondary wing feathers are black and chestnut, and the primaries are glossy black. The breast is grey-black with long, loose feathering on the upper portion, the belly and underparts are dark grey-black. The cheeks are white with a red flash extending along the sides of the hind-crown. The throat has a bright red wattle. The eyes are pale blue and the bill, legs and feet are black. The sexes are similar, the crest being less developed in the female. Resident. Size: 102cm.

Black Crake *(Amaurornis flavirostris)*

A shy but common species throughout the region, frequenting areas of dense reed and vegetation in swamps, marshes and around the margins of lakes and ponds. The plumage is entirely blue-black, with the eyes and orbital ring bright red. The bill is yellow and the legs, feet and long toes are bright pinkish-red. The sexes are alike. Immature birds have a plumage of olive brown, the bill is dull yellow-green, the eyes are orange-red and the legs and feet dull blood red. Often seen foraging around the waters edge taking insects from the water surface as well as preying on snails, small fish and amphibians. Resident. Size: 20cm.

Common Moorhen *(Gallinula chloropus)*

Common throughout much of the region, inhabiting freshwater lakes, swamps, marshes, streams and rivers. The head and neck are blue-black becoming slaty blue on the mantle, breast and belly. A conspicuous white streak is visible along the flanks. The wing coverts and flight feathers show variable amounts of brown-black. The tail is black with undertail coverts a prominent white particularly when the tail is flicked upwards in alarm. The bill is bright red at the base and has a bright yellow tip. An unfeathered shield extends from the base of the bill upwards over the forehead and onto the fore-crown. The legs and feet are yellowish-green with an orange-red band on the upper leg. The eyes are red to dark brown. The sexes are alike, the shield being less well developed in the female. Resident. Size: 33cm.

Purple Swamphen *(Porphyrio porphyrio)*

Found over much of East Africa in swamps, marshes and reedbeds. The head, neck and mantle are purple-blue. The plumage of both upper and underparts is iridescent purple with a wash of green on the back. The face and throat have a wash of light blue. The rump and tail are bronze-blue, the under tail coverts are white. The primary and secondary wing feathers are blackish-purple. The bill and frontal head shield are rich red, the eyes are deep blood red and the legs, feet and long toes are pinkish-red. The sexes are alike. Resident. Size: 46cm.

Red-knobbed Coot *(Fulica cristata)*

An inhabitant of open freshwater lakes, ponds and flood plains, often forming into large flotillas. The entire plumage is black with washes of brown on the rump and tail and with some grey on the underside. The bill and frontal shield is white often having a faint blue wash. At the apex of the shield are found two circular red knobs, these knobs become greatly reduced in size during periods of non-breeding. The eyes are dark rich red, the legs and feet darkish grey. The sexes are alike. Immature birds are dark brown above and pale grey below, with a variable amount of white on the throat and neck. They feed mainly on aquatic plant material as well as grasses, seeds, snails and insects. Resident. Size: 40cm.

Kori Bustard

(Ardeotis kori)

The largest of East Africa's bustards found in areas of open savannah, lightly wooded grasslands and dry bush country. The crown is black with a short crest extending from the rear. The face and neck are mid-grey finely barred with black, the mantle is black. The back and flight feathers are grey-brown finely marked with light and dark grey. The breast, belly and underparts are white. The wing coverts are white, often with a tinge of buff, broadly marked with black. The eyes are brown, the bill is grey with a wash of yellow, and the legs and feet are light grey. The sexes are similar, the female being smaller than the male. Usually encountered singly or in pairs walking in grassland areas feeding on disturbed insects, reptiles and small rodents. During courtship the male displays, to attract a female, by fanning and lifting the tail, dropping the wing tips to the ground and inflating the neck into a large whitish ball. Resident. Size: 100cm.

Crested Bustard

(Eupodotis ruficrista)

A small bustard of dry thorn bush, lightly wooded areas and open arid plains. The crown is buff-grey forming an erect crest during courtship and often when alarmed. The face and upper neck are soft orange-brown, the lower neck greyish becoming white on the upper breast. A black line extends from the chin down the centre of the throat and neck to the black breast, belly and underparts. The feathers of the back and wings have a mottled appearance of buff, black and grey. The tail is greyish brown, the eyes are pale yellow, the bill dark grey and the legs and feet pale yellow-grey. The female differs from the male in being paler and having the crown brown and in lacking the black chin to breast stripe. Resident. Size: 52cm.

White-bellied Bustard

(Eupodotis senegalensis)

A bird of open grasslands, arid bush and lightly wooded savannahs. The male has a black forehead and crown becoming blue-grey towards the rear. The face is white with black stripes extending from the base of the upper mandible across the upper cheek to a point below the eye and from the chin around the upper throat onto the sides of the blue-grey neck. The underparts are rufous-buff streaked and finely barred with dark brown. The breast is grey and the belly and underparts are white. The eyes are brown, the bill pink to yellow and the legs and feet pale yellow. The female is smaller than the male and lacks the dark crown, the black facial stripes and the blue-grey neck. Resident. Size: 60cm.

Black-bellied Bustard

(Eupodotis melanogaster)

An inhabitant of open areas of tall grassland and sparsely wooded savannahs. The forehead and crown are black flecked with tawny-buff. The face is grey with a black stripe extending from the eye to the nape. The neck is grey to tawny-buff, a broad black stripe edged with white, runs from the chin down the centre of the throat and neck to the black breast and underparts. The back and wings are tawny-buff heavily blotched and streaked with brown-black. The tail is buff-brown with dark brown bands. The eyes are brown, the bill, legs and feet dull yellow. The female differs from the male in having the chin white, the throat buff and underparts of grey-white. Resident. Size: 60cm.

Hartlaub's Bustard

(Eupodotis hartlaubii)

This species can easily be confused with the Black-bellied Bustard having similar plumage and occurring in the same types of habitat, although Hartlaub's often favours drier regions. The plumage is generally greyer than that of the Black-bellied and the rump and tail are black. A broad, well defined, black band extends from the chin to the breast and from the eye to the nape. The jet-black plumage of the breast and underparts arcs around the wings onto the shoulders. The female has all white breast and underparts, the fore neck, throat and chin are white and she lacks the head markings of the male. Found singly or in small groups and feeds on a wide variety of insects and vegetation. Resident. Size: 60cm.

African Jacana
(Actophilornis africanus)

Common throughout the region, frequenting areas of open water with an abundance of aquatic vegetation. The crown, nape and hind neck are black. A pale blue area of bare skin forms a frontal shield on the forehead. The chin, cheeks, throat and fore neck are white. The remaining plumage of both upper and underparts is chestnut brown. The eyes are dark brown, the bill is blue-grey and the legs and feet dull grey-brown. The toes are extremely long, spreading the birds weight as it walks on floating vegetation in search of insect food. The sexes are similar, the female being larger than the male. Resident. Size: 28cm.

Spotted Thick Knee
(Burhinus capensis)

Widespread throughout East Africa in savannah and grassland areas with bush and light tree cover, often around kopjes in the Serengeti and on arid stony hill sides. The plumage is pale buff to tawny brown heavily blotched and streaked with dark brown-black. The eyebrows, underparts and thighs are white. The bill is yellow at the base, tipped with black. The legs and feet are bright yellow. The large yellow eyes are very prominent. The sexes are alike. They are mainly active at night, being found during the daytime, usually in pairs or small flock, in communal roosts around scattered bushes. Resident. Size: 42cm.

Water Thick Knee
(Burhinus vermiculatus)

An inhabitant of lake side margins, riverbanks, estuaries and beaches. The crown, hind neck, mantle, back and wings coverts are grey-brown flecked and streaked with dark brown-black. The lower wing coverts are black at the base forming a distinct wing bar. The primary wing feathers are black. The eyebrows and cheeks are white as is the chin. The throat and breast are buff-white streaked with dark brown. The belly and underparts are white. The large prominent eyes are pale yellow. The bill is black with a yellowish tinge at the base, the legs and feet are pale yellow-green. The sexes are alike. Active mainly at night when they feed on molluscs and insects. Resident. Size: 36cm.

Long-toed Plover
(Vanellus crassirostris)

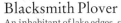

Found around lakes and ponds with floating aquatic vegetation. The forehead, fore-crown, face, chin and throat are white contrasting strongly with the black hind-crown, nape, hind neck, mantle and breast. The belly and underparts are white. The upperparts are grey-brown, the upper wing coverts are white being very conspicuous in flight. The tail is black with a white band at the base. The eyes are red with a crimson orbital ring. The bill is pinkish-red at the base, tipped with black. The legs, feet and long toes are dull red. The sexes are alike. Resident. Size: 30cm.

Blacksmith Plover
(Vanellus armatus)

An inhabitant of lake edges, swamps, marshes and riverbanks. The forehead and crown are white. The hind-crown, nape, face, chin, neck and breast are black. The hind neck, belly and underparts are white. The back and outer scapulars are black, the inner scapulars and wing coverts are silver-grey. The primary and secondary wing feathers are black, the rump and tail are white the latter having a terminal band of black. The eyes are a rich dark red, the bill, legs and feet are black. The sexes are alike. Resident. Size: 28cm.

Spur-winged Plover
(Vanellus spinosus)

A common and widespread species particularly in Uganda, Ethiopia, Somalia and Kenya inhabiting open bare ground around lakes, along riverbanks, on estuaries, beaches and soda flats. The upper portion of the head from a point below the eye is black. The lower portion of the head and the sides and back of the neck are white. The chin, throat, breast and upper belly are black, the remaining underparts are white. The mantle, back and wing coverts are greyish-brown, the primary wing feathers are black. The eyes are dark red, the bill, legs and feet are black. The sexes are alike. Resident. Size: 27cm.

Black-headed Plover
(Vanellus tectus)

A bird of open arid grasslands and bare ground near lakes, ponds and rivers. The forehead and chin are white. The crown is black and has a short crest. A thick band of white extends from behind the eye widening to cover the nape. A black collar extends from the hind neck to the upper throat, broadening to the base of the eye, from the throat it runs down the centre of the neck and breast. The sides of the breast, and the underparts are white. The upperparts and wing coverts are grey-brown. The primary and secondary wing feathers are black. The tail is white with a terminal black band. The eyes are bright yellow, the bill dull red with a black tip and legs and feet red. The sexes are alike. Resident. Size: 25cm.

Senegal Plover
(Vanellus lugubris)

A long legged, slender plover of open savannahs and burnt grassland areas. The forehead is white with the remainder of the head being brownish-grey. The chin is white, the neck and throat are light grey. The upperparts and wing coverts are brownish-grey, the secondary wing feathers are white and the primaries black. The tail is white tipped with black. The upper breast is grey, darkening to form a black band above the white belly and underparts. The eyes are golden yellow, the bill, legs and feet are black. The sexes are alike. Resident. Size: 25cm.

Black-winged Plover
(Vanellus melanopterus)

A species of restricted distribution, usually found on grasslands and on mountain slopes above 2,100m. The forehead, fore-crown and chin are white. The hind-crown and nape are grey-blue, the neck light grey becoming lighter in the region of the throat. Across the upper breast is a broad black band. The lower breast, and underparts are white. The upperparts including the scapulars are greyish-brown, the greater wing coverts are white. The secondary wing feathers are white at the base and black at the tips, the primaries are all black. The tail is white with a black band towards the tip. The eyes are yellow contrasting with a red orbital ring. The bill is dark grey-blue and the legs and feet are dull red. The female is browner than the male and has a smaller, less distinct, white forehead patch. Resident. Size: 28cm.

Crowned Plover
(Vanellus coronatus)

A common plover in areas of short grass savannahs and open plains. The forehead is black from which a stripe extends around the base of the head to the nape. Above this, around the base of the black crown, runs a white band. The chin is white and the cheeks, neck, upper breast and mantle are grey-brown becoming lighter on the throat and fore neck. The upperparts and wing coverts are a slightly darker grey-brown and the primary and secondary wing feathers are white at the base and black at the tips. The tail is white with a black band towards the base. The breast is grey-brown darkening to form a narrow black band on the lower breast. The belly and underparts are white. The eyes are bright yellow, the bill is pinkish-red at the base and black towards the tip. The legs and feet are bright red. The sexes are alike. Resident. Size: 28cm.

African Wattled Plover
(Vanellus senegallus)

Found on the open plains usually in the vicinity of water. A long legged, upright plover with a white forehead. The crown and hind neck are dark olive-brown finely speckled with brown-black. The cheeks, throat and fore neck are whitish heavily streaked with dark brown. The back and wing coverts are olive-brown and the tail is white. The chin and upper throat is black, the breast is buff and the underparts are white. The primary wing feathers are black. The eyes are pale yellow with a bright yellow orbital ring. At the base of the bill forward of the eyes are situated bright red and yellow wattles. The legs and feet are golden yellow. The sexes are alike. Resident. Size: 33cm.

Kittlitz's Plover
(Charadrius pecuarius)

A very small plover, well distributed throughout the region. Found on bare areas of ground around lakes and along river banks and tidal mudflats. The forehead is black, the fore-crown is black the hind-crown brown flecked with buff. A white band extends from above the eye to the nape and a black band extends from the base of the bill, through the eye to the mantle. The feathers of the upperparts and wing coverts are greyish-brown edged with buff. The lower cheeks, chin and throat are white. The breast is buff-yellow and the underparts are white. The eyes are dark brown, the bill, legs and feet are black. The sexes are similar. Resident. Size: 14cm.

Ringed Plover
(Charadrius hiaticula)

A winter visitor to coastal regions, inland lakes and riverbanks. The forehead is white, the fore-crown is black with the top and hind-crown olive brown. A black band extends from the base of the bill, through the eye, linking with the black fore-crown, then on across the cheeks to the sides of the nape. A white collar runs from the mantle around and across the upper breast. The lower breast and underparts are white. The back and wing coverts are olive-brown, the primary wing feathers are brown-black. Contrasting black and white plumage of the head and neck is much reduced during the non-breeding winter months. The eyes are dark brown with a yellow-orange orbital ring. The bill is red tipped with black (blackish during winter). The legs and feet are orange-red. Sexes are similar. Resident. Size: 19cm.

Little-ringed Plover
(Charadrius dubius)

A palearctic winter visitor to the margins of freshwater lakes, rivers and less commonly coastal regions. The forehead is white. The fore-crown, the sides of the face and head to the sides of the nape, are black. The remainder of the crown is brown. A broad black band extends from the mantle around and across the upper breast. The lower breast and underparts are white. The back and wing coverts are brown, the primaries are blackish. The eyes are brown with a bright yellow orbital ring. The bill is black and the legs and feet are yellow. The sexes are similar. Palearctic winter visitor. Size: 15cm.

Three-banded Plover
(Charadrius tricollaris)

A small plover encountered around the shores of lakes and ponds, on riverbanks and sand bars. Uncommon in coastal areas. The forehead is white, the crown and nape dark brown. A white stripe extends from above the eye around the crown to the nape. The chin, throat and face are greyish. Two black bands extend across the upper and lower breast separated by a band of white. The underparts are white. The back and wings are olive brown. The eyes are honey yellow with a bright red orbital ring. The bill is red at the base and black at the tip. The legs and feet are dull blood red. The sexes are alike. Resident. Size: 18cm.

Chestnut-banded Plover
(Charadrius pallidus)

Found only on Lake Magadi in Kenya and the alkaline lakes of northern Tanzania. The forehead and narrow eyebrows are white. The crown is dark chestnut-black at the fore and greyish brown elsewhere. A thin black stripe extends from the base of the bill to the eye. The cheeks, chin and throat are white with a wash of pale chestnut on the upper cheeks. The underparts are white with the exception of a broad chestnut band which extends across the upper breast. The mantle, back and wing coverts are greyish-brown. The primary wing feathers are brown-black. The eyes are dark brown, the bill is black and the legs and feet greenish-grey. The sexes are similar. Resident. Size: 15cm.

Caspian Plover
(Charadrius asiaticus)

A winter visitor from Asia, often found in flocks on short grasslands. In non-breeding plumage the forehead, chin, throat, sides of neck and eye stripe are buff-white. The crown is greyish brown. The hind neck, the sides of the lower neck and breast are buff flecked with grey-brown. The feathers of the mantle, back and wing coverts are tawny-brown edged with buff. The primary wing feathers are brown-black. Some birds may arrive for the winter and depart for the breeding grounds in spring having attained breeding plumage, when the face and fore neck are white and a rich chestnut breast band develops. The sexes are similar, the plumage of the female being generally duller. Palearctic winter visitor. Size: 20cm.

Pied Avocet
(Recurvirostra avosetta)

A bird of both freshwater and alkaline lakes, mudflats, flood plains and estuaries. The head and hind neck are black. The chin, cheeks, throat, fore neck, breast and underparts are white. The back, rump, tail and secondary wing feathers are white, the wing coverts and primaries black. The thin upturned bill which is specially adapted for feeding is black. The legs and feet are pale blue. The sexes are similar, the female occasionally having areas of black plumage tinged brown. A resident and palearctic winter visitor. Size: 43cm.

Black-winged Stilt
(Himantopus himantopus)

A widely distributed species, found in shallow waters, both freshwater and alkaline, marshes, estuaries and coastal mudflats. The head, neck, breast, underparts and tail are white, in non-breeding plumage the head and neck show a variable amount of dark grey-black. The wings are black. The eyes are deep red. The long thin bill is black. The bright pink-red legs are extremely long, extending beyond the tail in flight. The sexes are similar, the female usually showing a hint of brown on the mantle and scapulars. Resident and palearctic winter visitor. Size: 38cm.

Crab Plover
(Dromas ardeola)

A visitor to the coastal areas of Kenya and Tanzania from September to March. The head, neck, breast, underparts, back and scapulars are white, during non-breeding periods the crown, nape and hind neck are flecked and streaked with grey. The mantle and primary and secondary flight feathers are brown-black. The eyes are dark brown and the broad heavy bill is black. The legs and feet are pale blue-grey. The sexes are alike. Winter visitor. Size: 35cm.

Greater Painted Snipe
(Rostratula benghalensis)

A bird of lakes, marshes and swamps with dense banks of vegetation. In this species the female has the bright colourful plumage. The forehead and crown are dark brown with a buff central stripe extending to the nape. Patches of white, which extend towards the nape, surround the eyes. The chin, throat and upper neck are rich dark chestnut, the lower neck and upper breast are dark chestnut graduating to black on the lower breast. The underparts and sides of the breast around the wings are white. The wings and upperparts are dark green-bronze blotched and barred with black. The eyes are dark brown, the long slightly decurved bill is reddish brown and the legs and feet are greenish-yellow. The male lacks the rich plumage coloration of the female, having head and neck grey-buff streaked with brown, the breast is barred with brown and the wings are heavily blotched and barred with buffs and browns. Resident. Size: 27cm.

African Snipe
(Gallinago nigripennis)

A bird of swamps and flooded areas usually at altitudes in excess of 1,500m. The head is buff with a series of dark brown stripes extending from bill to hind neck, these stripes run along the sides of the crown, through the eyes and across the cheeks. The hind neck, throat and breast are buff heavily streaked with dark brown. The belly, flanks and underparts are white, the flanks being conspicuously barred with dark brown. The back is blackish-brown with buff flecking, the wing coverts and flight feathers are dark brown-black edged and barred with white and buff. The eyes are dark brown. The long straight bill is pinkish-brown and the legs and feet are brownish-green. Mainly nocturnal but also active at dawn and dusk feeding in areas of mud and shallow water. The sexes are alike. Resident. Size: 28cm.

Curlew Sandpiper
(Calidris ferruginea)

An abundant palearctic winter visitor particularly to coastal estuaries and mudflats but also found around the muddy edges of inland lakes both freshwater and alkaline. The forehead, crown and hind neck are grey-brown. The eyebrows, cheeks, throat, neck and underparts are white-buff. During the breeding season the face, breast and some wing coverts are rich chestnut, a hint of which may show in non-breeding and transitional plumages. The mantle and wing coverts are grey-brown edged with buff-white. The primary and secondary wing feathers are blackish-brown edged with white. The eyes are dark brown, the long slightly decurved bill is black as are the legs and feet. The sexes are similar. Winter visitor. Size: 19cm.

Little Stint
(Calidris minuta)

A small but common palearctic winter visitor to coastal mudflats, estuaries and muddy margins of inland waters. The forehead is white, the crown, hind neck and ear coverts are grey-brown. A white stripe follows the line of the eyebrow. The front and sides of the neck, breast, belly and underparts are white with some fine grey flecking on the breast. The feathers of the upperparts are grey-brown edged with white. The primary and secondary wing feathers are brownish-black edged with white. The eyes are dark brown and the bill, legs and feet are black. The sexes are alike. Palearctic winter visitor. Size: 13cm.

Sanderling
(Calidris alba)

A palearctic winter visitor to coastal beaches and occasionally to mudflats and inland waters. The forehead is white and the crown, hind neck and mantle are grey with streaks of brown. The cheeks. neck, centre of the breast and underparts are pure white, the sides of the breast are washed and streaked with grey-brown. The alula and primary and secondary wing feathers are blackish-brown. The wing coverts are grey-brown edged with white. The eyes are dark brown, the bill, legs and feet are black. The sexes are similar. Very active feeders, usually in small flocks darting about feeding along the tide line. Palearctic winter visitor. Size: 20cm.

Ruff
(Philomachus pugnax)

An abundant palearctic winter visitor throughout the region, favouring the surrounds of lakes, ponds, swamps and marshes only occasionally being found in coastal habitats. The forehead, cheeks and neck are white. The crown, nape and hind neck are tawny brown with fine darker brown flecking. The breast, belly and underparts are white with a variable amount of tawny brown mottling. The feathers of the mantle and wing coverts are dark brown edged with buff-white. The primary and secondary wing feathers are blackish-brown. The eyes are dark brown and the bill brownish-black. The legs and feet are pale orange. In non-breeding plumage the sexes are similar, during breeding periods the males develop a large and spectacular ruff around the head and neck which is extremely variable in colour, ranging from white-ochre to purple-black and chestnut. Palearctic winter visitor. Size: 23cm.

Black-tailed Godwit
(Limosa limosa)

A palearctic winter visitor usually in small flocks on marshes, lakesides, coastal estuaries, mudflats and lagoons. A large wader with long legs and an extremely long straight bill. The head, neck and breast are grey-brown slightly lighter on the cheeks, fore neck and centre of the breast. The underparts are white with a grey wash on the flanks. The feathering of the mantle and wing coverts is grey-brown edged with buff-white. The secondary wing feathers are dark brown edged with buff and the primaries are brownish-black. The tail is white at the base, the remainder being black tipped with a narrow band of white. The eyes are dark brown, the long straight bill is reddish-pink at the base becoming black at the tip. The legs and feet are black. The sexes are similar. Palearctic winter visitor. Size: 41cm.

Bar-tailed Godwit
(Limosa lapponica)

A palearctic winter visitor to coastal estuaries, mudflats and the muddy margins of inland lakes. Very similar in general size and shape to the Black-tailed Godwit (*Limosa limosa*) but has shorter legs, a heavily barred brown and white tail and the suggestion of an upturned bill. The forehead, crown and hind neck are greyish-brown streaked with dark brown. The chin, face and throat are white finely marked with grey-brown. The breast has a wash of pale tawny brown and the underparts are white. The wing coverts are greyish-brown streaked with dark brown and edged with white. The primary and secondary wing feathers are blackish-brown, the secondaries being edged with white. The eyes are dark brown. The bill is black at the tip and pinkish-red towards the base. The legs and feet are blackish. Palearctic winter visitor. Size: 38cm.

Ruddy Turnstone
(Arenaria interpres)

A winter visitor to coastal beaches and rocky shorelines, occasionally encountered on the surrounds of inland waters. The forehead, crown and hind neck are grey-brown streaked with dark brown. The face, cheeks, chin and upper neck are off-white. The lower neck and upper breast are heavily marked with blackish-brown. The lower breast and underparts are white. The feathers of the mantle, scapulars and wing coverts are dark brown edged with buff and tawny brown. The primary wing feathers are white at the base and blackish-brown at the tips, the secondaries are white which show as a conspicuous wing bar in flight. The tail is white at the base tipped with a broad black band. The eyes are dark brown, the bill is black and the legs and feet bright orange. The sexes are similar. Usually encountered in small flocks foraging among the rocks and debris along the tide line in search of insects and molluscs. Palearctic winter visitor. Size: 23cm.

Common Greenshank
(Tringa nebularia)

A bird of coastal mudflats and sandbars, the muddy surrounds of inland lakes both freshwater and alkaline, and exposed ground along riverbanks. The forehead, crown, nape and hind neck are greyish-white streaked with dark brown. The chin, face, breast and underparts are pure white with some fine dark brown streaking on the cheeks and across the breast. The feathers of the upperparts and wing coverts are greyish-brown, barred, blotched and streaked with dark brown and edged with white. The tail is white with brown-black barring, the rump and centre of the back are white, forming a distinctive wedge shape in flight. The secondary wing feathers are greyish-brown and the primaries are brownish-black. The eyes are dark brown. The long slightly upturned bill is grey-green at the base and black at the tip. The legs and feet are greenish-yellow. The sexes are alike. They are normally solitary but may form into flocks during migration. They usually depart for their breeding grounds in March or April with some birds returning as early as July. Palearctic winter visitor. Size: 31cm.

Common Redshank
(Tringa totanus)

A palearctic winter visitor mainly to coastal estuaries, mudflats and lagoons. A bird of uniform grey-brown appearance. The head, face and neck are brown with fine darker brown streaking, the sides of the face and neck are often paler. The throat, breast and flanks are white streaked with brown, the belly and underparts are white. The feathers of the mantle and wing coverts are brown with fine barring and streaking. The back, rump and secondary wing feathers are white. The primary flight feathers are dark brown. The tail is white finely barred with brown. The eyes are dark brown contrasting with a white orbital ring. The long bill is orange-red at the base and black towards the tip. The legs and feet are bright orange-red. The sexes are alike. They are often found feeding singly or in small flocks gathering together into larger flocks during periods of migration. When flushed they will usually utter a strident call, the wing beats are short and jerky. Palearctic winter visitor. Size: 28cm.

Spotted Redshank
(Tringa erythropus)

A wader that favours freshwater and alkaline inland lakes, pools and marshes. The forehead, crown, nape and mantle are grey-brown. The eyebrow stripe, face and neck are white, a dark brown stripe extends from the base of the bill through the eye towards the nape. The breast is white with a mottling of grey-brown. The belly and underparts are white. The feathers of the wing coverts are grey-brown edged with white and the primary wing feathers are brownish-black. The rump and tail are white, the latter finely barred with black. The eyes are dark brown with a white orbital ring, the bill has the upper mandible all black and the lower mandible orange-red at the base and black towards the tip. The long legs and feet are bright orange-red. The sexes are alike. The breeding plumage, which some birds acquire before migrating to the northern breeding grounds, is almost entirely black with white spotting on the wings and flanks. The back and rump remain white. Palearctic winter visitor. Size: 30cm.

Common Sandpiper
(Actitis hypoleucos)

A common palearctic winter visitor to coastal regions and inland waters. The forehead, crown and cheeks are olive brown streaked with dark brown. The upperparts and wings are olive brown finely barred with dark brown. The chin and throat are white with a wash of buff, the upper breast is olive brown with fine dark brown streaking. The remainder of the breast, belly and underparts are white. The white feathering extends onto the sides of the breast arcing around the line of the folded wings. The eyes are dark brown, the bill is grey-brown, the legs and feet pale greyish-yellow. The sexes are alike. Palearctic winter visitor. Size: 20cm.

Marsh Sandpiper
(Tringa stagnatilis)

A palearctic winter visitor to coastal mudflats, inland lakes, rivers and flood plains. The forehead is white, the crown, nape and hind neck are buff-grey streaked with dark brown. The face, throat, fore neck, breast, belly and underparts are white. The mantle and scapulars are tawny-buff streaked with dark brown. The wing coverts are grey-brown, the back and rump are white. The primary wing feathers are brown-black. The eyes are dark brown, the long slender bill is grey-black, and the legs and feet are greenish-yellow. The sexes are alike. Palearctic winter visitor. Size: 23cm.

Green Sandpiper
(Tringa ochropus)

A bird of freshwater lakes, ponds, rivers and streams throughout the region. The forehead and crown are olive brown heavily streaked with dark brown. The hind neck, sides of the neck and upper breast are whitish streaked and flecked with brown. The lower breast, belly and underparts are white. The wing coverts and primary and secondary wing feathers are dark olive brown barred and spotted with white. The tail is white with black barring, the rump is white contrasting strongly with the dark wings when seen in flight. The eyes are dark brown, the bill is greenish-yellow at the base and black at the tip. The legs and feet are greenish-grey. The sexes are alike. Palearctic winter visitor. Size: 23cm.

Wood Sandpiper
(Tringa glareola)

An abundant winter visitor to wetland areas. The forehead and eyebrows are white, the crown is olive brown boldly streaked with dark brown. The hind neck, cheeks and upper breast are greyish with brown mottling. The lower breast, belly and underparts are white. The wing coverts and secondary wing feathers are olive brown edged with white, the primaries are dark olive brown. The tail is white barred with black. The eyes are dark brown, the bill is blackish at the tip and yellow-green at the base. The legs and feet are yellow-green. The sexes are alike. Palearctic winter visitor. Size: 20cm.

Whimbrel
(Numenius phaeopus)

A large wader of coastal regions frequenting estuaries and rocky shorelines, occasional found on inland lakes. The forehead and crown have a buff central stripe, with a dark brown stripe either side extending to the nape. A dark brown stripe runs from the base of the bill through the eye. The cheeks and the sides and back of the neck are white streaked and flecked with dark brown. The chin, throat, fore neck and breast are whitish-buff streaked with dark brown. The belly and underparts are white. The wing coverts and primary and secondary wing feathers are dark brown edged with buff and white. The eyes are dark brown, the long decurved bill is blackish often with pinkish-red at the base. The long legs and feet are grey-blue. The sexes are alike. Palearctic winter visitor. Size: 40cm.

Eurasian Curlew
(Numenius arquata)

A winter visitor to coastal mudflats and estuaries. A very large long legged wader with long decurved bill. The head, neck and breast are buff-white heavily streaked with dark brown. The belly and flanks are white, the latter with bold blackish-brown streaks. The wing feathers are dark brown edged and tipped with buff-white, the primary flight feathers are brown-black. The eyes are dark brown, the bill is blackish and the legs and feet are pale blue-grey. The sexes are alike. Palearctic winter visitor. Size: 58cm.

Temminck's Courser
(Cursorius temminckii)

A bird of short grasslands, dry bush savannah and cultivated farmland, often in pairs or small flocks. The crown is bright chestnut, the white eyebrows extend to the nape and a black stripe extends from the rear of the eyes to the nape and downward to the hind neck. The neck, upper breast, mantle and upperparts are grey-brown. The lower breast is chestnut becoming blackish towards the belly, the remainder of the underparts are white. The primary wing feathers are black and the secondaries grey-brown. The eyes are dark brown, the slightly decurved bill is blackish. The legs and feet are pale grey. The sexes are alike. A very upright bird, feeds by pecking then running a few steps before pecking again, collecting invertebrates and seeds as it does so. Resident. Size: 20cm.

Somali Courser
(Cursorius somalensis)

An inhabitant of arid semi-desert regions, cultivated farmland and bare stony areas. A long legged, slender, upright bird with forehead and fore crown sandy rufous brown, the hind neck is grey-blue. The white eyebrows extend to the nape and downwards forming a 'V' at the top of the hind neck. The face, neck and throat are white with a wash of buff on the cheeks. The breast is sandy-brown and the belly and underparts are white. The mantle, back and wing coverts are buff sandy-brown. The primary and secondary wing feathers are black edged with buff. The eyes are dark brown, the decurved bill is black and the legs and feet are pale grey, almost white. The sexes are alike. Similar to Temminck's Courser but lacks the dark breast band and the bright chestnut crown. Usually encountered in small flocks of up to 30 birds running around on bare, arid patches of ground feeding on disturbed insects, on small lizards and seeds, often scratching in the loose surface soil to expose ants etc. Resident. Size: 21cm.

Two-banded Courser
(Rhinoptilus africanus)

A bird encountered on open bare patches of ground and short grassland areas, also often seen along dirt roads. The crown is pale buff finely streaked with brown-black. A black stripe extends from the base of the bill through the eye to the nape. The cheeks, chin and throat are buff-white, the neck is buff finely streaked and flecked with dark brown. The feathers of the back and wing coverts are sandy-brown with dark centres and broadly edged with white-buff. The rump is white and the tail black narrowly edged with white. The primary wing feathers are rufous brown to black and the secondaries are rufous to sandy-brown edged with white-buff. The upper breast is buff with a black band encircling the breast and mantle, a broader black band extends across the lower breast separated from the upper band by a band of sandy-buff. The lower breast, belly and underparts are whitish. The eyes are dark brown, the short bill is black and the legs and feet are pale grey. The sexes are alike. They are active mainly at dawn, dusk or through the night, when they feed on insects especially termites. Resident. Size: 20cm.

Collared Pratincole
(Glareola pratincola)

A resident and winter visitor to areas of open grassland, the surrounds of inland lakes and rivers as well as coastal regions. The crown, nape, face and sides and back of the neck are plain olive brown. The chin, throat and fore neck are creamy-yellow bordered by a narrow black band. The breast is buff-brown merging with the white belly and underparts . The wing coverts are olive brown, the primary and secondary wing feathers are black, the secondaries being tipped with white. The underwing coverts are chestnut which are conspicuous in flight. The rump is white and the black tail is deeply forked. The eyes are dark brown, the bill is black with red at the base, the legs and feet are blackish. During non-breeding periods the plumage is duller and the distinctive colour and markings of the throat and neck are much reduced. The sexes are alike. Resident and palearctic winter visitor. Size: 25cm.

Grey-headed Gull

(Larus cirrocephalus)

A common gull on inland freshwater and alkaline lakes and along rivers. The forehead, crown, face, chin and upper throat are soft grey, the neck, lower throat, breast, belly and underparts are white with a faint wash of pink. The wing coverts and secondary wing feathers are grey, the primaries are black the outermost feathers having distinctive white mirrors. The rump and tail are white. The eyes are pale yellow set in a bright red orbital ring. The bill is deep blood red and the legs and feet are bright red. In non-breeding plumage the grey head becomes paler and the pink flush is lost from the white feathering. The sexes are similar, the female being slightly smaller than the male. Usually encountered in flocks feeding from the surface of the water taking fish and insects, but will readily scavenge on rubbish tips. They will also take eggs and young from the nests of other waterbirds. Resident. Size: 40cm.

Lesser Black-backed Gull

(Larus fuscus)

A winter migrant to coastal estuaries and shorelines as well as to inland lakes and rivers. The entire head, neck, breast, belly and underparts are white. The back and wing coverts are dark blue-black, the primary wing feathers are black, the outermost primaries having white mirror spots. The eyes are pale yellow with a red orbital ring. The bill is yellow with a red patch on the lower mandible towards the tip. The legs and feet are yellow. The sexes are similar, the female being slightly smaller than the male. Immature birds have underparts streaked with dark brown, the feathers of the upperparts are grey-brown edged with buff. The tail has a broad black band, the bill is blackish, the eyes are dark brown and the legs and feet are dull pink. Adult plumage is not fully attained until the fourth summer, many first and second year birds remain in Africa even during the breeding season when adults fly north. Resident and palearctic winter visitor. Size: 55cm.

Black-headed Gull

(Larus ridibundus)

A winter visitor to coastal estuaries and beaches also encountered around inland lakes and along open riverbanks, on newly ploughed farmland and scavenging on rubbish tips. In non-breeding plumage the head, neck, breast, belly and underparts are white, the head having smudge-like patches of black around the eyes and in the region of the ear coverts. The mantle, back and the majority of the wings are soft grey-blue. The primary wing feathers are white tipped with black. The rump and tail are white. The eyes are dark brown and the bill is dull red at the base with a black tip. The legs and feet are dull red. Immature birds are similar to non-breeding adults but have a broad black band across the tail and show brown feathering on the mantle and the tertials. The base of the bill is yellowish tipped with black and the legs and feet are yellow-pink. Many immature birds remain year round in the region. Resident and palearctic winter visitor. Size: 38cm.

Sooty Gull

(Larus hemprichii)

A bird of coastal regions, rocky shores, beaches and mudflats. In breeding plumage the head and upper neck are dark brown-black, with the lower neck and short eyebrows white. The mantle, back and wing coverts are brown-grey, the primary and secondary wing feathers are brown-black, the outer primaries being tipped with white. The breast and flanks are grey-brown, the belly, underparts and tail are white. The eyes are dark brown set in a red orbital ring. The bill is yellowish-green at the base with a black band before the red and yellow tip. The legs and feet are yellowish-green. In non-breeding plumage the colours of the head and the bare parts are much reduced, the whole plumage becoming greyer. The sexes are similar, the female being slightly smaller than the male. They feed on fish and other aquatic creatures as well as the eggs and chicks of other seabirds. Very rarely recorded inland. Resident. Size: 45cm.

Whiskered Tern
(Chlidonias hybridus)

A bird of freshwater and alkaline lakes and marshes. In breeding plumage the forehead, crown and nape are black, the chin and cheeks are white. The upperparts including the wing coverts are grey, the primary wing feathers are grey edged with dark grey-brown. The throat is pale grey becoming darker on the breast and almost black on the belly and flanks. The eyes are dark brown, the bill is red with a blackish tip and the legs and feet are bright red. In non-breeding plumage the black of the forehead, crown and nape is lost, becoming grey with streaks and smudges of black, the bill, legs and feet become dark brown-black. The sexes are similar. Resident and palearctic winter visitor. Size: 25cm.

White-winged Tern
(Chlidonias leucopterus)

An abundant winter visitor to the Rift Valley Lakes, rarely found on the coast. In non-breeding plumage the forehead is white, the crown and nape are white streaked with grey-black. A smudge of black is present in the region of the ear coverts. The neck, breast and underparts are white. The upperparts including wing coverts and tail are pale grey. The eyes are dark brown, the bill blackish, often with a trace of red at the base, the legs and feet are dull red. Between plumages they can appear quite piebald. The sexes are similar. Palearctic winter visitor. Size: 24cm.

Gull-billed Tern
(Sterna nilotica)

An inhabitant of large inland lakes and rivers, coastal lagoons and estuaries. In breeding plumage the forehead, crown, nape and hind neck are black. The chin, cheeks, fore neck, breast and underparts are white. The mantle and wing coverts are silver-grey, the primary wing feathers are grey edged with black. The eyes are dark brown, the substantial bill is black, the legs and feet blackish. In non-breeding plumage the bird is generally paler with the forehead, crown and nape white with a variable amount of black streaking. The area around the eyes is dark grey. The sexes are similar. Resident and palearctic winter visitor. Size: 38cm.

Caspian Tern
(Sterna caspia)

Found on coastal estuaries, beaches and rocky shorelines, on inland lakes and large rivers. A very large tern with the forehead, crown and nape black, often with the impression of a short stiff crest on the hind-crown. The neck, breast and underparts are white. The mantle and wing feathers are pale soft grey, the primary wing feathers are mid-grey edged with dark grey. The eyes are dark brown. The heavy bill is bright orange-red, the legs and feet black. In non-breeding plumage the forehead, crown and nape become white-grey with a variable amount of black streaking. Usually feeds singly or in small groups flying a few metres above the water surface from where they plunge-dive for fish. Resident. Size: 53cm.

African Skimmer
(Rynchops flavirostris)

A bird found in the vicinity of large expanses of inland water and along the coastline of much of the region. Almost unmistakeable. The forehead, cheeks, sides and fore neck, breast and underparts are white. The crown, nape, hind neck, back and wing coverts are black-brown. The primary and secondary wing feathers are black-brown edged with buff and grey. The forked tail is white. The eyes are dark brown. The orange-red bill is specially adapted to suit the bird's unusual feeding method, the upper mandible is shorter than the lower mandible by some 25 mm. When feeding the bird skims over the surface of the water using short buoyant wing beats, with the lower mandible held just below the surface, when a prey item is detected the shorter upper mandible instantly snaps shut. Resident. Size: 35cm.

Chestnut-bellied Sandgrouse

(Pterocles exustus)

A bird of dry semi-desert areas, open grasslands and thorn bush country. The forehead, crown and hind neck are sandy-brown, the remainder of the head and neck is yellow-ochre. The throat and upper breast are sandy-brown, a thin black band extends across the breast from the fold of the wings. Below this band the lower breast becomes chestnut darkening to black on the belly and underparts. The scapulars and wing coverts are yellow-ochre with some white spotting, edged with buff-white and black. The primary and secondary wing feathers are dark brown, some of the primaries having white tips. The tail has long narrow central feathers. The eyes are dark brown set in a pale orbital ring. The bill is blue-grey and the legs and feet are blue-black. The female differs from the male in having the crown and hind neck streaked with dark brown, the breast spotted with dark brown and with narrow brown-black barring on the wings. The wing feathers also show more prominent sandy-buff spotting and barring. They feed in flocks mainly on seeds and plant material, but also take small quantities of beetles and other insects. Resident. Size: 30cm.

Black-faced Sandgrouse

(Pterocles decoratus)

An inhabitant of dry bush and semi-desert regions. The male has distinctive head markings consisting of a pale base to the upper mandible contrasting with a black forehead, chin and throat. The fore-crown is white and a white eye stripe bordered below by a narrow black stripe, extends from the fore-crown to the sides of the nape. The crown, nape and hind neck are ochre streaked with black. The cheeks, sides of the neck and the upper breast are buff-ochre, a black band extends across the breast below which the lower breast is white. The belly is dark brown. The feathers of the upperparts and wings are buff to ochre heavily streaked and barred with black-brown. The eyes are dark brown set in patches of bare yellow skin, the bill is orange-yellow and the legs and feet are dull orange. The female differs from the male in having no facial pattern, no eye stripe or breast band, the head and breast being streaked and barred with brown. Resident. Size: 28cm.

Lichtenstein's Sandgrouse

(Pterocles lichtensteinii)

Found in arid areas of hilly bush country, usually in pairs. The male has a white forehead and fore-crown separated by a broad band of black. The remainder of the crown and the nape are buff, heavily streaked with black. The chin and cheeks are buff-white with black speckling. The neck, throat and mantle are buff boldly barred with black. The breast is yellow-ochre broken by a narrow black band across the upper breast and a broader black band across the lower section. The belly and underparts are white with black barring. The back, rump and tail are buff-brown with black barring, the latter with a broad black band towards the yellow-ochre tip. The wing coverts, scapulars and secondary wing feathers are a mosaic of buff and ochre heavily blotched and barred with black and white. The primary wing feathers are black-brown narrowly edged with white. The eyes are dark brown surrounded by an area of bare pale yellow skin. The bill is orange-yellow, the legs and feet are yellow, and the thighs are feathered white. The female lacks the bold head markings and breast bands of the male, having the head and breast ochre-buff barred and streaked with black. Resident. Size: 28cm.

Yellow-throated Sandgrouse

(Pterocles gutturalis)

A bird of short grasslands usually close to water, encountered in pairs or small flocks. The male has the forehead, crown and nape olive brown and a creamy-yellow stripe extending from the base of the upper mandible to a point above and to the rear of the eye. The chin, throat and cheeks are creamy-yellow bordered below by a black band across the neck to the ear coverts. The lower neck and breast are plain dusky-buff, the belly and underparts are dark chestnut and black. The mantle and wing coverts are dusky-buff edged greyish, the primary wing feathers are dark brown-black edged with buff-white and the secondaries are olive-grey with a wash of chestnut brown. The eyes are dark brown set in an area of bare grey skin. The bill is slate-blue, the legs and feet brown. The female differs from the male in having the head, throat and neck buff-brown heavily streaked with dark brown, both upper and underparts are heavily spotted and barred with dark brown. Resident. Size: 33cm.

Speckled Pigeon
(Columba guinea)

A widespread species throughout the region found in a variety of habitats including open grasslands, woodlands, rocky slopes and cliffs, cultivated farmland and around human settlements, cities and suburban gardens. The head and upper neck are blue-grey, the eyes are surrounded by a large area of claret-red unfeathered skin. The neck and upper breast feathers are pale chestnut edged with grey. The breast, belly and underparts are plain blue-grey, the back and scapulars are chestnut. The wing coverts are chestnut boldly tipped with triangular white patches, the primary wing feathers are greyish-brown. The eyes are pale golden-yellow, the bill is blackish with a white cere, and the legs and feet are reddish-pink. The sexes are alike. They are usually found in small flocks of 4-6 birds but are sometimes encountered in flocks numbering several hundred feeding on the ground taking seeds, fruits and, when in season, many cultivated crops such as wheat, barley, millet and maize. Resident. Size: 40cm.

Red-eyed Dove
(Streptopelia semitorquata)

A common dove of woodland habitats usually close to water, forest edges, suburban gardens and parkland. The forehead is white becoming grey-blue on the crown and nape. The sides of the head and neck are mauve with a wash of pink. At the base of the nape is a black half collar that extends around the sides of the neck. The breast, belly and flanks are mauve-pink, the undertail coverts are greyish. The mantle, back and wings are brown, the primary wing feathers are dark brown finely edged with white. The eyes are orange-red surrounded by small patches of dark red unfeathered skin. The bill is blackish, the legs and feet are reddish-pink. The sexes are alike. Usually found singly, in pairs or small flocks feeding on a variety of seeds, berries and fruits. Resident. Size: 30cm.

African Mourning Dove
(Streptopelia decipiens)

A bird found over much of the region in acacia woodlands particularly those close to water, cultivated farmland, parks and suburban gardens. The forehead, crown and cheeks are blue-grey, the neck is mauve-pink with a distinctive black half collar extending from the hind neck around the sides of the neck, this collar has narrow white edging. The chin and throat are off-white, the breast is mauve-pink becoming greyish-white on the belly, flanks and undertail coverts. The mantle, back, rump and wing coverts are brown, the primary and secondary wing feathers are dark brown finely edged with buff-white. The eyes are yellow surrounded by a circular patch of pink-red unfeathered skin. The bill is black and the legs and feet are pinkish-red. The sexes are alike. Usually forages alone or in small flocks, often in association with other doves eating grain, seeds, berries, fruits and occasionally some insects. Resident. Size: 28cm.

Ring-necked Dove
(Streptopelia capicola)

A very widespread dove found in a variety of habitats including acacia woodlands, dry thorn bush, around human habitations and on cultivated farmland, parks and in suburban gardens. The head is blue-grey, usually paler on the forehead and cheeks. The chin and throat are pale grey, the neck is grey with a flush of mauve-pink and has a black half collar around the hind neck. The breast is mauve-grey, the belly and underparts pale grey-white. The mantle, scapulars and wing coverts are grey-brown. The tail is grey-brown above and black below. The primary and secondary wing feathers are dark brown finely edged with grey-white. The eyes are dark brown, the bill is black and the legs and feet are dull flesh-pink. The sexes are alike. Often feeds singly or in pairs and freely associates with other dove species foraging for seeds, plant material and occasionally invertebrates including earthworms and termites. They often gather in large flocks around waterholes during the dry season. Resident. Size: 25cm.

Laughing Dove
(Streptopelia senegalensis)

A common and widespread dove throughout the region in areas of acacia woodland and thorn bush, cultivated farmland and around human habitations. The head and upper neck are pale grey with a flush of pink. The fore neck has a broad half collar of rufous flecked with black. The breast is pinkish-grey becoming white on the belly and underparts. The mantle and scapulars are rufous brown, the wing coverts are greyish-blue, the primary wing feathers are brown-black and the secondaries are blue-grey edged with black. The back and rump are blue-grey and the tail is brown-black. The eyes are dark brown, the bill is blue-black and the legs and feet are dull red. The sexes are similar. Resident. Size: 24cm.

Namaqua Dove
(Oena capensis)

The smallest of East Africa's doves with a long pointed tail, found in areas of thorn bush and dry scrub, lightly wooded savannah and on cultivated farmland. The male has forehead, face, chin, throat and breast black, the remainder of the head and neck being pale grey. The belly and underparts are white. The mantle and back are grey-brown, the tail is brown-black. The wing coverts are pale grey, the primary wing feathers are rufous brown edged with black and the secondaries are grey-brown edged with black. The eyes are dark brown, the bill is reddish at the base and orange-yellow at the tip. The legs and feet are pinkish-red. The female differs from the male in lacking the black facial markings and breast bib, instead being pale grey-brown. The primaries are grey-brown. Resident. Size: 21cm.

Emerald-spotted Wood Dove
(Turtur chalcospilos)

A small dove of woodlands, forests and cultivated farmland. The head is grey, the nape and hind neck light brown. The face and fore neck are greyish, the breast, belly and underparts are buff-white with a wash of pink on the former. The mantle, back and rump are brown, the wing coverts are brown with several large oblong metallic green patches. The primary wing feathers are rufous brown, being very pronounced in flight, tipped and edged with black-brown, the secondaries are dark brown-black. The eyes are dark brown, the bill is blackish and the legs and feet are dull pinkish-red. The sexes are alike. Resident. Size: 20cm.

African Green Pigeon
(Treron calva)

A bird of woodlands, forests and cultivated farmland usually in the vicinity of fruit trees particularly fig. The head, neck, breast, belly and underparts are yellow-green. The mantle, back, wing coverts and rump are olive-green, a patch of lilac-mauve appears at the carpal joint of the folded wing. The primary and secondary wing feathers are grey-brown edged with yellow. The eyes are pale blue-green, the bill is pinkish-red with a grey tip and the legs and feet are bright pink-red. The sexes are alike. Normally found in small parties feeding high in the canopy of fig and other fruiting trees, where they are not easily spotted their plumage blending so well with the foliage. They rarely feed on the ground occasionally doing so to feed on seeds. Resident. Size: 30cm.

Olive Pigeon
(Columba arquatrix)

A bird of forests and woodlands mainly found at altitudes above 1,400m. The forehead and fore crown are purple, the hind crown and nape are blue-grey. The throat and neck are mauve-grey, the breast feathers are dark purple-red tipped with white, the belly is maroon heavily spotted with white. The mantle is purple-brown with some white spotting, the back and rump are dark brown. The wing coverts and scapulars are maroon boldly spotted with white. The primary and secondary wing feathers are dark brown, the tail is blackish. The eyes are brownish-yellow with a bright yellow orbital ring. The bill, legs and feet are bright yellow. The sexes are alike. Resident. Size: 38cm.

African Orange-bellied Parrot   *(Poicephalus rufiventris)*

A parrot of dry acacia woodland and thinly foliated trees particularly baobabs. The male has the head, neck and upper breast dusky-brown the cheeks and ear coverts are finely streaked with white. The lower breast and belly are bright orange, the thighs and undertail coverts are bright yellow-green. The mantle, back and wing coverts are dusky-brown, the primary wing feathers and tail are brownish-black. The eyes are dark orange-red surrounded by an area of dark brown unfeathered skin. The bill, legs and feet are blackish. The female differs from the male in having the lower breast and underparts yellow-green not orange. Usually found in small parties, the flight is fast during which they usually utter a shrill squawk. Resident. Size: 25cm.

Brown Parrot   *(Poicephalus meyeri)*

Found in savannah woodlands. The head, neck and mantle are dark brown, the crown of the head bearing a pronounced band of yellow. The breast, belly and underparts are darkish blue-green, the thighs are yellow. The wing coverts are dark brown with the carpal area of the folded wing bright yellow. The primary wing feathers and tail are dark brown, the back and rump are bluish-green. The eyes are rich deep red surrounded by an area of black unfeathered skin. The bill, cere, legs and feet are blackish. The sexes are alike. They occur in pairs or small parties feeding mainly on seeds, nuts and occasionally fruit. Resident. Size: 25cm.

Fischer's Lovebird   *(Agapornis fischeri)*

Restricted in distribution to north western Tanzania and west to Rwanda and Burundi where they favour areas with acacia and baobab trees. The forehead, cheeks and chin are orange-red, the hind neck and breast are golden-yellow merging on the belly to yellow-green. The mantle and back are green, the uppertail coverts blue and the tail blue-green at the base permeating through yellow-green to a yellow tip with a black band on the outer feathers. The wing coverts are rich leaf green, the primary wing feathers dark green. The eyes are dark brown set in a prominent white orbital patch. The bill is bright red, the cere is white and the legs and feet are pinkish-grey. Resident. Size: 14cm.

Yellow-collared Lovebird   *(Agapornis personatus)*

Restricted in distribution to a wide band extending north to south through central Tanzania, inhabiting acacia woodlands and areas of baobab trees. Several feral populations have established themselves outside the normal breeding range on the Tanzanian coast. The head, chin and throat are dark brown. The nape, hind neck and breast are yellow, the belly and underparts are green. The mantle, back and wing coverts are green, the uppertail coverts are blue and the tail is green with a flush of orange and a black bar towards the tip. The primary wing feathers are green-brown. The eyes are dark brown with a pronounced white orbital patch, the bill is red with a whitish cere, and the legs and feet are grey. The sexes are alike. Resident. Size: 15cm.

Fischer's Lovebird / Yellow-collared Lovebird Hybrid

Fischer's Lovebird and Yellow-collared Lovebirds hybridise and several populations are well established within the region, the principle locations being Nairobi and Lake Naivasha in Kenya. The forehead is reddish-peach, the crown and face are darkish-brown merging with the bright yellow nape, neck and breast, the latter often with a flush of orange. The belly and underparts are bright yellow-green. The back is yellow-green becoming blue-green on the rump and uppertail coverts. The wing coverts are dark green and the primary wing feathers are brownish. The eyes are dark brown, the bill is bright red with a narrow white cere and the legs and feet are grey. The sexes are alike. Resident. Size: 14cm.

Hartlaub's Turaco

(Tauraco hartlaubi)

A common turaco of highland forests in Kenya and Tanzania. The forehead, crown and nape feathers are dark blue and take the form of a fan-shaped crest. A white patch appears in front of the eye which is surrounded by a red orbital ring. A white stripe extends from below and to the rear of the eye to the ear coverts. The sides of the face, chin, throat, neck and breast are leaf green. The belly and underparts are greyish-black. The mantle, back and wing coverts are green becoming dark blue on the secondary wing feathers. The primary wing feathers are edged with rich red. The tail is dark blue. The eyes are dark brown, the bill is red and the legs and feet are black. The sexes are alike. Resident. Size: 40cm.

White-bellied Go-away-bird

(Criniferoides leucogaster)

Found throughout much of the region in dry acacia and riverine woodlands. The head, neck, breast and upperparts are grey, the forehead exhibits a long erectile crest of grey feathers tipped with black. The belly and underparts are white. The wing coverts are grey broadly tipped with black which form bars across the folded wing. The primary wing feathers are black with white at the base. The tail is grey above and black below with a broad white central band. The eyes are dark brown, the bill, legs and feet are blackish. The sexes are alike. Resident. Size: 50cm.

Bare-faced Go-away-bird

(Corythaixoides personata)

A bird of thickets, bush and open woodlands, also favouring forests and woodlands with fig trees. The forehead exhibits a long crest of buff-grey feathers, the neck and breast are white, the latter with a flush of green in the centre. The chin and the face, to a point to the rear of the eyes, are black. The belly is pale buff-grey becoming white on the thighs and undertail coverts. The mantle, back, wings and tail are buff-grey. The eyes are dark brown, the bill, legs and feet are black. The sexes are alike. Resident. Size: 50cm.

Schalow's Turaco

(Tauraco schalowi)

A reasonably common turaco in the dense forests of southern Tanzania. The head, neck, mantle and breast are green, the forehead and crown exhibit a long erectile crest of green feathers tipped with white. A white stripe extends from the gape to the apex of the eye and a second stripe runs from below the eye to the ear coverts. A small black patch is present in front of and below the eye. The belly and underparts are blackish. The upperparts and wing coverts are dark green. The primary and secondary wing feathers are bright red tipped with black. The tail is green-blue. The eyes are red-brown, the bill is red and the legs and feet are blackish. The sexes are alike. Resident. Size: 40cm.

Fischer's Turaco

(Tauraco fischeri)

A bird with distribution limited in East Africa to forests and woodlands of the coastal regions of Kenya, Tanzania and Somalia. The forehead, face, sides of the neck and the breast are green. The feathers of the forehead, crown and nape form an erectile crest, green at the base with crimson towards the black and white tips, the crimson extends down the hind neck. Two white stripes extend from the gape, one to a point in front of the eye and the second running below the eye to the ear coverts. A patch of bare red skin surrounds the eyes. The upperparts are green-blue, the flight feathers are red tipped with black. The eyes are dark brown, the bill red and the legs and feet blackish. The sexes are alike. Resident. Size: 40cm.

Ross's Turaco

(Musophaga rossae)

A bird of savannah woodlands and forests in Uganda, western Kenya and western Tanzania. The overall plumage coloration is glossy blue-black. The forehead and crown have a short erectile crest of crimson. An area of bright yellow unfeathered skin surrounds the eyes. The primary and secondary wing feathers are crimson. The eyes are dark brown, the broad bill is bright yellow and the legs and feet are blackish. The sexes are alike. Resident. Size: 50cm.

Red-chested Cuckoo
(Cuculus solitarius)

A cuckoo of woodlands, forests and thickets. The male has the head, mantle and upperparts slaty-grey, the chin and throat pale grey and the neck and upper breast rufous red. The lower breast and belly are creamy-buff boldly barred with black, the undertail coverts are plain buff-white. The wing coverts are slaty-grey and the primary wing feathers grey with some white barring. The tail is dark grey to black spotted and barred with white. The eyes are dark brown with a yellow orbital ring. The bill is black at the tip and yellowish at the base, the legs and feet are bright yellow. The female differs from the male in having a less well-developed rufous breast with black barring. Immature birds have the head, neck and upperparts black streaked and spotted with white, the nape is white. The breast, belly and underparts are whitish barred with black. The tail is black heavily spotted with white. Resident. Size: 30cm.

Great Spotted Cuckoo
(Clamator glandarius)

An inhabitant of dry savannah with sparse trees and bushes. The head is mid-grey with a paler silver-grey crown forming a slight crest. The chin, throat and sides of the neck are creamy-yellow merging to white on the breast, belly and underparts. The hind neck and back are grey-brown, the wings are greyish-brown with scapulars, wing coverts, primaries and secondaries tipped and edged white. The eyes are dark brown with a grey orbital ring, the bill is blackish and the legs and feet are grey. The sexes are alike. Resident and palearctic winter visitor. Size: 41cm.

Eurasian Cuckoo
(Cuculus canorus)

A palearctic winter visitor throughout the region favouring areas of savannah woodland and forest edges. The male has the head, hind neck, mantle, wing coverts and upperparts slaty-grey. The chin and throat are white with the lower fore neck and upper breast pale grey. The lower breast, belly and underparts are white barred with dark grey. The tail is blackish, spotted, barred and tipped with white. The eyes are yellow, the bill is blackish. The legs and feet are yellow. The sexes are similar but the female has the upper breast barred with grey-black. This species could easily be confused with the African Cuckoo (*Cuculus gularis*) which is paler on the breast, has fainter barring on the flanks and has a yellow base to the bill. Palearctic winter visitor. Size: 33cm.

Diederik Cuckoo
(Chrysococcyx caprius)

A widespread cuckoo found in a variety of habitats including woodland and forest edges, thorn bush country and semi desert areas. The forehead, crown, ear coverts and nape are metallic green. A white eye strip extends from the base of the upper mandible over the eye to the hind-crown and a dark green-black stripe extends from the gape under and to the rear of the eye. The chin, throat and fore neck are white with a dark green moustachial stripe. The breast, belly and underparts are white with a wash of buff on the breast and dark green barring on the flanks. The wing coverts are metallic green, the primary and secondary wing feathers are dark green boldly spotted and barred with white. The eyes are dark red, the bill is blackish and the legs and feet are grey. The sexes are similar, but the female is duller and has white streaking over much of the plumage. Resident. Size: 19cm.

White-browed Coucal
(Centropus superciliosus)

A common species throughout the region in areas of thickets and tall rank grasses on savannah and in woodland clearings. The feathers of the head, nape and hind neck are earth-brown streaked with white. A prominent white eye stripe extends from the base of the bill along the sides of the crown to the nape. The chin, throat and fore neck are white, the breast, belly and underparts whitish with some barring on the sides of the breast and the flanks. The wings are rich chestnut, the feathers of the mantle and scapulars are chestnut boldly streaked with white-buff. The long tail is blackish-brown narrowly tipped white. The eyes are crimson, the bill black and the legs and feet grey-black. The sexes are alike. Resident. Size: 40cm.

Marsh Owl

(Asio capensis)

Found in a variety of habitats throughout the region from coastal marshes, savannah grasslands, marshes and mountain moorlands. The facial disc is buff with dark brown patches around the eyes, the remainder of the head, neck and mantle are plain mid-brown, short ear tufts are usually visible. The breast is brown finely barred and flecked with buff. The belly and underparts are plain buff. The scapulars and wing coverts are mid-brown with buff barring and spotting, the primary and secondary wing feathers and the tail are dark brown with broad buff bars and tips. The eyes are dark brown, the bill is blackish and the legs and feet are feathered buff with black claws. The sexes are similar, the females being paler. Resident. Size: 36cm.

Verreaux's Eagle Owl

(Bubo lacteus)

A very large owl of thick woodland, riverine forest and wooded savannah throughout the region. The head and face are pale grey-buff with prominent ear tufts, the facial disc is bordered with a broad black line. The breast, belly and underparts are buff-white with fine dark brown barring on the breast and flanks. The upperparts are grey-brown finely barred with white and dark brown. The scapulars are edged with white which produces a white wing stripe. The primary wing feathers and the tail are dark brown-grey with broad bands of light brown-buff. The eyes are dark brown with pink eyelids, the bill is grey-white, and the legs and feet are feathered white-buff with black claws. The sexes are similar, the females being larger than the males. Resident. Size: 65cm.

Spotted Eagle Owl

(Bubo africanus)

An owl of arid bush, rocky slopes and cliffs, and lightly wooded savannah. The head, breast and underparts are pale buff-white smudged, spotted and finely barred with grey-brown. The facial disc is bordered with a prominent black line and the ear tufts are tipped black. The mantle, back, tail and wing coverts are dark grey-brown finely barred with buff-white. The primary wing feathers are dark brown barred and banded with buff-white. The eyes are yellow (the race *cinerascens* present in northern Kenya and northern Uganda has dark brown eyes). The bill is blackish, the legs and feet are feathered pale buff-white with black claws. The sexes are alike. Resident. Size: 50cm.

Pearl-spotted Owlet

(Glaucidium perlatum)

A small owl of savannah and riverine woodlands and dry bush and scrub throughout the region. The head is grey-brown finely spotted with white, the face is white streaked with brown. The throat, breast, belly and underparts are white heavily blotched and streaked with rufous and dark browns. The mantle, back and tail are dark grey-brown with prominent white spots. The scapulars and wing coverts are brown-grey spotted and edged with white, the primary wing feathers are dark brown spotted with buff and white. The eyes are bright yellow, the bill is pale yellow, the legs are feathered white and the feet are pale yellow with grey-black claws. The sexes are alike. Resident. Size: 20cm.

White-faced Scops Owl

(Otus leucotis)

A very distinctive owl of woodlands and acacia bush country. The head is mid-grey with fine dark grey-black streaking, the facial disc is white with sparse grey flecking bordered with a broad black line. The ear tufts are mid-grey edged with black. The breast, belly and underparts are pale grey streaked and barred with darker greys. The wings are grey-brown barred and streaked with dark brown, the scapulars have white tips which produces a narrow wing stripe. The tail is grey-brown with dark brown banding. The eyes are golden yellow, the bill is pale yellow and the legs and feet are feathered whitish-buff with black claws. The sexes are alike. Resident. Size: 27cm.

Eurasian Nightjar *(Caprimulgus europaeus)*

A palearctic winter visitor inhabiting woodlands, thickets and scrub. A nocturnal species that spends the daytime roosting motionless in trees or on the ground. The head and neck are grey-brown finely streaked and flecked with buff-white and black. A white moustachial stripe extends from the gape across the lower cheek. The breast, belly and underparts are grey-brown flecked, streaked and barred with dark brown. The mantle, back and tail are grey-brown finely streaked with black, the latter also having dark brown barring and white outer tips. The wings are dark brown with extensive grey and buff barring and spotting, the primaries having some white spots. The eyes are dark brown, the small bill is black and the short legs and feet blackish. The sexes are similar but the female lacks the white on the tail and primaries. Palearctic winter visitor. Size: 27cm.

Slender-tailed Nightjar *(Caprimulgus clarus)*

A resident species throughout Kenya, Uganda and northern Tanzania inhabiting acacia woodlands and areas of bush and scrub as well as grasslands. The head is grey-brown with black streaking, a faint rufous brown half collar extends from the hind neck onto the sides of the neck, and the face is brown with pale flecking. A narrow buff-white moustachial stripe extends from the gape and a small white patch is present on the sides of the throat. The breast and underparts are brown-buff with black flecking. The wing coverts are grey-brown streaked with black and spotted with buff. The primary wing feathers are dark brown with white patches. The tail is grey-brown with blackish banding, the central tail feathers are up to 2cm longer than the outer feathers. The eyes are dark brown, the short bill and the legs and feet are blackish. The sexes are similar, the female being duller in appearance. Resident. Size: 28cm.

Alpine Swift *(Apus melba)*

A large swift which can be seen wheeling around the sky hawking for insects in central parts of Kenya and northern Tanzania. The head, neck and upper breast band are dark brown as are the forked tail, the undertail coverts and the underwings. The plumage of the upperparts is entirely dark brown. The lower breast and belly are white and a white patch also usually shows on the chin and throat, but this can be almost absent in some individuals. The eyes are dark brown, the bill is black and the short legs and feet pinkish. The sexes are alike. Palearctic winter visitor. Size: 22cm.

Eurasian Swift *(Apus apus)*

Aerial over most habitats including lakes, forests, grasslands, coasts and mountains. The plumage is almost entirely dark brown-black with patches of pale grey on the forehead, chin and upper throat. The tail is forked. The eyes are dark brown, the bill is black and the legs and feet are grey-black. The sexes are alike. Palearctic winter visitor. Size: 16cm.

Little Swift *(Apus affinis)*

A common swift of towns and cities, where they breed and roost on buildings often in large congregations. For the most part the plumage is dark brown, the exceptions being the very prominent white rump and a white chin and throat patch, there is also some white flecking on the head and face. The end of the tail is square not forked. The eyes are dark brown, the bill, legs and feet are blackish. The sexes are alike. Resident. Size: 13cm.

African Palm Swift *(Cypsiurus parvus)*

A very thin narrow swift with long wings and a deeply forked tail, encountered hawking for insects over arid bush, woodlands and towns. The plumage on the upperparts is olive-brown with darker brown primary and secondary wing feathers. The underparts are grey-brown slightly paler on the chin and throat. The eyes are dark brown, the bill, legs and feet are blackish. The sexes are alike. Resident. Size: 13cm.

Speckled Mousebird

(Colius striatus)

A common species over much of the region found in a wide range of habitats from woodlands, areas of bush and scrub, parks, gardens, towns and cultivated farmland. The forehead, face and chin are black, the crown with its short crest, and the hind neck are grey-brown, the ear coverts are white. The throat and fore neck are buff-brown flecked with black, the breast, belly and underparts are buff-brown with darker brown barring on the breast. The mantle, back and wing coverts are grey-brown, the primary wing feathers are darkish brown. The tail is grey-brown the central feathers being very long, the outer feathers are edged white. The eyes are dark brown, the bill is greyish-black, and the legs and feet are red. The sexes are alike. They are usually encountered in small family flocks foraging among vegetation for fruits, buds and other plant matter. Easily recognised in flight with the long tail and short wings which beat rapidly between short intervals of gliding. Resident. Size: 33cm.

White-headed Mousebird

(Colius leucocephalus)

A bird of dry areas restricted in distribution to north, east and south-eastern Kenya, southern Somalia and north-eastern Tanzania. The forehead, crown, crest and nape are white, the ear coverts and upper cheeks are greyish-white surrounding a dark eye patch. The throat, neck, mantle, back and wing coverts are buff grey-white boldly barred with black. The breast, belly and underparts are buff. The primary and secondary wing feathers are grey-buff. The very long tail is grey above and grey-brown below. The uppertail coverts are grey with fine black barring. The eyes are dark brown, the bill is blue-grey at the base and black at the tip, the legs and feet are red. The sexes are alike. Resident. Size: 31cm.

Blue-naped Mousebird

(Urocolius macrourus)

Normally encountered in small flocks inhabiting areas of bush and scrub, thickets and vegetation along rivers and streams. The forehead, crown, crest and face are grey, the nape is bright turquoise blue. An area of bright red unfeathered skin surrounds the eyes. The mantle, back and neck are grey-brown, the breast is grey merging to buff on the belly and underparts. The wing coverts are grey-brown and the primary and secondary wing feathers are dark brown edged with grey and buff. The extremely long tail is bluish-grey darkening towards the tip. The eyes are red, the bill is black with the base of the upper mandible red. The legs and feet are pinkish-red. The sexes are alike. Immature birds lack the turquoise blue nape and have a greenish-grey bill. They are usually encountered in small flocks of 4-6 individuals feeding on fruits and leaves. Resident. Size: 36cm.

Giant Kingfisher

(Megaceryle maxima)

The largest of Africa's kingfishers well distributed in southern Kenya, Uganda and Tanzania always in the vicinity of water, favouring the wooded banks of streams and rivers, lakes and ponds. Often well concealed in overhanging foliage from where they plunge-dive for fish, crabs and amphibians. The male has the forehead, crown and nape black spotted with white, the feathers being loosely arranged to form a spiky crest. The chin, throat and lower cheeks are white broken by a narrow moustachial stripe. The breast is a rich chestnut, the belly and underparts are white boldly spotted with black. The wings and tail are black boldly spotted and barred with white. The eyes are dark brown, the bill greyish-black and the legs and feet are grey-brown. The female differs from the male in having the breast white boldly spotted with black and the belly and underparts rich chestnut. Resident. Size: 42cm.

Pied Kingfisher
(Ceryle rudis)

The only black and white kingfisher in East Africa, often seen hovering over water. The forehead, crown, nape and hind neck are black. A white stripe extends from the upper mandible above the eye to the nape and a black stripe extends from the gape through and below the eye to the black ear coverts. Chin, throat and fore neck are white, the breast, belly and underparts are white with two black bands extending across the breast of the male; in the female a single band fails to join at the centre of the breast. The wings, back and tail are black irregularly spotted and barred with white. Eyes are dark brown, bill, legs and feet are black. Resident. Size: 25cm.

Malachite Kingfisher
(Alcedo cristata)

One of East Africa's most colourful birds, found along rivers and streams, coastal estuaries and mangroves. The forehead, crown and nape are iridescent greenish-blue barred with black. The chin, throat and centre of the breast are white merging with bright rufous cheeks, sides of the breast and underparts. A white patch is present at the base of the ear coverts. The mantle and tail are dark blue, the back and rump are iridescent azure blue. The scapulars and wing coverts are dark blue spotted with azure, the primary wing feathers are dark blue-black. The eyes are dark brown, the bill, legs and feet are bright red. The sexes are alike. Resident. Size: 14cm.

African Pygmy Kingfisher
(Ispidina picta)

One of the smallest of Africa's kingfishers, found in woodlands, riverside forests, along rivers and streams and in areas of lush tall grasses. The forehead and crown are dark blue barred with black, the hind neck, sides of neck, cheeks and face are orange with a flush of violet in the region of the ear coverts, below which is a prominent white patch. The chin and throat are white, the breast, belly and underparts are orange. The mantle, scapulars and rump are dark iridescent blue, the primary and secondary wing feathers and the tail are blackish. The eyes are dark brown, the bill, legs and feet are orange-red. The sexes are alike. Resident. Size: 11cm.

Woodland Kingfisher
(Halcyon senegalensis)

A bird of wooded savannah, parks and gardens. The forehead, crown, nape and hind neck are greyish-white with a flush of blue. A black patch extends from the base of the upper mandible to encircle the eye. The chin and throat are white, the sides of the neck and breast are pale grey, and the belly and underparts are white with a wash of grey-blue on the flanks. The scapulars, back, rump and upper tail are bright azure blue. The wing coverts are black, the primary wing feathers are azure broadly edged with black, and the secondaries are azure tipped with black. The eyes are dark brown, the bill is unusual in having the upper mandible bright red and the lower mandible black. The legs and feet are blackish. The sexes are alike. Resident. Size: 20cm.

Striped Kingfisher
(Halcyon chelicuti)

A rather dull kingfisher found in areas of light woodland and on grasslands and savannah. The forehead, crown and nape are brown-black finely streaked with grey-white. A black stripe extends from the base of the bill through the eye to the sides of the nape. The hind neck and sides of the neck are grey-white with sparse dark brown speckling. The chin, throat, breast, belly and underparts are white, the breast having a wash of buff and being lightly streaked with brown, the flanks are heavily streaked with brown. The wing coverts are dark brown-black edged with white, the primary wing feathers are dark brown and the secondaries are brown broadly edged with azure blue. The back and rump are azure blue and the tail is grey-blue. The eyes are dark brown, the bill is blackish the lower mandible being red towards the base. The legs and feet are dull pink-red. The sexes are alike. Resident. Size: 16cm.

Grey-headed Kingfisher
(Halcyon leucocephala)

Commonly found in woodlands, riverine forests and lightly wooded savannah. The head, neck, chin, throat and breast bib are greyish-white. The sides of the breast, the belly and underparts are rich chestnut. The scapulars and wing coverts are black, the primary wing feathers are black broadly edged with bright azure blue. The back, rump and tail are azure blue. The eyes are dark brown, the bill, legs and feet are bright red. The sexes are alike. Resident. Size: 20cm.

Madagascar Bee-eater *(Merops superciliosus)*

Found over much of the region. The forehead is white extending around the head to form a white stripe above the eye. The crown is olive green. A black stripe bordered below with white, extends from the gape through the eye to the sides of the nape. The chin is pale yellow becoming orange-red on the throat. The breast, belly and underparts are leaf green. The mantle and back are green, the wing coverts olive green and the primary wing feathers are green edged with brown. The eyes are deep red, the bill is black and legs and feet are greyish-black. The sexes are alike. Resident. Size: 29cm.

Blue-cheeked Bee-eater *(Merops persicus)*

A winter visitor to East Africa usually found close to water where they frequent papyrus reedbeds and lakeside trees. The forehead is white with a faint wash of blue. The crown, nape, back and long tail are leaf green. A broad black stripe extends from the gape through the eye to the ear coverts and is bordered above and, to a lesser extent, below with pale blue. The cheeks are pale blue-white. The chin is pale yellow graduating to orange-red on the throat. The breast, belly and underparts are yellowish-green. The wings are leaf green, the primaries being edged with dark brown-black. The eyes are deep red, the bill is black and the legs and feet are brown-black. The sexes are alike. Palearctic winter visitor. Size: 30cm.

Eurasian Bee-eater *(Merops apiaster)*

A palearctic winter visitor found over a wide range of habitats. The forehead is white, the crown, nape and mantle are chestnut. A black patch extends from the gape and covers the eye and ear coverts bordered below with white, becoming yellow on the chin and throat. A narrow black band separates the throat from the blue-green breast, belly and underparts. The scapulars, back and rump are golden yellow. The wing coverts are green and chestnut, the primaries are blue-green tipped black. The tail is green. The eyes are rich red, the bill is black and the legs and feet are blackish-brown. The sexes are similar, the female being duller above and paler below. Palearctic winter visitor. Size: 28cm.

Carmine Bee-eater *(Merops nubicus)*

Easily recognised by the bright carmine red plumage. The forehead, crown, chin and throat are iridescent blue-green, a black band extends from the gape to the ear coverts. Nape, neck, breast and belly are bright reddish-pink, undertail coverts are pale blue-green. The mantle and scapulars are reddish-pink. Wings and tail are carmine red, the tertials are edged blue, the primaries and secondaries are edged and tipped black, and the long central tail feathers darken towards the tip. Uppertail coverts are blue-green. Eyes are dark red; bill, legs and feet are black. The sexes are alike. Resident. Size: 37cm.

White-throated Bee-eater *(Merops albicollis)*

Encountered in a range of lightly wooded habitats. The forehead is white extending as a stripe around the head to the nape, the crown is black. A black stripe extends from the gape through the eye to the ear coverts. The chin, throat and cheeks are white. A broad black band extends across the upper breast bordered below with a band of pale blue, becoming pale green on the lower breast. The belly and underparts are white. The nape is orange-buff merging into green on the mantle and back. The wing coverts are green-blue, the primaries and secondaries are bluish. The tail is green-blue with very long blackish central streamers. The eyes are dark red, the bill is black and the legs and feet are greyish. The sexes are similar. Resident. Size: 28cm.

Cinnamon-chested Bee-eater *(Merops oreobates)*

A bird of woodland edges and clearings. The forehead, crown, nape, back, mantle and wing coverts are bright green. A black stripe extends from the gape to the ear coverts and is narrowly bordered below with white. The chin and throat are yellow and a broad black band extends across the upper breast. The lower breast is rich cinnamon red merging to yellow-buff on the belly and underparts. The primary and secondary wing feathers are green edged with black. The tail is square, bright green above with a black band towards the tip. The eyes are dark red, the bill, legs and feet are blackish. The sexes are alike. Immature birds lack the black breast band and have finely streaked underparts. Resident. Size: 22cm.

Little Bee-eater
(Merops pusillus)

The commonest and most widely distributed of East Africa's bee-eaters. The forehead, crown and upperparts are rich leaf green. A black stripe extends from the gape through the eye to the ear coverts. The eyebrow line is metallic ultramarine blue. The chin and throat are pale yellow, a black band is present in the centre of the upper breast, the remainder of the breast being rich orange-red becoming paler on the belly and underparts. The wings are green the primary wing feathers being edged with olive and the secondaries with rufous-black. The central tail feathers are green the outer feathers rufous tipped black, the tail is slightly forked. The eyes are red, the bill, legs and feet blackish. The sexes are alike. Resident. Size: 15cm.

Somali Bee-eater
(Merops revoilii)

Found in the north of the region. The feathers of the forehead and crown are pale olive green and have a spiky appearance. A black stripe runs from the gape through and beyond the eye above which is a bright blue eyebrow stripe. The chin and throat are white, the breast and belly are buff and the undertail coverts are pale blue. The nape is buff blending with the green mantle and back. The wings are green the primaries and secondaries edged with brown. The tail is blue-green. The eyes are red, the bill is black and the legs and feet are greyish. The sexes are alike. The bird usually has an unkempt appearance. Resident. Size: 16cm.

White-fronted Bee-eater
(Merops bullockoides)

The distribution of this species in East Africa is mainly restricted to the Rift Valley in Kenya and to southern Tanzania. The forehead is white becoming buff to pale orange on the crown and nape. A black stripe extends from the base of the bill through the eye to the ear coverts below which is a white band from the ear coverts to the chin. The throat is bright scarlet red. The breast and belly are orange-buff, the undertail coverts blue. The upperparts including the wings and tail are green-blue. The eyes are brown, the bill, legs and feet are blackish. The sexes are alike. Resident. Size: 23cm.

Lilac-breasted Roller
(Coracias caudata)

East Africa's commonest roller, found mainly in savannah habitats. The forehead and eyebrow are white, the crown and nape are pale green. A narrow black stripe runs through the eye, the cheeks are rufous with a wash of lilac. The chin is white, the throat and breast are lilac streaked with white. The belly and underparts are turquoise blue. The mantle, back and scapulars are brown, the rump is dark blue with turquoise blue uppertail coverts. The tail is azure blue with long central streamers darkish blue and brown. The wing coverts are dark and azure blue, the primaries are bright azure blue and black. Eyes are dark brown, bill is blackish and legs and feet yellowish-pink. The sexes are alike. Resident. Size: 40cm.

Eurasian Roller
(Coracias garrulus)

A palearctic winter visitor throughout the region in most habitats. The head, neck, breast, belly and underparts are pale turquoise blue, whitish on the forehead and cheeks. There is a narrow black stripe through the eye. The mantle, back and scapulars are rufous brown, the rump and uppertail coverts are dark green-blue. The tail is azure blue with darker blue central feathers. The wing coverts are dark blue to bright azure, the primaries are blue-black. The eyes are dark brown, the bill is black and the legs and feet are dull yellow-pink. The sexes are alike. Palearctic winter visitor. Size: 30cm.

Rufous-crowned Roller
(Coracias naevia)

An inhabitant of dry woodlands and lightly wooded savannah. The forehead and eyebrow are white, the crown, nape and hind neck are dull cinnamon-brown, the latter having a central white patch. The chin is white, the cheeks, throat, breast and belly are dark lilac heavily streaked with white. The mantle and scapulars are olive brown with a flush of green, the back is lilac blending to dark purple-blue on the rump and uppertail coverts. The tail is purple-blue with the central tail feathers olive brown. The wing coverts are dark purple at the carpal joint blending into lilac and rufous brown on the greater coverts, the primaries are dark blue edged with blue-green. The eyes are dark brown, the bill is blackish and the legs and feet are dull ochre. The sexes are alike. Resident. Size: 33cm.

Hoopoe
(Upupa epops)

A bird of wooded savannah, cultivated land, pastures and short grassy areas in park and gardens. Difficult to confuse with any other species. The head, neck, mantle, breast and belly are bright rufous, and the undertail coverts are buff-white. The feathers of the forehead and crown form a crest which, when erect, is fan-shaped, these feathers are tipped with black. The wings are black with broad white bands, the primary and secondary feathers are black with a white band towards the tips. The tail is black with a broad white band across the centre. The eyes are dark brown, the long decurved bill is blackish and the legs and feet are grey-black. The sexes are similar, the female being duller and slightly smaller. Resident. Size: 28cm.

Green Wood Hoopoe
(Phoeniculus purpureus)

A species found in most types of woodland, usually encountered in noisy flocks foraging from tree to tree in search of insects. A slender bird with the bulk of the plumage dark green-blue with an iridescent sheen showing purple and violet. The primary coverts and wing feathers have white bars which are very prominent in flight, as are the white spots that are present towards the end of the very long tail. The eyes are dark brown, the decurved bill and the legs and feet are bright red. The sexes are similar, the female being slightly smaller. Resident. Size: 40cm.

Common Scimitarbill
(Rhinopomastus cyanomelas)

Found over much of the region in woodlands, dry thorn bush areas and in lightly wooded savannah. The entire plumage is dark iridescent blue-black with washes of violet on the throat, breast and rump. The primary wing feathers and the very long tail have some prominent white spots. The eyes are dark brown, the very long decurved bill and the legs and feet are black. The female shows brown-black on the throat and breast and the primaries are faintly tipped greyish. Usually encountered in small groups of about 6 birds foraging on the trunks and branches of trees in search of a wide variety of insect foods. Resident. Size: 28cm.

White-headed Barbet
(Lybius leucocephalus)

A species found throughout Uganda, central and southern Kenya and northern Tanzania, inhabiting woodlands, favouring areas with fig trees, cultivated farmland and parks and gardens. The head, mantle, neck, breast and rump are white. The belly is brownish-black streaked with white and the undertail coverts are white. The back is brownish-black, the wing coverts are black with white spots and the primary wing feathers are black finely edged with white. The tail is black-brown. The eyes are dark brown, the heavy bill and the legs and feet are blackish-grey. The sexes are alike. Resident. Size: 16cm.

Red & Yellow Barbet
(Trachyphonus erythrocephalus)

A species that favours dry bush country, lightly wooded savannah and scrub areas usually in the vicinity of termite mounds in which they breed. The male has the forehead and crown black and the nape red and yellow spotted with black. The chin and the centre of the throat are black, the sides of the throat are yellow and the cheeks are red. The breast, belly and underparts are yellow, the former with a necklace of black feathers spotted with white. The back is black spotted with white and yellow, the rump is yellow and the uppertail coverts are red tipped with yellow. The tail is black heavily barred with yellow-white. The wing feathers are blackish boldly spotted with white. The eyes are brown, the bill is orange-red darker at the tip, the legs and feet are dark grey. The female lacks the black throat patch and the black crown, and is generally not so bright as the male. Resident. Size: 23cm.

D'Arnaud's Barbet
(Trachyphonus darnaudii)

A species that favours areas of arid bush, open woodlands, acacia scrub and lightly wooded grasslands. The head, neck and throat are yellow heavily speckled with dark brown-black, the breast is yellow with an irregular black patch in the centre and with fine black flecking. The belly is pale yellow-white, the undertail coverts are white tipped with bright red. The mantle, back, wings and tail are black-brown boldly spotted and barred with yellow and white. The eyes are brown, the bill, legs and feet are blackish. The sexes are alike. Resident. Size: 16cm.

African Grey Hornbill *(Tockus nasutus)*

A species of open woodlands and lightly wooded savannah. The head and neck are dark grey with a white stripe extending from just above the eye, along the edge of the crown and down the hind neck. The breast is buff-brown fading to white on the belly and underparts. The mantle and back are brown, the latter with a white central stripe. The tail is dark brown tipped white. The wing coverts and primaries are dark brown edged with buff and white. The eyes are dark brown, the large decurved bill is blackish with a white stripe along the upper side of the lower mandible, and the legs and feet are black-brown. The female differs from the male in having the upper mandible creamy-yellow at the base and red at the tip. A small patch of bare skin on the throat is pale yellow-green. Resident. Size: 48cm.

Red-billed Hornbill *(Tockus enythrorhynchus)*

A common species in arid bush regions and in open woodlands. The forehead, crown and nape are black, the remainder of the head and neck are white with grey smudges on the ear coverts and the sides of the neck. The breast, belly and underparts are white. The mantle and back are black-brown with a white central stripe, the long tail is black, the outer feathers with white edging. The wing coverts and primaries are black with bold white spots. The eyes are dark brown, the decurved bill is red with the basal, section of the lower mandible blackish. The legs and feet are blackish-brown. The female is smaller than the male and has less black on the bill. Resident. Size: 45cm.

Von Der Decken's Hornbill *(Tockus deckeni)*

A bird of bush areas and acacia woodlands. The crown and nape are black, the rest of the head, neck, breast and underparts are white. A black patch surrounds the eyes and the ear coverts are streaked with grey-black, the sides of the throat have patches of bare pink-red skin. The back is black with a white central stripe, the rump and tail are black with the outer tail feathers showing much white from midway to the tips. The wing coverts and primaries are black, the secondaries are white. The eyes are dark brown, the large decurved bill is red at the base and dull yellow towards the tip. The legs and feet are black. The female has an all black bill and is smaller than the male. Resident. Size: 49cm.

Eastern Yellow-billed Hornbill *(Tockus flavirostris)*

A bird of arid bush country and lightly wooded savannah. The forehead, crown and nape are black, the head and neck are white with a black patch around the eye and black streaking on the ear coverts and the sides of the neck. The throat has a patch of bare pink skin, the breast, belly and underparts are white. The black back has a broad white central stripe, the rump and tail are black the outer tail feathers with white tips and a broad white midway band. The wing coverts and primaries are black spotted with white. The eyes are yellow, the large decurved bill is yellow and the legs and feet are black-brown. Resident. Size: 50cm.

Silvery-cheeked Hornbill *(Bycanistes brevis)*

A large hornbill of mountain and coastal forests. The plumage is mainly black, the belly and underparts are white, along with the rump and uppertail coverts, the tail is tipped white and the cheeks are streaked with grey. The eyes are dark brown with a blue orbital ring, the enormous bill has a yellow band at the base, is brownish-black with a large creamy-yellow casque. The legs and feet are black. The female is smaller than the male and the bill casque is much reduced. Resident. Size: 70cm.

Southern Ground Hornbill *(Bucorvus leadbeateri)*

A very large bird found on open and lightly wooded grasslands and savannah, spending most of the day on the ground in search of food which consists of snakes, amphibians, rodents and a variety of insects. The plumage is almost entirely black, the exception being the white primary wing feathers. A patch of bright red unfeathered skin surrounds the eyes and extends on to the sides of the neck and the throat. The eyes are yellow, the large decurved bill is black with a short casque at the upper base. The legs and feet are black. The female is smaller than the male and has a throat patch of blue-grey and red. Immature birds have brown-black plumage, primaries streaked with black, pale yellow-grey eyes and facial and throat patch greyish-yellow. Resident. Size: 107cm.

Crowned Hornbill
(Tockus alboterminatus)

Commonly found in woodlands and forest edges over much of the region. The male has the head, neck, back, wings and upper breast brown/black. A variable amount of light streaking appears on the upper head. The lower breast and underparts are white. The tail is brown/black with white tips to all but the outer and central feathers. The eyes are yellow set in an orbital patch of black skin. The bill is red and has a clearly developed casque; the base of the bill is yellow. The legs and feet are black. The female is similar to the male but is smaller and has the bill casque less well developed. Immature birds resemble adults but are duller and have a yellow bill which lacks a casque and greyish eyes. Resident. Size: 55cm.

Nubian Woodpecker
(Campethera nubica)

A bird of open woodlands and bush. The male has the forehead, crown and nape red, the remainder of the head and neck are white with blackish flecks and streaks. The chin is white and the moustachial stripe is red bordered with black. The breast, belly and underparts are creamy white with black spots on the breast and undertail coverts and black barring on the flanks. The scapulars and wing coverts are green-brown barred with creamy-yellow. The back, rump and uppertail coverts are greenish-brown barred and spotted with white. The tail is greenish barred with brown. The primary wing feathers are brown barred with white. The eyes are dark red, the bill, legs and feet are greyish-black. The female has the forehead and crown black, spotted with white and the moustachial stripe is black finely flecked with white. Resident. Size: 18cm.

Cardinal Woodpecker
(Dendropicos fuscescens)

Found throughout the region in areas of arid bush and most types of woodland and forest. The forehead and fore crown are buff-brown, the hind crown and the nape are red. The sides of the head are white finely flecked and streaked with grey-brown. A black moustachial stripe extends from the base of the bill to the lower neck. The chin, throat and breast are white boldly marked with brown-black streaks. The belly and underparts are creamy-white streaked and barred with brown-black. The upperparts are dark brown barred with white, the uppertail coverts are tipped with red. The eyes are reddish-brown, the bill, legs and feet are blackish. The female differs from the male in having black-brown nape and crown. Immature birds are a duller version of the adults and have a red crown patch. Resident. Size: 13cm.

Grey Woodpecker
(Dendropicos goertae)

A bird of woodland and forest edges and acacia woodlands and clearings, often foraging on the ground. The forehead, cheeks and ear coverts are grey, the crown and nape are red edged with white. The neck, chin, throat and breast are grey and the underparts are greyish with a tinge of yellow. A patch of yellow-orange appears on the belly and some grey barring is visible on the flanks. The back and wing coverts are yellowish-green, the primary and secondary wing feathers are dark brown edged with green and barred with white. The rump and uppertail coverts are red. The tail is dark brown barred with white. The eyes are darkish brown, the bill is black and the legs and feet are greyish. The female lacks the red crown and nape of the male, the head being all grey. Resident. Size: 18cm.

Greater Honeyguide
(Indicator indicator)

A widespread species over much of the region. This species is famous for its guiding behaviour, whereby it leads humans and Honey Badgers to bee nests, feeding on the wax once the nest is broken open. This species is also a brood parasite, laying its eggs in the nests of other species which then act as foster parents to the young. Hole nesting species such as Barbets and Woodpeckers are usually chosen, but the authors have recently seen Ruppell's Long-tailed Starlings feeding newly fledged young. The male has the head, nape and back grey-brown with a prominent grey/white cheek patch. The throat is brown/black, the breast is light brown/grey while the remainder of the underparts are pale grey-white. The secondary flight feathers are grey/brown edged with grey/white with a patch of bright yellow on the shoulder. The primary flight feathers are grey/brown. The bill is pale, often with a pink flush. The legs and feet are black. The female lacks both the grey-white cheek patch and the dark throat and is generally duller than the male. Juveniles (*illustrated*) have the chin, throat and upper breast yellow while the upperparts are uniform brown. Resident. Size: 18cm.

Rufous-naped Lark
(Mirafra africana)

A common resident species on open plains and in bushy terrain throughout much of the region. The feathers of the forehead and crown are greyish brown streaked with black, the nape feathers are usually rufous but there is a certain amount of regional variation. The face, chin and throat are buff-white, the cheeks and ear coverts are mid-brown. The breast, belly and underparts are buff with a wash of rufous on the upper breast and flanks. The breast is spotted with dark brown. The wings are rounded, dark brown with streaks of rufous and black. The back, rump and tail feathers are dark brown streaked with black and edged with buff. The eyes and bill are brown, the legs and feet are flesh pink. The sexes are alike. Resident. Size: 17cm.

Red-winged Lark
(Mirafra hypermetra)

Found throughout most of the region in areas of open grassy plains interspersed with bushes. They can usually be located singing from the tops of low bushes and shrubs, the song consisting of a short series of clear repeated whistles. They can be distinguished from the Rufous-naped Lark by their larger size and longer tail. The forehead, crown, nape and mantle are greyish brown, boldly streaked with black. The face is buff-white with some irregular speckling, a pale stripe extends above the eye from the forehead to the hind-crown. The chin and throat are white, the breast is buff. The sides of the neck and the breast are heavily spotted with dark brown and black. The primary and secondary flight feathers are rufous edged and tipped with brown and buff. The rump and tail are brown edged with grey and buff. The eyes are brown, the bill is dark brown/black, paler at the base, and the legs and feet are grey/pink. The sexes are alike. Resident. Size: 23cm.

Crested Lark
(Galerida cristata)

A locally common species in northern Kenya and southern Ethiopia. The forehead and crown are pale buff streaked with brown/black, the feathering of the crown forming an erectile crest. The nape, mantle and sides of the neck are buff streaked and speckled with mid-brown. The chin, throat and breast are buff, heavily streaked with dark brown, the belly and underparts are whitish with a wash of buff on the flanks. The back, wing coverts and flight feathers are brown edged with buff. The tail is dark brown and rufous, paler on the outer edges. The eyes are deep brown. The bill is dark brown/black, paler at the base. The legs and feet are flesh coloured. The sexes are alike. Resident and partial migrant. Size: 16cm.

Red-capped Lark
(Calandrella cinerea)

A bird favouring areas of short dry grassland. A medium-sized slender lark with the forehead and erectile crest feathers rufous. The nape, mantle, cheeks and sides of the neck are brown/buff. A pronounced white stripe extends from above the eye to the hind-crown. The chin and throat are white, the breast is brownish buff with prominent rufous patches on the sides, and the belly and underparts are white. The back is brown merging to rufous on the rump and becoming dark brown on the tail, the outer edges of which are whitish-buff. The wing coverts and flight feathers are dark brown edged and tipped with pale brown and buff. The eyes are dark brown, the bill is black and the legs and feet are brownish-black. The sexes are alike. Resident. Size: 14cm.

Fischer's Sparrow Lark
(Eremopterix leucopareia)

A small rather finch-like lark of south-western Kenya, north, central and western Tanzania and north-eastern Uganda. The adult male has the forehead, crown, nape and neck chestnut brown. The face is black with one black stripe extending from the eye to the hind-crown and another extending from the chin, down the throat and around the sides of the neck and running down the centre of the breast, belly and underparts. The cheeks and ear coverts are creamy white. The sides of the breast, the belly and the flanks are white with a wash of buff. The wing coverts and flight feathers are dark brown, broadly edged with grey, buff and rufous. The tail is dark brown edged with grey and rufous. The female lacks the bold markings of the male having a grey-brown head streaked with dark brown and a hint of rufous brown around the neck. The breast is buff and a broad central band of brown extends down the centre of the white belly and underparts. The eyes are brown, the thickish bill greyish blue-black and the legs and feet brown. Resident. Size: 11cm.

Banded Martin
(Riparia cincta)

Found in areas of open grassland and bush, often in small parties. The plumage of the upper side of the body, from the forehead to the tail is a uniform dark chocolate brown. A short narrow stripe extends from the base of the upper mandible to the eyebrow. The chin, throat and sides of the neck are buff-white, a broad chocolate brown band extends across the upper breast, while the lower breast, belly and underparts are white. In flight the primary and secondary wing feathers appear slightly darker than the rest of the upper plumage and contrast strongly with the white under wing coverts. The tail is unforked. The eyes, legs and feet are dark brown and the bill is black. The sexes are alike. Resident. Size: 16cm.

Rock Martin
(Hirundo fuligula)

A widely distributed species around kopjes, cliffs, mountains, rocky hillsides and human habitations. The plumage is almost entirely dark brown, slightly darker above than below, occasionally with a faint wash of grey on the wings and tail. The chin and throat are pale rufous. The unforked tail has a series of white spots towards the tip which are only visible when the tail is spread in flight. The eyes are dark brown, the bill is black and the legs and feet are greyish-brown. The sexes are alike. Resident. Size: 13cm.

Wire-tailed Swallow
(Hirundo smithii)

A common species throughout the region on savannahs, along rivers, and around lakes and human habitations. The forehead and crown are bright rufous, the face, nape, mantle, back and wing coverts are glossy, dark violet blue. The chin, throat, breast, belly and underparts are white, a violet blue patch extends from the sides of the neck to the sides of the breast and a similar patch extends from the rear of the flanks around the sides onto the undertail coverts. The primary and secondary flight feathers are purple-black above and whitish-grey below. The rump and tail are purple-black, the outermost tail feathers form into long thin wire-like streamers. The eyes are dark brown, the bill, legs and feet are black. The sexes are similar, the female having less well-developed tail streamers. Resident. Size: 15cm.

Mosque Swallow
(Hirundo senegalensis)

The largest swallow in East Africa. An inhabitant of open country, light woodlands, river edges and coastal bush over much of the region. The forehead, crown, nape, mantle, back, wings and tail are deep blue-black. The cheeks, ear coverts, rump, belly and underparts are rufous, the chin, throat and breast are whitish merging into the rufous feathering of the belly. The underwing coverts are whitish and the underside of the flight feathers are greyish. The outermost tail feathers are elongated, resulting in a deeply forked tail, particularly noticeable in flight. The eyes are dark brown, the bill, legs and feet are black. The sexes are alike. Resident. Size: 23cm.

Red-rumped Swallow
(Hirundo daurica)

A bird of open grasslands, rocky hillsides and human habitations. The upper plumage resembles that of the Mosque Swallow, with the forehead, crown, nape, back and wing coverts dark, glossy blue-black. The sides of the neck and the rump are rufous. The chin, throat, breast, belly and underparts are off-white with faint streaks of dark grey. The primary and secondary wing feathers are dark blue-black. The tail is blue-black and deeply forked. The eyes are dark brown, the bill is black and the legs and feet brownish-black. The sexes are alike. Resident and winter migrant. Size: 18cm.

Lesser Striped Swallow
(Hirundo abyssinica)

A common and well-distributed species throughout the region, inhabiting areas of open grassland, cultivated farmland, human habitations and woodland edges. One of the prettiest of East Africa's swallows, with the forehead, crown, nape, sides of the neck and rump rusty red. The chin, throat, cheeks, breast, belly and underparts are white boldly streaked with black. The flight feathers are black with a wash of brown. The tail is bluish-black and deeply forked. The eyes are dark brown, the bill, legs and feet are black. The sexes are similar, the female having shorter outer tail feathers. Resident. Size: 18cm.

African Pied Wagtail
(Motacilla aguimp)

A common species over most of the region. The forehead, crown, nape, back, wing coverts and cheeks are black. A broad tail band extends across the upper breast. The chin, throat, lower breast, belly and underparts are white. The primary wing feathers are black edged and tipped with white. The central tail feathers are black and the outer feathers white. The eyes are dark brown, the bill is black and the legs and feet dark grey-black. The sexes are similar. Resident. Size: 20cm.

Yellow Wagtail
(Motacilla flava)

A widely distributed and common species throughout the region. Several races of yellow wagtail occur during periods of migration, when they exhibit great variation in head plumage from white to yellow, grey and black. In most races the remainder of the plumage is similar. The throat, breast, belly and underparts are bright yellow. The back and wing coverts are olive green and the primary and secondary wing feathers are black edged with whitish-buff. The tail is brown-black with the outermost feathers white. The eyes are dark brown, the bill, legs and feet are black. The females are less well marked around the head and generally duller. Winter visitor and passage migrant. Size: 16cm.

Grassland Pipit
(Anthus cinnamomeus)

A common and widely distributed species, found in areas of open grasslands and savannahs. The plumage of the upperparts is buff-brown with dark streaking. A broad off-white stripe follows the line of the eyebrow while the chin, throat, cheeks and ear coverts are off-white with some buff streaking. The narrow eye and moustachial stripes are dark brown. The breast, belly and underparts are buffish with some dark streaking on the upper breast. The wing feathers are brown edged with buff. The tail is darkish-brown, the outermost feathers being edged with white. The eyes are dark brown, the bill is black with some yellowish-brown at the base and the legs and feet are warm brown. The sexes are alike. Resident. Size: 15cm.

Golden Pipit
(Tmetothylacus tenellus)

A bird of the dry bush and scrub. The forehead, crown, nape, mantle and ear coverts are olive green streaked with black. The face, chin, throat, breast and underparts are brilliant chrome yellow. A broad black band extends across the breast. The wing coverts are yellow edged with dark brown, the secondary wing feathers are yellow and the primary wing feathers yellow edged and tipped with black. The central tail feathers are dark brown while the outer feathers are bright yellow. Eyes and bill are dark brown, legs and feet are pale flesh pink. The female lacks much of the colour found in the male, being buff-brown above streaked with dark brown and having much of the underside buffish; lacks the black breast band. Resident. Size: 15cm.

Yellow-throated Longclaw
(Macronyx croceus)

A reasonably common bird in grassland and savannah regions. The forehead, crown and nape are mid-brown streaked with dark brown. A band of yellow follows the line of the eyebrow and the chin, throat, lower breast, and underparts are the same bright yellow. A narrow black moustachial stripe extends down the sides of the neck, joining a broad black breast band, some black spotting occurs on the breast below this band. The wing coverts are brown edged with buff and the primary and secondary wing feathers are brown edged with yellow and buff. The tail is dark brown tipped with white. The eyes and bill are dark brown, the legs and feet are dull yellow-pink. The female has a duller appearance than the male. Resident. Size: 20cm.

Rosy-breasted Longclaw
(Macronyx ameliae)

A bird of moist areas. The forehead, crown, nape, mantle and wing coverts are warm brown streaked with dark brown-black. The face is buff-white with a brown eye stripe thickening at the rear to cover the ear coverts. A narrow black moustachial stripe extends down the sides of the neck before linking with a broad black breast band. The chin and throat are bright rosy-red, the lower breast and upper belly are washed pink and the remainder of the underparts are buff-white. The primary and secondary wing feathers are warm brown edged with buff. The tail is dark brown tipped and edged with white. The female is generally duller in appearance. Resident. Size: 18cm.

Common Bulbul

(Pycnonotus barbatus)

Probably the commonest bird in East Africa, being found throughout the region in a wide variety of habitats. The head, face and chin are black, becoming dark brown on the throat, breast, ear coverts and the slightly crested nape. The belly and flanks are off-white and the feathers of the undertail are bright yellow. The upperparts including the wing coverts are grey-brown. The primary and secondary wing feathers are darkish grey-brown edged with buff. The tail is dark brown with a variable amount of white at the tip. There are several races found within the region, some of which show white on the sides of the neck and ear coverts, the yellow on the undertail coverts is also variable or absent. The eyes are dark brown, the bill, legs and feet are black. The sexes are alike. Resident. Size: 18cm.

Northern White-crowned Shrike

(Eurocephalus rueppelli)

A bird of dry thorn bush country, locally common throughout the region. The forehead and crown are white, a black band extends from the base of the bill through the eye before broadening to cover the ear coverts and the nape. The chin, throat, breast, belly and underparts are white, a brown patch is visible on the sides of the breast. The mantle and wing coverts are greyish-brown. The primary and secondary flight feathers are dark brown. The rump is white and very conspicuous in flight, the tail is dark brown. The eyes, which have a narrow white orbital ring, are dark brown, the bill, legs and feet are black. The sexes are alike. Resident. Size: 23cm.

Rosy-patched Bush Shrike

(Rhodophoneus cruentus)

A locally common bird in regions of dry thorn bush and scrub, often encountered on top of a bush from where they issue a loud, piping call. The male has the forehead, crown, nape, mantle and wing and ear coverts greyish-brown. A broad band of crimson red extends from the chin down the centre of the throat and breast, this band is bordered by white feathering which also covers the belly and underparts. The sides of the breast and the flanks have a wash of tawny-buff. The primary and secondary wing feathers are dark grey-brown, the rump is crimson red and the tail is black with white tips on the outermost feathers. The eyes are dark brown, the bill is black and the legs and feet are grey. The female differs from the male in lacking the crimson band on the white chin and upper throat, but has a broad black band across the lower throat and a crimson band extending from it down the centre of the belly. Resident. Size: 23cm.

Tropical Boubou

(Laniarius aethiopicus)

A widely distributed species in areas of forests, woodlands, scrub and thickets. Rather shy birds that are usually in pairs skulking in dense vegetation, often being located as a result of hearing the bell-like calls produced as a duet by a male and female. The head, mantle, wings and tail are black with a sheen of blue, in some individuals white is visible on the wing coverts. The chin, throat, breast, belly and underparts are white, often with a wash of peach-buff on the breast and flanks. The eyes are dark brown, the bill, legs and feet are black. The sexes are alike. Resident. Size: 23cm.

Grey-headed Bush Shrike

(Malaconotus blanchoti)

A large, robust shrike with startling plumage, found in woodlands, riverine forests and areas of scrub and bush. The head is a slaty blue-grey, the chin and throat are bright yellow merging to chestnut on the breast then back to bright yellow on the belly and underparts. The mantle, back, wings and tail are a bright rich green with some yellow spotting on the wing coverts, secondary wing feathers and tail. The eyes are yellow, the large, hooked bill is black and the legs and feet are grey-blue. The sexes are alike. Resident. Size: 25cm.

Magpie Shrike
(Urolestes melanoleucus)

A very conspicuous shrike with a very long tail, usually encountered in pairs or small parties hunting insects from a vantage point on top of small bushes and rank vegetation. Locally common over much of the region, favouring areas of open grassland with scattered scrub and woodland edges. The plumage is almost entirely glossy black, the exceptions being a broad white edge to the scapulars showing as a distinctive wing bar, white bases to the primary wing feathers, a white patch on the flanks, a variable amount of white on the tip of the tail and a grey rump. The eyes are dark brown, the bill, legs and feet are black. The sexes are alike. Resident. Size: 38cm.

Red-backed Shrike
(Lanius collurio)

Found over much of the region in a variety of habitats but preferring thorn bush country and woodland edges. The male has a black band extending from the forehead, through the eye to the ear coverts, as if wearing a 'highwayman's mask'. The remainder of the head, nape and the rump are grey-blue. The chin and throat are white, the breast, belly and underparts are white with a hint of pink. The mantle, wing coverts and secondary wing feathers are rich chestnut, the primary wing feathers are dark brown edged with chestnut. The tail feathers are black, the outermost feathers being white edged. The eyes are dark brown, the bill, legs and feet are black. The female lacks the splendour of the male, having a brown head, mantle and wing coverts, the underparts are off-white with crescents of brown on the sides of the throat, breast, belly and flanks. Winter visitor. Size: 17cm.

Common Fiscal Shrike
(Lanius collaris)

A widespread and common species over much of the region, often encountered around human habitations, cultivated farmland and woodland edges. The head, mantle and back are glossy black, the chin, cheeks, throat, breast, belly and underparts are white. The scapulars are black broadly edged with white resulting in a conspicuous wing bar. The rump is grey, the central tail feathers are black tipped with white and the outermost feathers are black with broad white outer edges. The eyes are dark brown, the bill, legs and feet are black. The female is similar to the male, but is occasionally brownish-black above and with some chestnut on the flanks. Resident. Size: 23cm.

Long-tailed Fiscal Shrike
(Lanius cabanisi)

A widespread and locally common species, inhabiting grasslands and areas of scrub and bush. The forehead, crown and nape are black, the chin, cheeks, throat, breast and underparts are white. The mantle and scapulars are greyish, the wings are black with a small white patch at the base of the primary flight feathers. The rump is white, the very long tail is black tipped with white. The eyes are dark brown, the bill, legs and feet are black. The sexes are alike. Resident. Size: 30cm.

Grey-backed Fiscal Shrike
(Lanius excubitoroides)

A bird of thorn bush and acacia scrub, found in Uganda, western Tanzania and western Kenya from the rift valley lakes. A broad black band extends from the forehead, through the eye, ear coverts and down the sides of the neck. The crown, nape and mantle are silver-grey. The chin, cheeks, throat and underparts are white, as is the rump. The wings are black with a distinctive white patch at the base of the primary flight feathers. The long, broad tail is black tipped with white and the outermost feathers are white towards the base. The eyes are dark brown, the bill, legs and feet are black. The sexes are similar. Resident. Size: 25cm.

Taita Fiscal Shrike
(Lanius dorsalis)

A reasonably common bird in areas of dry bush country, often perching conspicuously on the upper most branches of bushes from where they drop on prey items. The forehead, upper face, crown and nape are black, the chin, cheeks, breast, belly and underparts are white. The mantle is grey merging with the white of the back and rump. The wings are totally black, the broad tail is black narrowly tipped and edged with white. The eyes are dark brown, the bill, legs and feet are black. The sexes are alike. Resident. Size: 20cm.

Common Stonechat
(Saxicola torquata)

A reasonably common species at elevations of 1,500m or more. The male has the head, nape, mantle, chin and throat black, the centre of the breast is rich chestnut. The sides of the neck and breast are white, as are the belly and underparts. The wing coverts are black edged with white forming a distinctive wing bar when perched. The primary and secondary wing feathers are black, the uppertail coverts and rump show white, the tail is black. The eyes are dark brown, the bill, legs and feet are black. The female has the upper plumage warm brown-black. Resident. Size: 13cm.

Schalow's Wheatear
(Oenanthe lugubris)

Quite common in highland areas, on rocky hillsides, cliffs or bare stony ground. The forehead, crown and nape are creamy-white, the chin, throat, face, neck, mantle and wings are black. The breast, belly and underparts are white, often with a wash of buff. The rump is whitish, the tail is black with white on the basal half of the outer feathers. The eyes are dark brown, the bill, legs and feet are black. The female has the upper plumage grey-brown and the chin and throat greyish. Resident. Size: 15cm.

Northern Wheatear
(Oenanthe oenanthe)

A common winter visitor over much of the region on short grass plains and savannahs, dry rocky areas and cultivated farmland. The male has the forehead, crown, nape and mantle greyish. A black band extends from the base of the bill through the eye before broadening to cover the ear coverts. (In breeding plumage this area of black also covers the chin and breast). The chin is white, the throat and breast are white washed with warm buff. The belly and underparts are greyish-white. The primary and secondary wing feathers are black edged with buff. The rump is white and the tail is black, tipped with white and with the basal portion of the outer feathers white. The eyes are dark brown, the bill, legs and feet are black. The female has the upperparts buff-brown and has the black facial patch of the male replaced with pale olive-brown. Palearctic winter visitor. Size: 15cm.

Isabelline Wheatear
(Oenanthe isabellina)

A winter visitor to areas of semi-desert and open plains in Kenya, Uganda and northern Tanzania. A bird with almost uniform sandy-brown plumage both above and below. A faint eye stripe is present and the belly and underparts have a creamy wash. The primary and secondary wing feathers are dark brown edged with buff. The rump is white and the tail feathers are white at the bases and black at the tips. The eyes are dark brown, the bill, legs and feet are black. The sexes are alike. Palearctic winter visitor. Size: 16cm.

Pied Wheatear
(Oenanthe pleschanka)

A common winter visitor over much of the region. The forehead, crown and nape are brownish on arrival in the autumn, becoming whiter throughout the winter in readiness for their spring migration north. The face, cheeks, chin, throat and upper breast are black-brown. The lower breast, belly and underparts are buff-white, the lower breast sometimes showing traces of creamy-yellow. The wings are black-brown, and the rump is white. The basal half of the central tail feathers are white with the remaining half black, while the outer feathers are almost completely white with black tips. The eyes are dark brown, the bill, legs and feet are black. The female has the upperparts mottled brown and the throat and breast greyish-brown. Palearctic winter visitor. Size: 14cm.

Capped Wheatear
(Oenanthe pileata)

A common species on short grass plains and savannahs in central and southern Kenya and throughout Tanzania. The forehead is white with a band following the line of the eyebrow. The crown is black, merging with the chocolate brown of the nape, mantle, back and wing coverts. The cheeks and sides of the neck are black, joining with a black breast bib. The chin, throat, belly and underparts are white with a wash of cream-buff on the flanks. The wing feathers are dark brown-black edged with buff. The rump is white, the tail is predominantly black with white at the base. The eyes are dark brown, the bill is black and the legs and feet are greyish-black. The sexes are alike. Resident. Size: 16cm.

Northern Anteater Chat
(Myrmecocichla aethiops)

A very common species in south-western and central Kenya, particularly in the Masai Mara and in the highlands of northern Tanzania. They are often encountered along the margins of roads and tracks. A sturdy bird with the entire plumage brownish-black, the only exception being the primary wing feathers which are white at the base, showing as a very conspicuous wing bar in flight. The flight itself is rather weak and laboured. The eyes are dark brown, the bill, legs and feet are black. The sexes are alike. It is possible to confuse this species with the Sooty Chat (*Myrmecocichla nigra*) which has white wing coverts not primaries, the female and immature Sooty Chat have no white in the wings at all. Resident. Size: 20cm.

Sooty Chat
(Myrmecocichla nigra)

A bird of open plains and grasslands with scattered bush and scrub, in south-western Kenya, north-western and southern Tanzania and throughout most of Uganda. The plumage of the male is entirely black with the exception of the wing coverts which are white. The female and immature birds are dark brown and have no white in the wings at all. The eyes are dark brown, the bill, legs and feet are black. This species may be confused with the Anteater Chat (*Myrmecocichla aethiops*) which has the base of the primary wing feathers white. Resident. Size: 18cm.

Cliffchat
(Thamnolaea cinnamomeiventris)

As its name implies this species can be found on cliffs, escarpment edges and rocky hillsides. The male has the head, mantle, chin, throat and breast glossy black. A narrow white band separates the black breast from the rich orange-red of the belly and underparts. The wing coverts are white, the remainder of the wings are black. The rump is orange-red and the tail is black. The female has the head, mantle, chin, throat and breast dark slaty-grey and, unlike the male, shows no white on the wing coverts. The eyes are dark brown, the bill, legs and feet are black. Resident. Size: 20cm.

Common Redstart
(Phoenicurus phoenicurus)

A winter visitor to many parts of East Africa. The male has the forehead white and the crown, mantle and wing coverts slaty-grey. The face, chin and throat are black, the breast is orange-red becoming paler on the belly and underparts. The primary and secondary wing feathers are dark brown edged and tipped with buff-white. The rump and outer tail feathers are orange-red, the central tail feathers are black. The female has grey-brown upper plumage, sandy brown below with white on the belly. The rump and tail are orange-red with the central tail feathers black as in the male. The eyes are dark brown, the bill, legs and feet are black. Palearctic winter visitor. Size: 14cm.

White-browed Scrub Robin
(Cercotrichas leucophrys)

A species found over much of the region in areas of bush, open woodland and dense thickets and scrub. The forehead, crown and nape are grey-brown. A white stripe follows the line of the eyebrow from the base of the bill, the chin and throat are white with a black moustachial stripe. The breast is white, boldly streaked with dark grey, the belly and underparts are white with a wash of warm buff on the flanks. The wing coverts and secondary wing feathers are dark brown-black broadly tipped with white. The primary wing feathers are black edged with russet brown. The rump and tail are russet brown, the latter tipped black and white. The eyes are dark brown, the bill, legs and feet are black. The sexes are alike. Resident. Size: 15cm.

Spotted Morning Thrush
(Cichladusa guttata)

A shy, secretive inhabitant of dry bush, scrub, thickets and dense undergrowth in savannahs, parks and gardens. The forehead and crown are brown streaked with grey-white, the nape, mantle, back, rump and tail are russet brown. A narrow white stripe follows the line of the eyebrow and the cheeks, chin and throat are buff-white with a black moustachial stripe. The breast, belly and underparts are buff-white, the breast, belly and flanks being boldly spotted with black. The wings are brown with the primary and secondary feathers edged russet brown. The sexes are alike. Resident. Size: 17cm.

White-browed Robin Chat *(Cossypha heuglini)*

Distributed over much of the region, favouring woodlands and gardens with dense undercover. A rather shy, secretive species, often seen skulking about under bushes and shrubs. The forehead, crown and nape are black and a broad white band follows the line of the eyebrow to the side of the nape. The face, upper cheeks and ear coverts are black. The chin, lower cheeks, throat, neck, breast and underparts are rich orange-red. The mantle, back and scapulars are olive-brown, the wing coverts and primary and secondary wing feathers are slaty-brown. The rump is orange-red. The central tail feathers are olive brown and the outer feathers are dull orange-red. The eyes are dark brown, the bill is black and the legs and feet are mid-brown. The female is occasionally browner on the mantle and back, otherwise the sexes are alike. It is easy to confuse this species with Ruppell's Robin Chat (*Cossypha semirufa*) which has the wings dark olive brown and the central tail feathers black. Resident. Size: 20cm.

Ruppell's Robin Chat *(Cossypha semirufa)*

A bird of forests, thickets and the dense undergrowth of woodlands and gardens in the highlands of central and southern Kenya and north-central Tanzania. The forehead, crown and nape are black, a white stripe extends from the sides of the forehead above the eye to the hind-neck. The face, cheeks, sides of the neck and ear coverts are black. The chin, throat, breast, belly and underparts are orange-red. The mantle, back and scapulars are olive brown, the wing coverts and primary and secondary wing feathers are dark brown edged with olive. The rump and outer tail feathers are orange-red, the central tail feathers are black. The eyes are dark brown, the bill is black and the legs and feet are mid-brown. The sexes are alike. This species could easily be mistaken for the White-browed Robin Chat (*Cossypha heuglini*) which is larger and has slaty-brown wings and olive brown central tail feathers. Resident. Size: 18cm.

Olive Thrush *(Turdus olivaceus)*

A bird of forests, woodlands, hillsides and gardens with trees, bushes and dense undergrowth. Somewhat shy and secretive they spend much of their time skulking in deep vegetation. The head, back, mantle and wing coverts are olive brown, paler on the cheeks and sides of the neck. The chin and throat are white streaked with dark brown, the breast is grey brown often with dark brown and whitish streaks. The sides of the belly and the flanks are orange-red, the centre of the belly and underparts showing some white. The wing coverts are greyish-brown and the primary and secondary wing feathers are dark brown edged with olive. The tail is greyish-brown. The eyes are dark brown, with a bright yellow-orange orbital ring. The bill, legs and feet are orange-yellow. The sexes are alike. Immature birds have the chin, throat, breast and flanks spotted with black. Resident. Size: 23cm.

Bare-eyed Thrush *(Turdus tephronotus)*

One of East Africa's most attractive thrushes, found in areas of dry bush and scrub particularly along the coasts of Kenya, northern Tanzania and southern Somalia, also inland as far as the central highlands. The head, nape, mantle, wing coverts and upper breast are slaty blue-grey. The chin and throat are white boldly streaked with black. The lower breast, belly and underparts are orange-red. The primary and secondary wing feathers are blackish edged with grey-blue. The tail is slaty blue-grey. The eyes are dark brown surrounded by an area of bare yellow-orange skin. The bill is bright orange and the legs and feet are yellow-orange. The sexes are alike. Immature birds have the breast streaked and spotted black. Resident. Size: 21cm.

Arrow-marked Babbler *(Turdoides jardineii)*

A bird of bush, scrub, light woodlands, swamp edges and dense undergrowth throughout much of the region. Usually encountered in small but noisy parties, foraging from bush to bush. The feathers of the head and neck are dark brown edged with buff-white, the lores are dark. The chin, throat, breast and belly are greyish-brown, the chin, throat and breast having the feathers tipped with white. The central tail and primary wing feathers are dark brown, the remainder of the tail and wings are ashy-brown. The eyes are bright yellow-orange, the bill is black and the legs and feet are grey. The sexes are alike. Resident. Size: 23cm.

Black-lored Babbler *(Turdoides sharpei)*

Locally common in woodlands, bush, scrub and areas of dense vegetation around swamp and lake edges. Often encountered in small, noisy parties. The head, neck, chin and throat feathers are dark grey broadly edged, tipped and streaked with grey-white. The lores are black, contrasting quite strongly with the remainder of the head. The feathers of the breast, belly and underparts are ashy-brown edged with grey. The wings and tail are ashy-brown. The eyes are cream-white, the bill, legs and feet are black. The sexes are alike. Resident. Size: 23cm.

Rufous Chatterer *(Turdoides rubiginosus)*

A species found in dry thickets, bush and scrub over much of the region, often foraging through the undergrowth in small parties. The forehead, crown, nape and ear coverts are grey-brown, the forehead often being streaked with white. The feathers of the chin, throat and centre of the breast are pale rust-red with narrow white streaks. The outer breast, belly and underparts are rusty-red. The mantle, wings and long tail are ashy-brown. The eyes are cream-white, the bill, legs and feet are flesh-grey. The sexes are alike. Resident. Size: 19cm.

Sedge Warbler *(Acrocephalus schoenobaenus)*

A common winter visitor to East Africa, frequenting swamps, reed beds and other waterside vegetation. The forehead, crown and nape are brown streaked with black, a broad whitish band extends from the base of the bill, over the eye to the side of the nape. The chin, throat and central upper breast are off-white, the remainder of the breast, the belly and underparts are off-white with a wash of buff, darkest on the flanks. The mantle, scapulars and wings are ashy-brown with dark brown streaks and edges. The rump is rufous brown and the rounded tail is dark brown. The bill is black and the legs and feet are flesh-grey. The sexes are alike. Palearctic winter visitor. Size: 13cm.

Eurasian Reed Warbler *(Acrocephalus scirpaceus)*

A winter visitor to the region, where they inhabit areas of swamp and lake edges. Usually quite secretive, skulking in reedbeds and other thick waterside vegetation. They also occupy areas of acacia bush and scrub. The upper plumage is a uniform olive-brown/grey, often with a rusty coloured rump, the primary and secondary flight feathers are a darker brown/grey. A lighter eyebrow stripe and eye ring are discernible at close quarters. The eyes are dark brown, the bill is dark brown/grey and pale yellow at the base, the legs and feet are flesh grey. The sexes are alike. Palearctic winter visitor. Size: 13cm.

Willow Warbler *(Phylloscopus trochilus)*

A winter visitor throughout much of the region, found in a wide variety of habitats. The forehead, crown, nape, mantle, wings and tail are plain olive-brown, lighter on the rump. A pale whitish stripe follows the line of the eyebrow from the base of the bill. The chin, throat, breast, belly and underparts are whitish with a wash of pale yellow-buff on the sides of the breast, belly and flanks. The eyes are dark brown, the bill is brown-yellow and the legs and feet are grey-brown. The sexes are alike. Palearctic winter visitor. Size: 11cm.

Winding Cisticola
(Cisticola galactotes)

A locally common species throughout the region, favouring swamps, marshes and areas of dense rank grasses, usually in the vicinity of water. The forehead, crown and nape are russet brown, the ear coverts are buff/brown. The chin, throat and breast are white, the underparts are white with a wash of buff. The mantle and back are grey streaked with black. The wing coverts and the primary and secondary flight feathers are dark brown/black edged with russet brown and buff. The rump is plain grey, the tail feathers are brown/black edged with russet brown and with bold white spots towards the tip. The eyes are brown, the bill dull grey and the legs and feet pale flesh pink. The sexes are alike. Resident. Size: 13cm.

Rattling Cisticola
(Cisticola chiniana)

Found throughout much of the region in areas of open grassland, savannah and acacia scrub. The forehead, crown and nape are buff-brown, streaked with darker brown. The upperparts and wing coverts are pale grey-brown with darker brown streaking. The chin, throat and underparts are buff and the primary and secondary wing feathers are mid-brown, edged with buff. The eyes are reddish brown, the bill is black and the legs and feet are pale brown. The sexes are alike. Resident. Size: 14cm.

Black-collared Apalis
(Apalis pulchra)

A bird of highland forests and woodlands throughout Uganda and western and central Kenya. They usually carry their tails 'cocked' upwards towards the back, fanning and waving them from side to side. The forehead, crown, nape and back are dark slaty-grey. The chin and throat are white and a broad black band extends across the upper breast. The lower breast is white and the flanks, belly and underparts are a rich chestnut brown. The wings are dark slaty-grey. The rump and tail are grey, the latter tipped white. The eyes are dark brown, the bill, legs and feet are grey/black. The sexes are alike. Resident. Size: 13cm.

Grey-capped Warbler
(Eminia lepida)

A rather shy stocky warbler widely distributed and usually encountered in dense, luxuriant undergrowth along the edges of lakes, rivers and streams. The forehead and crown are blue/grey bordered by a broad black band extending from the lores, through the eye to the nape. The chin, breast, belly and underparts are pale grey and the centre of the throat has a prominent patch of chestnut. The mantle, back, wings, rump and tail are rich olive-green, a patch of chestnut is sometimes visible on the shoulder of the wing. The eyes are dark brown, the bill is black and the legs and feet are dull red. The sexes are alike. Resident. Size: 15cm.

Grey-backed Camaroptera
(Camaroptera brachyura)

A shy, secretive little bird that spends much of its time skulking in dense bush and scrub. They usually carry the tail 'cocked' upwards towards the back. Widely distributed over much of the region. The head, mantle, rump, tail and underparts are grey. The chin, throat and breast are pale grey. The wing coverts and flight feathers are rich olive-green. The eyes are red, the bill is black and the legs and feet are dull brown/red. The sexes are alike. Resident. Size: 10cm.

Southern Black Flycatcher
(Melaenornis pammelaina)

A species found in dry woodlands, forest clearings and areas of bush and scrub. Adult birds have uniformly black plumage with a bluish gloss to the head, inner wings and tail. The primary and secondary wing feathers are dull brownish black. The eyes are dark brown, the bill, legs and feet are black. Immature birds are dark brown/black with small spots of dark buff on the head, neck, mantle, breast and underparts. Resident. Size: 21cm.

African Dusky Flycatcher
(Muscicapa adusta)

A widely distributed species favouring areas of open forests and woodlands, also often encountered in large parks and gardens. They can often be seen hawking for insects from a favoured perch. The head, nape, mantle, back and wing coverts are plain greyish-brown. The chin, throat, breast, belly and underparts are white, the flanks and sides of the breast having a wash of grey/buff. The flight and tail feathers are dark grey/brown. The eyes are dark brown, the bill, legs and feet are dark grey/black. The sexes are alike. Immature birds have the upperparts spotted with buff and some dark streaking below. Resident. Size: 10cm.

Spotted Flycatcher
(Muscicapa striata)

A common winter visitor over much of the region in areas of thorn bush and scrub. The forehead and crown are pale grey/brown streaked with dark brown. The ear coverts and cheeks are pale brown. The chin, throat and breast are white, streaked with brown, the belly and underparts are white. The mantle, back, scapulars and rump are grey/brown. The primary and secondary flight feathers are dark brown, narrowly edged with buff and white. The tail feathers are dark brown. The eyes are dark brown, the bill, legs and feet are black. The sexes are alike. Palearctic winter visitor. Size: 13cm.

White-eyed Slaty Flycatcher
(Melaenornis fischeri)

Found over much of the region in highland forests and woodlands as well as in parks, gardens and areas of cultivated land. Typical of flycatchers they can often be seen hawking for insects from a favoured perch. The head, mantle, back and wings are slaty-grey. The chin and throat are pale grey, the breast, belly and underparts are white with a wash of grey/buff along the flanks. The most prominent identification feature is the broad white eye-ring. The eyes are dark brown, the bill, legs and feet are dark grey/black. The sexes are alike. Immature birds have the upperparts spotted with white. Resident. Size: 15cm.

African Grey Flycatcher
(Bradornis microrhynchus)

Found in areas of dry thorn bush and savannah woodlands throughout Ethiopia, Uganda, Kenya and Tanzania. A rather drab flycatcher with the plumage of the upperparts a rather uniform dull grey. The forehead and crown have some indistinct dark streaking. The chin, throat, breast, belly and underparts are whitish-grey. The eyes are dark brown, the bill, legs and feet are dark grey/black. The sexes are alike. Immature birds have white/buff spotting and streaking over the upper plumage and some dark streaking on the breast. Resident. Size: 13cm.

Common Wattle-eye
(Platysteira cyanea)

A bird of forests and woodlands in western Kenya, Uganda and northern Tanzania. A very striking flycatcher with the male having the forehead, crown, nape, mantle and back blue/black. The chin, throat, lower breast, belly and underparts are white, with a broad blue/black band extending across the upper breast. The female has a greyish-blue/black head and mantle, while the throat and upper breast are a rich chestnut brown. Both sexes have a prominent red eye-wattle. A white wing bar is present across the secondary flight feathers, the primary wing and tail feathers are black edged with white. The eyes are dark brown, the bill, legs and feet are black. Resident. Size: 13cm.

African Paradise Flycatcher
(Terpsiphone viridis)

A widespread and common species throughout the region in woodlands, thickets and areas of scrub. The head and neck are blue/black, merging to slaty-grey on the chin, throat and breast, becoming white on the belly and underparts. The eyes have a blue orbital ring. The mantle, back, wing coverts and tail are rich chestnut red. The central tail feathers of the male become elongated during the breeding season making identification even easier. The secondary flight feathers are chestnut edged with white, the primary flight feathers are black. In some regions, principally eastern Kenya, a white phase occurs. This affects the males only, to the extent that all areas of chestnut plumage found in the nominate phase are white. The eyes are dark brown, the bill, legs and feet are grey/black. Resident. Size: male including tail 33cm, female 20cm.

Scarlet-chested Sunbird *(Nectarinia senegalensis)*

Encountered in a wide variety of habitats. The male has the upper plumage dark brown/black. The crown, chin and throat are bright metallic green and the breast is vivid scarlet. The belly and underparts are dark brown/black. The female lacks the bright plumage of the male: dusky-olive above with a flush of dark brown on the wings and tail. Underparts are pale yellow/buff streaked with brown. Eyes are dark brown, the long, decurved bill and the legs and feet are black. Resident. Size: 15cm.

Hunter's Sunbird *(Nectarinia hunteri)*

A bird of dry thorn bush country. The male has the upper plumage glossy black, which often shows a sheen of metallic violet/purple. The forehead, crown and moustachial stripe are bright metallic green, the chin, throat, belly and underparts are black. The breast is a vivid scarlet. The female lacks the bright iridescent plumage of the male, being ashy-brown above and pale yellow/buff below with some brown streaking on the breast, throat and chin. The eyes are dark brown, the decurved bill, the legs and the feet are black. Resident. Size: 14cm.

Variable Sunbird *(Nectarinia venusta)*

A common species over much of the region. The male has the upper plumage bright metallic blue/green, the primary and secondary flight feathers are brown. The chin, throat and upper breast are dark purple/blue, the lower breast, belly and underparts are yellow. There is, however, much regional variation in the plumage of the underparts, ranging from white, through yellow to pale orange. The female has the upper plumage ashy-grey, often showing a pale eyebrow stripe, and is yellow/white below. The eyes are dark brown, the decurved bill and the legs and feet are black. Resident. Size: 9cm.

Bronze Sunbird *(Nectarinia kilimensis)*

A common bird of Uganda and the highland regions of Kenya and Tanzania, favouring forest and woodland edges, areas of scrub, gardens and cultivated farmland. The male has the head and neck dull metallic green, the remainder of the upper plumage being dull metallic bronze. The wings and elongated tail are dull purple/black. The chin and throat are bronze, merging to purple/black on the breast, belly and underparts. The female has the upper plumage olive/ashy-grey, while the underparts are yellowish streaked with bronze-grey. The female lacks the elongated tail feathers of the male. The eyes are dark brown, the decurved bill is black and the legs and feet are greyish-black. Resident. Size: male 23cm, female 14cm.

Beautiful Sunbird *(Nectarinia pulchella)*

A locally common species away from coastal districts. The male, in breeding plumage, has the head, neck, mantle, back and wing coverts bright metallic green. The chin, throat and upper breast are metallic green, the centre of the lower breast is bright scarlet being bordered on either side by patches of bright yellow. The belly and underparts are metallic green/black. The primary and secondary flight feathers are blue/black. The tail is blue/black with the elongated central feathers edged with metallic green. In non-breeding plumage males appear similar to females but retain the long central tail feathers and the dark flight feathers. The female has the upper plumage ashy-grey. The chin and throat are white, becoming pale yellow on the breast, belly and underparts. The female lacks the elongated tail feathers of the male. The eyes are dark brown, the decurved bill, the legs and feet are black. Resident. Size: male 15cm, female 11cm.

Eastern Violet-backed Sunbird *(Anthreptes orientalis)*

A locally common species of semi-desert country. The male has the head, mantle, back, tail and wing coverts metallic violet/blue. The flight feathers are dark brown/black. Rump and shoulders of the wings are metallic green. Chin and upper throat are blue/black, the lower throat, breast, belly and underparts are white. A small patch of yellow is present on the sides of the breast. The female is ashy-grey above with a pale eyebrow stripe, the tail is purple/black and the wings are brownish-grey. The chin, throat, breast, belly and underparts are white, occasionally with a faint wash of yellow. The eyes are dark brown, bill is brown/black, and the legs and feet are black. Resident. Size: 11cm.

Golden-breasted Bunting
(Emberiza flaviventris)

A widely, but locally distributed species, inhabiting dry areas of forest, woodland and scrub. The head is black, with white stripes extending above and below the eyes and down the centre of the head from the forehead to the nape. The chin is white, the throat and breast are orange/yellow, and the belly and underparts are white with a wash of grey. The mantle and back are rufous brown, the rump is grey, the wing coverts are rufous tipped with white and the primary and secondary wing feathers are brown/black edged with white. The tail is black, the outer feathers being edged with white. The eyes are dark brown. The bill has the upper mandible black and the lower mandible pale pink. The legs and feet are flesh-pink. The sexes are similar, the female being slightly duller and having those areas of black plumage found in the male replaced with brown. Resident. Size: 15cm.

White-bellied Canary
(Serinus dorsostriatus)

Similar in size to the Yellow-fronted Canary (*Serinus mozambicus*), but inhabiting drier areas throughout the region. The forehead is yellow, the crown, nape, back and wing coverts are dull yellow streaked with brown. A dull brown eye stripe extends from the base of the bill through the eye and ear coverts to the sides of the nape. A similar molar stripe extends from the lower mandible across the cheek. The chin, throat and breast are yellow and the belly is white. The primary and secondary flight feathers are dull brown edged with yellow and buff. The tail feathers are dark brown edged with yellow. The eyes are dark brown and the legs and feet are brown/black. The sexes are similar; the female is usually duller and paler in plumage than the male. Resident. Size: 11cm.

Yellow-fronted Canary
(Serinus mozambicus)

Locally distributed throughout the region favouring woodlands, areas of scrub, cultivated farmland and parks and gardens. The forehead and eyebrow stripe are bright yellow, the crown, nape, mantle, back and wing coverts are olive green streaked with black. They have a black moustachial stripe and a dark stripe extending from the base of the bill through the eye. The rump is bright yellow, the tail feathers are dark, the outer feathers being edged with olive green/yellow. The primary and secondary wing feathers are blackish, edged with yellow/green. The eyes are dark brown, the bill pale brown and the legs and feet brown/black. The sexes are similar, the female usually having a browner head and mantle. Resident. Size: 11cm.

African Citril
(Serinus citrinelloides)

A species distributed over much of the region inhabiting forest and woodland edges and clearings, cultivated farmland, grasslands with some bush and scrub cover and gardens. The forehead, face, cheeks, chin and upper throat are black. They have a yellow eyebrow stripe. The lower throat, breast, belly and underparts are lemon yellow, with a variable amount of dark streaking usually heaviest on the flanks. The crown, nape, mantle and wing coverts are olive green streaked with black. The tail and the primary and secondary flight feathers are blackish edged with greenish-yellow. The eyes are dark brown, the bill is blood red/black, and the legs and feet are black. The female lacks the black facial feathering of the male. Resident. Size: 11cm.

Streaky Seed-eater
(Serinus striolatus)

A common, well-distributed species throughout the region inhabiting woodland and forest edges, areas of scrub and bush, cultivated farmland and parks and gardens. The forehead, crown, nape, mantle and wing coverts are mid-brown streaked with black. A white stripe follows the line of the eyebrow from the base of the bill to the ear coverts. The chin and throat are buff/white, the moustachial stripe is brown/black. The breast, belly and underparts are white/buff, heavily streaked with black. The tail and the primary and secondary wing feathers are dark brown edged with buff and white. The eyes are dark brown, the bill is pink/yellow and the legs and feet are blackish. The sexes are alike. Resident. Size: 15cm.

Common Waxbill
(Estrilda astrild)

A common species encountered in areas of rank grassland. The male has the forehead, crown and nape dark brown closely barred with grey/brown. A broad red stripe extends from the base of the bill, through the eye to the ear coverts. The cheeks, chin and throat are white. The centre of the breast and belly are pale red, the sides of the breast and the flanks are buff/white closely barred with dark brown. The remainder of the underparts are black. The mantle, back, wings and tail are dark brown, barred with grey/buff. The female has less red and black on the breast, belly and underparts. The eyes are dark brown, the bill is red (black in the immature) and the legs and feet are black. Resident. Size: 10cm.

Purple Grenadier
(Uraeginthus ianthinogaster)

A species found in areas of dry thorn bush, thick scrub and open bush habitats over much of the region. A bird of striking plumage, the male has a narrow iridescent blue band across the forehead which extends onto the sides of the head to encircle the eyes and cover the cheeks. The crown, nape, neck, chin, throat and upper breast are rich russet brown. The lower breast, belly and underparts are violet blue. The mantle, back and wings are brown, the rump is violet blue and the tail is black. The female has the area around the eyes pale blue/white and the breast, belly and underparts dull russet brown with white spots and barring. The eyes are dark red, the bill is bright pinkish-red and the legs and feet are black. Resident. Size: 14cm.

Red-cheeked Cordon-bleu
(Uraeginthus bengalus)

Distributed over much of the region, favouring grasslands with some bush cover, woodland and forest edges, cultivated farmland and overgrown areas in parks and gardens. Usually encountered feeding on or near the ground in small flocks. The forehead, crown, nape, mantle and wings are sandy-brown. The face, chin, throat, sides of the breast, belly and underparts are azure blue. A bright scarlet patch covers the ear coverts. The centre of the breast, belly and underparts are buff/brown. The rump and tail are bright blue. The female is generally duller in appearance than the male and lacks the scarlet patch on the ear coverts. The bill is pink with a black tip, the legs and feet are flesh-pink. Resident. Size: 13cm.

Red-billed Firefinch
(Lagonosticta senegala)

Widely distributed within the region. Often seen in pairs or small non-breeding flocks feeding on the ground. The male has the entire head, neck, mantle, chin, throat and breast red. Generally a few white spots are discernible on the sides of the breast. The belly and underparts are sandy-brown. The wing coverts are red, the primary and secondary wing feathers are dull brown. The rump and outer tail feathers are red, the central tail feathers are brown. The female lacks the red plumage of the male except on the lores, the rump and the tail, being earth-brown above and buff below with white spots on the sides of the breast and flanks. Eyes are dark red, the bill is red and the legs and feet are greyish-pink. Resident. Size: 9cm.

African Silverbill
(Lonchura cantans)

A common species often encountered feeding together in small flocks in dry bush country throughout Uganda, Kenya and northern Tanzania. The head, chin and throat are dark brown finely streaked with ashy-brown. They have a pale blue orbital ring. The breast, belly and underparts are white. The wing coverts and secondary flight feathers are dark brown with ashy-grey vermiculations. The primary flight feathers, the rump and the pointed tail are black. The eyes are dark brown, the thick bill is blue/grey and the legs and feet are flesh pink/grey. The sexes are alike. Resident. Size: 10cm.

Bronze Mannikin
(Lonchura cucullata)

Commonly found in a wide variety of habitats. The forehead, crown, cheeks, chin and throat are glossy black, merging to bronze on the ear coverts, neck and nape. The breast, belly and underparts are white with black barring on the flanks and under tail coverts. The mantle, back and wing coverts are ashy-brown, the flight feathers are dark brown. The rump is white boldly barred with black, the tail is black. The eyes are dark brown, the bill is blue/black and the legs and feet are blackish. The sexes are alike. Resident. Size: 9cm.

Pin-tailed Whydah
(Vidua macroura)

A parasitic species laying its eggs in the nests of Waxbills, Finches and Cisticolas. The breeding male is almost unmistakable, the forehead, crown and chin are black and the nape, neck, breast, belly and underparts are white. The mantle, shoulders and back are black, the wing coverts are white and the primary and secondary wing feathers are black edged with buff/white. The outer tail feathers are black edged with white, the black central tail feathers are elongated, measuring almost twice the length of the body. In non-breeding dress the males look similar to females, having the forehead and crown tawny-brown with bold black stripes extending from the bill to the nape. The throat, breast, belly and underparts are white with a wash of buff. The mantle, back and wings are tawny-brown broadly streaked with black. The tail is brown/black edged with white and lacks the elongated central feathers. The eyes are dark brown, the bill is pink/red and the legs and feet are flesh pink. Resident. Size: breeding male 32cm, female 12cm.

Paradise Whydah
(Vidua paradisaea)

A parasitic species, laying its eggs in the nests of Green-winged Pytilia. The breeding male has the entire head, chin, throat and upper breast black, the nape is buff and forms a collar around the neck to the breast. The lower breast is chestnut merging to buff/white on the belly and underparts. The mantle, back, wings and tail are black. The central tail feathers are relatively short but extremely broad, the outer feathers are greatly elongated being almost twice the length of the body. The non-breeding plumage of the males resembles that of the females, having the head creamy-buff with broad black stripes extending from the bill to the nape. The throat, breast, belly and underparts are buff/white, with dark streaking on the flanks and the sides of the breast. The mantle, back and wing coverts are tawny streaked with black, the flight feathers and tail are brown/black finely edged with buff. The eyes are dark brown, the bill is black and the legs and feet are brown/grey. Resident. Size: breeding male 40cm, female 13cm.

Reichenow's Weaver
(Ploceus baglafecht reichenowi)

Locally distributed inhabiting forest and woodland edges, scrub, cultivated farmland, parks, gardens and human habitations. The male has the forehead and fore-crown bright golden yellow, the hind-crown and nape are black. A broad black facial mask covers the lores, the eyes and the ear coverts. The chin, throat, breast, belly and underparts are bright yellow. The mantle, back and wing coverts are black. The primary and secondary wing feathers are black broadly edged with yellow. The tail is black. The female lacks the golden yellow forehead and crown, having the entire head black. The eyes are pale yellow, the bill is black and the legs and feet are flesh pink. Resident. Size: 15cm.

Golden Palm Weaver
(Ploceus bojeri)

A common species in coastal regions as well as inland in eastern Kenya and north-eastern Tanzania. The male has the head, neck, chin, throat and upper breast bright orange/yellow, the remainder of the plumage being bright yellow. The primary and secondary wing feathers and the tail are dark brown broadly edged with yellow. The female is yellow below the upper plumage being yellow washed with olive and finely streaked with olive-brown. The eyes are dark brown, the bill is black in the male and yellow/grey in the female, the legs and feet are flesh pink. Resident. Size: 15cm.

Northern Masked Weaver
(Ploceus taeniopterus)

A weaver of lake edges and swamps with limited local distribution. The breeding male has the forehead black, becoming chestnut on the fore-crown, the hind-crown, nape, sides of the neck, breast, belly and underparts are bright yellow. A black facemask covers the lores, eyes, cheeks, chin and upper throat. The mantle and wing coverts are yellow with a wash of olive. The primary and secondary wing feathers are dark brown, broadly edged with yellow. The rump is bright yellow and the tail is olive-brown edged with yellow. In non-breeding plumage the males are similar to the females, having the head olive/yellow finely streaked and flecked with black, the breast, belly and underparts are buff/white. The mantle and wing coverts are brown/black edged with buff. The eyes are deep red, the bill is black and the legs and feet are flesh pink. Resident. Size: 15cm.

Speke's Weaver   *(Ploceus spekei)*

An abundant species found in a variety of habitats including light woodlands, swamps, farmland and around human habitations. The male has the forehead, crown, nape and neck yellow. The chin, throat, face and cheeks are black, the breast, belly and underparts are yellow, often with a wash of orange on the lower throat and upper breast. The feathers of the back and wing coverts are dark brown broadly edged with yellow, the primary and secondary flight feathers are dark brown finely edged with pale yellow. The rump is olive yellow and the tail feathers are dark brown edged with olive. The female is grey brown above streaked with dark brown, the underparts are pale yellow/white. The eyes are yellow, the bill, legs and feet are blackish with a hint of pink/red. Resident. Size: 15cm.

Black-headed Weaver   *(Ploceus cucullatus)*

Encountered over much of the region in areas of bush and scrub, light woodlands and in the vicinity of human habitations. The male has the head, chin, throat and centre of the upper breast black. The hind neck, lower breast, belly and underparts are bright yellow. The wing coverts are dark brown/black broadly edged with yellow. The primary and secondary flight feathers are black narrowly edged with pale yellow/white. The tail is dark olive brown. The female is olive brown above with darker brown streaking and off-white below with a wash of pale yellow on the throat and upper breast. The eyes are red, the bill is black and the legs and feet are dull reddish/black. Resident. Size: 16cm.

Black-capped Social Weaver   *(Pseudonigrita cabanisi)*

As its name suggests this is a very social species, nesting in large colonies in acacia trees. They inhabit dry, open bush country and are particularly common in Samburu Game Reserve in Kenya. The head is black while the nape, back and wings are pale brown. The chin, throat, breast and underparts are white with black streaks along the sides of the breast and flanks. A black streak also extends from the base of the breast through the belly. The tail is black, the eyes are rich red, the bill is pale yellow and the legs and feet are pale brown. Juvenile birds lack the black markings of the adults and have dark brown eyes. The sexes are alike. Resident. Size: 13cm.

Jackson's Golden-backed Weaver   *(Ploceus jacksoni)*

A bird of scrub, bush and thickets in the immediate vicinity of lakes, rivers and swamps. The male has the entire head, including the chin and throat black, the breast and flanks are rich dark chestnut, and the belly and underparts are yellow. The mantle and back are bright yellow, the wings and tail are olive brown narrowly edged with yellow. The female is olive yellow above with a variable amount of darker streaking, while below the breast is yellow becoming paler, almost white, on the belly and underparts. The eyes are crimson red, the bill, legs and feet are black. Resident. Size: 15cm.

Red-headed Weaver   *(Anaplectes rubriceps)*

Widely distributed over the region, favouring acacia woodland and scrub. The male has the head, neck, lower throat, breast and upper belly bright crimson red. The lower belly and underparts are white. (The amount of white is variable and in some instances covers most of the breast as well as the belly). The face, cheeks, ear coverts, chin and upper throat are black. The wings and tail are grey/black, the outer edges of the flight and tail feathers are edged with crimson. The female is grey above and white below, with crimson edges to the flight and tail feathers. The eyes are dark brown, the bill is pinkish/red and the legs and feet are flesh pink. Resident. Size: 15cm.

Red-billed Buffalo Weaver

(Bubalornis niger)

Distributed throughout much of the region favouring areas of acacia thorn bush and savannah. A large weaver, usually encountered in small parties. During the breeding season several pairs establish individual nesting chambers within a communal mass of sticks placed high in an acacia or other suitable tree. The plumage appears entirely black, but the basal section of much of the feathering is white, which shows whenever the plumage is disarranged. The primary and secondary flight feathers are narrowly edged with white. The females and immature birds are browner than the males. The eyes are dark brown, the bill is bright red and the legs and feet are blackish. Resident. Size: 25cm.

White-billed Buffalo Weaver

(Bubalornis albirostris)

Found over much of the region in acacia woodlands and, like the Red-billed Buffalo Weaver (*Bubalornis niger*), has the plumage all black with white basal sections to the feathers, which show when the plumage is ruffled. The outer edges of the primary and secondary flight feathers are white. The bill is white during the breeding season, becoming black at other times. The female is similar to the male but has a blackish bill at all times. The eyes are dark brown, the legs and feet are greyish/black. Resident. Size: 25cm.

White-headed Buffalo Weaver

(Dinemellia dinemelli)

A species found throughout much of the region in areas of dry bush and acacia scrub and woodland. The head, neck, chin, throat, breast and belly are pure white. A small black patch encircles the eye. The mantle, back and wing coverts are dusky brown. The primary and secondary flight feathers are dark brown/black, boldly edged with white. The rump and under tail coverts are bright red, being very conspicuous in flight. The tail is dark brown/black, narrowly edged with white. The eyes are dark brown, the bill, legs and feet are black. The sexes are alike. Resident. Size: 23cm.

White-browed Sparrow Weaver

(Plocepasser mahali)

Locally common throughout much of the region favouring areas of dry thorn bush and scrub. The forehead, crown and face are dark brown, a broad white stripe extends from above the eye to the nape. The ear coverts, nape, mantle and wing coverts are earth brown. The chin, throat, breast, belly and underparts are pure white. They have a dark brown/black moustachial stripe which extends down the sides of the neck. The wing coverts are blackish, broadly edged with white, the primary and secondary flight feathers are dark brown/black. The rump is pure white and the tail dark brown finely edged with white. The eyes are dark brown, the bill is black and the legs and feet are dull red. The sexes are alike. Resident. Size: 15cm.

Rufous-tailed Weaver

(Histurgops ruficaudus)

A species that occurs locally, mainly in northern Tanzania, being very common in areas of the Serengeti, particularly around Ndutu and Naabi Hill. A large weaver with the feathers of the head, mantle, back and wing coverts dark brown boldly edged with buff/grey. The chin, throat, breast, belly and flanks are grey/buff streaked and spotted with dark brown. The primary and secondary flight feathers are dark brown and chestnut narrowly edged with buff. The central tail feathers are dark brown, the outer feathers are rich chestnut. The eyes are very pale blue, the bill is black and the legs and feet are greyish/black. The sexes are alike. Resident. Size: 22cm.

144

Grey-capped Social Weaver
(Pseudonigrita arnaudi)

A small weaver encountered throughout much of the region in areas of dry scrub and light acacia woodland. The forehead and crown are pale grey, the remainder of the head, neck, mantle and the whole of the underside are grey/buff. The wing coverts and inner portion of the secondary flight feathers are dark brown, the outer portion of the secondaries are grey/buff. The primary flight feathers are dark brown/black, the short tail is brown/black narrowly edged with buff. The eyes are dark brown, the bill, legs and feet are blackish with a flush of dull red. The sexes are alike. Resident. Size: 13cm.

Speckle-fronted Weaver
(Sporopipes frontalis)

A very gregarious species found in areas of dry bush and scrub, woodland and cultivated farmland. The forehead and fore-crown are black, finely speckled with white, the hind-crown, nape and sides of the neck are rufous. The face, ear coverts, chin, throat and underside are grey/white. They have a prominent black moustachial stripe. The mantle and wing coverts are ashy-brown, the primary and secondary flight feathers and the tail are dark brown edged with buff/grey. The eyes are dark brown, the bill, legs and feet are dull grey/black. The sexes are alike. Resident. Size: 13cm.

Rufous Sparrow
(Passer rufocinctus)

A species favouring open acacia thorn bush and light woodland as well as cultivated farmland and human habitations. The male has the forehead and crown grey. A rufous band extends from the rear of the eyes around the ear coverts and the sides of the neck, bordered along the front edge by a band of black. The chin and throat are black, the cheeks, breast, belly and underparts are white/grey. The back, rump and wing coverts are rufous streaked with black, the tail and primary and secondary flight feathers are dark brown edged with buff. The female has the chin and throat grey not black. The eyes are dark brown, the bill, legs and feet are blackish. Residents. Size: 14cm.

Grey-headed Sparrow
(Passer griseus)

A common local resident over much of the region. The head and neck are grey, the chin, throat and upper breast are white merging to grey on the lower breast, belly and underparts. The mantle, rump and wing coverts are grey/rufous, the primary and secondary flight feathers are earth brown edged with buff. The eyes are dark brown, the bill is black and the legs and feet are dull grey/red. The sexes are alike. Resident. Size: 15cm.

Yellow-spotted Petronia
(Petronia pyrgita)

Locally distributed in areas of dry bush and savannah as well as patches of cultivated farmland. The male has the head, neck and mantle plain grey, the chin and throat are white. A patch of pale yellow is present in the centre of the lower throat. They have a faint grey/buff eyebrow stripe. The breast, belly and underparts are grey/white. The tail and the primary and secondary flight feathers are dark brown edged with grey/white. The female is similar to the male but the yellow throat spot is often very faint. The eyes are dark brown, the bill is buff/grey and the legs and feet are grey/black. Resident. Size: 15cm.

Red-billed Quelea
(Quelea quelea)

A very gregarious species often encountered in enormous flocks feeding in areas of bush, scrub, grassland and cultivated farmland where they can cause considerable damage to crops. In breeding plumage the male usually has the forehead, face, chin and throat black, although occasionally the head is rufous. The crown, nape, sides of the neck and the breast are buff with a wash of pink, the belly and underparts are whitish. The feathers of the back, wings and tail have dark brown centres edged with buff/white. The female has the head grey/brown finely streaked with dark brown and a buff/white eye stripe. Immature birds and males in non-breeding plumage resemble females. The eyes are dark brown, the bill is bright red and the legs and feet are dull orange/yellow. Resident. Size: 13cm.

Fan-tailed Widowbird
(Euplectes axillaris)

An inhabitant of swamps, marshes, lake edges and riverbanks wherever there are tall reeds and grasses. In breeding plumage the male is entirely black with the exception of very prominent orange-red shoulder patches which are very conspicuous in flight. The eyes are dark brown, the bill blue-grey and the legs and feet are dark brown almost black. In non-breeding plumage the upper black feathering becomes extensively streaked with buff, the underparts become pale buff-white with dark buff-brown streaking while the orange-red shoulder patches are retained. Females and juveniles are smaller but, in plumage, are similar to non-breeding males, although the shoulder patches are less prominent. Resident. Size: 16cm.

Red-collared Widowbird
(Euplectes ardens)

Locally common throughout the region encountered in areas of rank grassland, scrub and bush. In breeding plumage the male has a long flowing tail, the entire plumage being black with the exception of a broad scarlet breast band. In the highlands of Kenya, Tanzania and Uganda this species also has the crown, nape and sides of the neck scarlet. The primary and secondary flight feathers are edged with buff/white. The female has the upper plumage dark brown boldly edged and streaked with tawny/buff. The chin and throat are yellowish/buff, the breast is buff, the belly and underparts white. In non-breeding plumage the male has similar plumage to the female but is larger and more heavily streaked above. The eyes are dark brown. The bill of the breeding male is black and at other times is buff/grey like that of the female. The legs and feet are blackish. Resident. Size:: Breeding male 28cm, female 13cm.

Yellow Bishop
(Euplectes capensis)

Locally distributed throughout the region in areas of scrub, bush and rank vegetation. During the breeding season the male has predominantly black plumage, with a bright yellow shoulder patch and loose bright yellow feathering on the rump. The primary and secondary flight feathers are edged with buff. The female has the upper feathering dark brown broadly edged with yellow/buff and the rump olive yellow finely streaked with brown. The underside is buff/white streaked with earth-brown. During non-breeding periods the upper plumage of the male resembles that of the female. He is, however, larger, has a yellow rump, is more heavily streaked above and has darker wings and tail. The eyes are dark brown. The bill of the breeding male is blackish with some white on the lower mandible and on the female is grey/buff. The legs and feet are blackish. Resident. Size: 15cm.

Northern Red Bishop
(Euplectes franciscanus)

A species with local distribution frequenting reedbeds and other areas of aquatic vegetation around the margins of lakes. The male in breeding plumage has the forehead, crown, upper face, breast and belly black. The nape, cheeks, neck, chin and throat are bright red. The mantle, wing coverts, under tail coverts and elongated upper tail coverts are also bright red. The tail and flight feathers are dark brown. The female has the upper feathering dark brown, broadly edged and streaked with buff, while the underside is buff/white with some faint streaking on the breast. Immature birds and males in non-breeding plumage resemble females. The eyes are dark brown, the bill is black and the legs and feet are dusky red. Resident. Size: 10cm.

Jackson's Widowbird

(Euplectes jacksoni)

A species of highland regions at elevations over 1,500m in western and central Kenya and northern Tanzania. The male in breeding plumage has a long decurved tail and almost entirely black feathering, the only exceptions being a yellow/brown shoulder patch and the flight feathers having brown edges. Males are often seen displaying, leaping several feet into the air from deep grass. The female has the upper feathering dark brown boldly edged and streaked with buff. The underside is buff with darker streaking on the breast and flanks. In non-breeding plumage the male is similar to the female but is generally browner. The eyes are dark brown, the bill of the breeding male is blue/grey, and the bill of the female is yellow/grey. The legs and feet are black. Resident. Size:: Breeding male 36cm, female 14cm.

Red-winged Starling

(Onychognathus morio)

Distributed over much of the region, favouring hillsides, rocky outcrops and gorges, woodlands and, in some areas, towns and cities. A large starling with a long tail, the male has glossy violet blue/black plumage with a trace of green on the cheeks. The primary flight feathers are rich chestnut tipped with black, the chestnut being most prominent when the bird is in flight. The plumage of the female is similar to that of the male but the head, neck, chin, throat and upper breast are washed with dark grey and heavily streaked with black. They mate for life and, during the breeding season, can be encountered in pairs or small parties. Outside the breeding season flocks of several hundred have been recorded. The eyes are dark red/brown, the bill, legs and feet are black. Resident. Size: 30cm.

Bristle-crowned Starling

(Onychognathus salvadorii)

A bird mainly encountered in northern Kenya and north eastern Uganda, where they inhabit rocky hill sides and gorges as well as lake and riverside forests and woodlands. A large starling with a very long, graduated tail. The male has glossy blue/black plumage with a wash of violet on the head and neck. A patch of raised, bristle-like feathers are present on the forehead, noticeable even at a considerable distance. The primary flight feathers are rich chestnut tipped with black, the chestnut being much more apparent in flight than when perched at rest. The female resembles the male but has a faint wash of grey on the head and neck. The eyes are deep red, the slightly decurved bill is black and the legs and feet are blackish. Resident. Size: 40cm.

Greater Blue-eared Starling

(Lamprotornis chalybaeus)

A common and well-distributed species throughout the region, inhabiting woodlands, lightly wooded savannahs, cultivated farmland and city parks and gardens. A robust starling with wonderful iridescent plumage, the colours of which change constantly as the bird alters position in strong sunlight. The entire plumage is rich metallic blue/green, the crown, ear coverts, belly and underparts showing darker iridescent blue. The shoulders of the wings often show as violet patches and the tips of the wing coverts and the secondary flight feathers are boldly tipped with black. The eyes are golden yellow, the bill, legs and feet are black. The sexes are alike. Resident. Size: 23cm.

Ruppell's Long-tailed Starling

(Lamprotornis purpuropterus)

A common and conspicuous bird over much of the region in areas of open savannah, bush, scrub, cultivated farmland and human habitations. They are often common and very tame in the grounds of safari lodges and hotels. They are usually encountered in pairs or small parties. A large long-tailed Starling with striking iridescent plumage when viewed in bright sunlight, usually when seen in poor light the entire plumage appears black. The head, neck, chin and throat are glossy black with a flush of metallic bronze. The nape, breast, belly, underparts and tail are metallic violet blue. The wing coverts and primary and secondary flight feathers are rich metallic green. Immature birds are duller than adults. The eyes are pale creamy-white, the bill, legs and feet are black. The sexes are alike. Resident. Size: 36cm.

Hildebrandt's Starling
(Lamprotornis hildebrandti)

A bird of southern Kenya and northern Tanzania inhabiting areas of bush, lightly wooded savannah and cultivated farmland, often being encountered in small flocks foraging on the ground. A typical starling with very attractive plumage. The upperparts, wings and tail are a metallic blue, as are the chin, throat and upper breast. The tips of the wing coverts and the secondary flight feathers are black. The lower breast, belly and underparts are rich chestnut/orange. The eyes are bright red, the bill, legs and feet are black. This species can easily be confused with the Superb Starling (*Lamprotornis superbus*), which although similar has a narrow white breast band, white undertail coverts and creamy-white eyes. Resident. Size: 18cm.

Superb Starling
(Lamprotornis superbus)

A small starling with stunning plumage, being a widespread and common species throughout much of the region. They are present in a wide range of habitats including lightly wooded savannahs, woodlands, areas of bush and scrub and human habitations. Common and usually extremely tame in the grounds of safari lodges and hotels. The forehead, crown, face, chin and throat are black, the nape, mantle, wings and tail are metallic blue, often with a flush of green, particularly on the wings. The tips of the wing coverts and the secondary flight feathers are black. The upper breast is blue/black and is separated from the chestnut/orange lower breast and belly by a narrow band of white. The undertail coverts are white. The eyes are creamy-white, the bill, legs and feet are black. The sexes are alike. Immature birds show little of the narrow white breast band, are generally duller and have dark brown eyes. This species can easily be confused with Hildebrandt's Starling (*Lamprotornis hildebrandti*) which lacks the narrow white breast band, has chestnut/orange undertail coverts and bright red eyes. Resident. Size: 18cm.

Golden-breasted Starling
(Cosmopsarus regius)

This species is possibly the most beautiful of the starlings found in East Africa. A slender, long-tailed bird encountered over much of the region, frequenting areas of dry thorn bush and scrub. A rather shy and wary species. The forehead, crown, nape and neck are iridescent metallic green, the chin, throat and cheeks are metallic blue. The upper breast is metallic purple, the remainder of the breast, belly and underparts are rich golden yellow. The mantle, rump and wings are deep metallic blue, washed with purple. The long graduated tail is violet blue with a strong wash of bronze. The eyes are creamy-white, the bill, legs and feet are black. The sexes are alike. Immature birds are duller than adults. Resident. Size: 36cm.

Ashy Starling
(Cosmopsarus unicolor)

A locally common species in areas of acacia woodland and lightly wooded grasslands, particularly in the vicinity of baobab trees. There are many in and around Tarangire National Park in Tanzania. Compared with other starling species of the region, the Ashy Starling has rather dull uninteresting plumage, being almost uniform ashy-brown. The cheeks, chin, throat and the primary and secondary flight feathers are usually a slightly darker brown and the very long graduated tail often shows faint vermiculations. The eyes are pale yellow, the bill, legs and feet are black. Immature birds are usually greyer than adults. The sexes are alike. Resident. Size: 30cm.

Wattled Starling
(Creatophora cinerea)

A common and widely distributed species throughout the region, occurring in areas of open grassland, bush and scrub and acacia woodlands. They are very gregarious and often associate with plains game animals, feeding on the insects disturbed by the grazing herds. The head, neck, mantle and the whole of the underside are light grey. The wing coverts are light grey at the base and white at the tips, the primary and secondary flight feathers and the tail are black. The rump is white. In breeding plumage the male has a patch of bright yellow skin covering the ear coverts and extending around the eye to the back of the crown. The front of the head, face and chin are black, with large black wattles on the forehead, crown and throat. During periods of non-breeding the wattles disappear, being replaced by grey and black feathering. The eyes are dark brown, the bill, legs and feet are dull flesh pink. The female is similar to the male in non-breeding plumage. Resident. Size: 21cm.

Magpie Starling

(Speculipastor bicolor)

A species often found in small flocks in areas of dry thornbush, scrub and savannah woodlands. The male has the head, neck, mantle, wings and tail coverts black, with a blue sheen. The tail is black. The sides of the upper breast and the lower breast and underparts are buff-white. A conspicuous white patch is visible at the base of the primary wing feathers when the bird is perched. The bill is black, the eyes are rich red and the legs and feet are black. The female is similar to the male, but has the head, neck, mantle, wings and tail coverts buff to grey-brown with dark brown mottling. Resident. Size: 18cm.

Red-billed Oxpecker

(Buphagus erythrorhynchus)

Locally common throughout much of East Africa in areas of open grassland, bush and scrub and light woodlands. They are particularly numerous on the open plains where they associate with herds of plains game, feeding by climbing all over the animals picking off ticks and other blood sucking insects. The head, neck, wings, rump and tail are earth-brown, the breast, belly and underparts are buff. The eyes are bright red, surrounded by a bright yellow orbital ring. The bill is bright red, the legs and feet are black. The sexes are alike. This species may be confused with the Yellow-billed Oxpecker (*Buphagus africanus*) which has a bright yellow base to the bill and a pale buff rump. Resident. Size: 18cm.

Yellow-billed Oxpecker

(Buphagus africanus)

Widely distributed throughout the region frequenting areas of open grasslands and light bush and scrub. Like the Red-billed Oxpecker (*Buphagus erythorhynchus*) this species is dependent on large herds of plains game or domestic stock, feeding on a range of ticks and other blood-sucking insects that they pluck from the animal hides. The head, neck, wings and tail are dark brown, the rump is pale buff. The breast, belly and underparts are buff/brown. The eyes are bright red, the bill is bright yellow at the base and red at the tip, the legs and feet are black. The sexes are alike. This species may be confused with the Red-billed Oxpecker (*Buphagus erythorhynchus*) which has an all red bill, a darker rump and a bright yellow orbital ring. Resident. Size: 19cm.

Black-headed Oriole

(Oriolus larvatus)

A common species found in forests, woodlands and areas of bush and scrub. The head, neck, chin, throat and upper breast are black. The mantle, lower breast, belly and underparts are bright chrome yellow, the wing coverts are olive yellow and the primary and secondary flight feathers are black edged with yellow and white. The central tail feathers are olive yellow, the outer tail feathers are golden yellow. The eyes and the bill are deep red, the legs and feet are blackish. Immature birds have yellow streaking on the head and some black streaking on the breast. The sexes are alike. Resident. Size: 23cm.

Common Drongo

(Dicrurus adsimilis)

A common species throughout the region, inhabiting a wide range of habitat types including woodlands, areas of scrub and bush, lightly wooded savannahs and parks and gardens. They can often be seen perched on a branch overlooking a clearing from where they hawk for insects which they capture in mid-flight. The entire plumage is glossy black, with a hint of brown on the edges of the primary and secondary flight feathers. The long, broad tail is deeply forked, less so in the female. The eyes are deep red, the bill, legs and feet are black. The sexes are alike. Resident. Size: 25cm.

Square-tailed Drongo

(Dicrurus ludwigii)

Widely distributed but locally common throughout much of East Africa. A bird of dense forests and woodlands, often seen hawking for insects from a perch overlooking a forest clearing. The entire plumage is glossy black which, under some lighting conditions shows a flush of deep blue. The tail is shorter than that of the Drongo (*Dicrurus adsimilis*) and lacks the deep fork, being almost square. The eyes are deep red and the bill, legs and feet are black. The female is generally duller in appearance than the male. Resident. Size: 18cm.

Pied Crow
(Corvus albus)

A locally distributed but common species in East Africa, being found in a wide variety of habitat types including open grasslands, lake and river edges, cultivated farmland and towns and cities. The head, throat and upper breast are glossy black, the mantle, the sides of the neck and the lower breast are white. The belly, underparts, wings and tail are glossy black. The eyes are dark brown, the legs and feet are black. The sexes are alike. Resident. Size: 46cm.

White-naped Raven
(Corvus albicollis)

A bird encountered on rocky slopes, on hillsides, in gorges and in the vicinity of human habitations, where they perform the role of scavenger. With the exception of a broad white crescent-shaped band on the hind-neck, the entire plumage is glossy blue/black. The eyes are dark brown, the large, thick bill is black with a white tip. The legs and feet are black. The sexes are alike, although the female has a smaller bill. Resident. Size: 56cm.

Fan-tailed Raven
(Corvus rhipidurus)

A common species around inland cliffs, gorges and hill sides in northern Kenya, northern Uganda and Somalia. They are often quite common and reasonably tame in and around safari lodges. The entire plumage is glossy black often showing a purple or blue iridescence, particularly on the wings. When the bird is at rest the folded wings extend 2-3cm beyond the end of the short tail. The eyes are dark brown, the bill, legs and feet are black. Immature birds are duller in appearance than adult birds. The sexes are alike. Resident. Size: 46cm.

Cape Rook
(Corvus capensis)

A slender built crow, widely distributed in East Africa, favouring areas of open plains and grasslands, cultivated farmland, pastures and human habitations. The plumage is entirely black which, if viewed in good light, often has a sheen of blue and bronze. The black bill is, for a crow at least, long and slender. The eyes are dark brown, the legs and feet are black. Immature birds are often duller and have a browner appearance than do the adults. The sexes are alike. Resident. Size: 43cm.

House Crow
(Corvus splendens)

A species introduced from Asia towards the end of the nineteenth century, which is now well established and quite numerous in the coastal regions of Kenya and Tanzania. The hind-crown, neck and breast are dusky-grey, the upper plumage is glossy blue/black with a sheen of purple on the wings. The belly and underparts are blue/black with a wash of grey. The eyes are dark brown, the bill, legs and feet are black. Immature birds lack the plumage gloss of the adults. The sexes are alike. Resident. Size: 33cm.

Piapiac
(Ptilostomus afer)

A bird of western and northern Uganda, usually encountered in small flocks on grasslands and pastures, where they associate with large game animals and domestic stock, feeding on the insects disturbed by the grazing herds. The plumage in mainly black with a wash of brown on the wings and the long graduated tail. The eyes are dark brown, the bill, legs and feet are black. The sexes are alike. Resident. Size: 35cm.

MAMMALS

Bush Pig
(Potamochoerus porcus)

A typical hog, with a long face and a short rotund body. The coat is long and coarse and varies in colour from reddish to dark brown. Along the back the hair is longer, forming a dorsal crest. The head has a conspicuous pattern of black and white markings which are extremely variable and in some instances appears white. The tail is long and thin, measuring up to 40cm in length. The hooves have four toes. Very young animals have a spotted pelage of buff on dark brown, but these spots are replaced, at about six months old, by a rufous brown coat and the longer hair of the dorsal crest. Males are larger and heavier than females.

An animal of forests, woodlands, thick bush, and other areas offering sufficient cover and water. Bush Pigs are gregarious animals living in family groups usually consisting of a boar with several sows and offspring, numbering on average 15-20 pigs in all, although congregations of over 40 animals have been recorded. The boar is the dominant family member, leading and protecting his group. The sows give birth at anytime of the year in a nest prepared in advance, usually in dense vegetation. The sow will keep the piglets well hidden for the first two months of their lives, leaving them in the nest while away foraging. Bush Pigs are omnivorous, eating a wide variety of vegetation as well as insects, reptiles, birds eggs, seeds and fruits which they search out by rooting around and digging with their snouts. Occasionally their feeding habits bring them into conflict with man, as a foraging group can do vast damage to crops.

Giant Forest Hog
(Hylochoerus meinertzhageni)

The largest of East Africa's pig species. A huge, heavily built animal with long black body hair. The head is large, with patches of light hair on the long face. They have a broad snout and large distended ridges below the eyes. Mature males are much larger than females and have tusks which can be as long as 30cm, emerging in a backward direction from the mouth, the tusks are much smaller in the female. The ears are small and pointed. The young are uniform brown in colour. The tail is long and thin, measuring up to 45cm in length.

An animal usually associated with dense forest and very often those of high mountains. Mainly nocturnal, they usually remain in deep cover during the daytime and are most likely to be seen foraging at dusk in forest glades. They feed on grasses, sedges, leaves, berries and fallen fruits. Although they will eat certain plant roots they do very little digging or rooting for food with the snout. They live in family parties of 4-12 animals, consisting of a mature boar, a sow and several generations of offspring. Sows give birth to average litters of 2-6 piglets in a nest of dry grass and other vegetation prepared in advance and sited in dense cover. At birth the young are uniform buff in colour, however, the fur soon darkens to brown, becoming black on reaching full maturity.

Warthog
(Phacochoerus aethiopicus)

Often regarded as ugly, the Warthog is the most common of the African pigs. They have little in the way of fur, just a few bristles and whiskers on the body of grey skin. They do, however, have a long black mane of hair on the neck and shoulders. Coloration can vary greatly due to their habit of wallowing in muddy pools. The tail is long and thin, measuring up to 50cm in length and is carried vertically when running. They have a large flat face on which are found two sets of 'warts', one set immediately below the eyes and the other on the sides of the face between the eyes and the mouth. They have tusks, which emerge from the mouth in a semi-circle outwards and upwards. The tusks and warts are less prominent in the sow than in the boar.

An animal of open savannahs and woodlands, living in family groups consisting of a boar, a sow and the offspring from several litters. They can be found during daylight hours grazing, which they often do while kneeling on their front legs. During the hottest part of the day they will seek shade or cover. They feed mainly on short grasses, but will take leaves, roots, fruits and tubers. Sows give birth in burrows and hollows which are lined with grass. The young will remain in the nest for 6-7 weeks. Whole families will sleep together in burrows often excavated originally by Aardvark and later enlarged by the hogs. To defend themselves against predators they enter the burrow backwards, this enables them to make good use of their formidable tusks if threatened.

Hippopotamus
(Hippopotamus amphibius)

Second in weight only to the Elephant, this unmistakeable amphibious mammal has a bulbous body, short legs and a large head which broadens at the muzzle. The eyes, ears and nostrils are placed high on the head in order to remain clear of the water when the animal has its body submerged. The coloration is pink, grey/purple and brown. The body is devoid of fur, having just a few bristles on the tail, head and face. The tail is short and thick. They have well developed incisor teeth which are used when fighting and serve no purpose at all with regard to feeding, which is accomplished by use of the large lips in a ripping motion. In isolated cases they have been recorded feeding on rotting flesh of other animals (see bottom pic.)

An animal of rivers and swamps across much of East Africa. During the daytime they usually remain partially submerged to avoid the effects of overheating, sunburn and dehydration. At night time they leave the water to graze, preferring short grassy pastures. They use well-defined pathways from the water to their feeding areas, and during the course of the nights foraging; they may cover a distance of 8-10km. They have been recorded, in isolated cases, feeding on the rotting flesh of other animals. They will usually gather together in herds of 10-50 animals, but during periods of drought densities can increase dramatically to 200 or more. Adults are capable of remaining completely submerged for periods of up to 5 minutes. When giving birth cows will isolate themselves from the herd, remaining alone with their calves for about 6 weeks. Calves are capable of suckling underwater as well as on land.

Masai Giraffe

(Giraffa camelopardalis)

As the world's tallest animal, reaching heights over 5m, the giraffe is unmistakeable. The immense neck, sloping body and long legs aid easy identification. The coat pattern is that of irregular brown blotches on a yellow-buff background. The coat colour of the males has a tendency to darken with age. The underparts are light with faint blotches and spots. A mane of stiff hair extends from the nape, down the neck to the shoulders. The tail is long and thin, terminating in an abundance of long black hair. The amount and size of horns is very variable, but normally they possess a principle pair on the upper forehead and signs of a much smaller pair on the crown. In addition they often have a single knob of horn in the centre of the lower forehead. The horns are skin covered with tufts of hair at the tips in some females and younger animals. Females are smaller than males.

An inhabitant of bush and lightly wooded regions south of the Sahara, where they feed by browsing to a height denied to all other herbivores. They will strip leaves and shoots from even the most thorny trees and bushes with ease, by use of prehensile lips and a very long 45 cm tongue. They remain active for much of the day, seeking shade during the hot midday period. They are found in herds of between 6-12 animals on average. They need to drink every 2-3 days when water is available and during the dry season they are seldom too far from a permanent source, they will disperse over a much wider area during the rains. In order to drink they have to splay out the forelegs and it is at these times they are most susceptible to attack by lions. They walk with a slow amble moving both legs of the same side of the body together; this is known as 'pacing' and is quite unusual among animals. When they run or gallop they give the impression of 'slow motion' but are capable of speeds up to 60km/h.

Reticulated Giraffe

(Giraffa camelopardalis reticulata)

A sub-species of Masai Giraffe.
The coat pattern of this sub-species is very striking. Crisp, liver-coloured geometric patches, conspicuously defined by narrow white lines running between them, produces a 'crazy paving' appearance. These markings become paler on the inner flanks, legs and underparts. The coat colour of the male has a tendency to darken with age. Females are smaller than males. A distribution overlap brings Reticulated Giraffes into contact with Masia Giraffes resulting in a variety of hybrid types within certain areas. An inhabitant of dry bush country in north-eastern Kenya, particularly in Samburu Game Reserve, and into Somalia.

Rothschild's Giraffe

(Giraffa camelopardalis rothschildi)

A sub-species of Masai Giraffe.
The coat pattern of this sub-species is similar to that of the Reticulated Giraffe but with the 'crazy paving' effect less well defined. There is no patterning at all below the knees or hocks, these areas being almost pure white. The body patterning, although fainter, does extend to the inner flanks, upper legs and underparts. Females are smaller than males.

An inhabitant of bush and lightly wooded areas of western Kenya. A fine herd of Rothschild's Giraffe can be found in the Lake Nakuru National Park in Kenya.

Common Duiker

(Sylvicapra grimmia)

A medium-size, slender Duiker, with long legs, large ears and pointed horns. The horns are usually only present in the male, ranging from 7-18cm in length. The pelage coloration ranges from grizzled grey to yellowish brown with a black streak running from the top of the russet forehead to the nose. The underparts are white tinged with grey and the legs are grey having a black band just above the hooves. The short tail is black above and white below. Females are generally larger than males.

They are mainly found in woodland habitats with scattered bush and scrub, avoiding arid desert regions, as well as areas of open plains and dense forest. They feed mainly on the leaves and shoots of bushes, as well as tree bark, fruits and seedpods, rarely do they eat grass. They also consume insects and other animal matter from time to time, including frogs, small mammals and birds. They obtain the vast majority of their water requirement from their food and are able to survive for very long periods without drinking. Females give birth to single calves in dense cover, the newborn are able to run within 24 hour. They remain in dense cover sucking from the female 2 or 3 times a day growing very rapidly and by 6 months are as large as adults.

Kirk's Dik Dik

(Madoqua kirkii)

The commonest Dik Dik in East Africa. A small delicate antelope, with a grizzled grey and brown coat, the legs are rufous/grey. The head, neck and shoulders sometimes show a flush of rufous brown. White patches encircle the large dark eyes and the males have short, spiky horns, measuring 6-11cm in length. The elongated nose is a distinctive feature, serving as a very effective cooling device. They have prominent preorbital scent glands. Female Dik Dik are slightly larger than the males.

A relatively common inhabitant of arid regions with bush or scrub cover. Dik Dik live in pairs and are very territorial, each male guarding his own 'patch' against other males. Territorial boundaries are marked by a succession of dung/urine sites, which are re-stated daily by both males and females. As well as dung sites the animals mark their territory by using preorbital scent glands. These glands exude a secretion which the animals spread on twigs, branches and grass stems. They are active during both the day and night, but seek shade during the hottest period of the day. They have extremely sensitive eyesight and hearing, seeking cover at the slightest sign of danger.

Steinbok
(Raphicerus campestris)

A small, slender antelope with a reddish coat. The underside and the insides of the large ears are white. The horns, which are present only in the male, are straight spikes, measuring between 9-19cm in length. They have long legs and the appearance of being higher at the hindquarters than at the shoulder. They have a pale patch around the eyes, contrasting with dark areas surrounding the preorbital scent glands. A triangular patch of black fur extends up the muzzle from the black nose. The young have a heavier, fluffier coat than the adults, but retain the same coloration.

An animal of dry savannah and wooded hill sides, they graze on grass and browse trees, bushes and shrubs, as well as scraping with their hooves to expose roots and tubers. They are able to subsist without water, obtaining their entire fluid requirement from their food. They are active during both the day and night in undisturbed areas, but will avoid the midday heat by seeking shade in regular resting places. Females will produce young throughout the year, the newborn, weighing about 1 kilo at birth; will suckle from its mother almost immediately. The young commence grazing at about 2 weeks old and are weaned at 3 months. There are reports that from time to time Steinbok may take refuge underground in old Aardvark burrows, both for resting and for nursing young.

Oribi
(Ourebia ourebi)

A small, slender built antelope with long legs and neck, the hindquarters are rounded and slightly higher than the forequarters. They have large pointed ears below which is situated a scent gland which appears as a patch of bare black skin. The coat is of silky fine hair, reddish to fawn above and white below. The chin is white and the dark eyes contrast strongly with the white eyebrows. The legs are reddish-fawn with tufts of slightly longer hair at the knee joints. The horns, which feature in the male only, have rings on the lower third, are curved backwards and grow to a length of 8-19cm. The rufous tail is very short and has a black tip. Females are slightly larger than males.

An antelope of open grassland regions, where they require short grasses for feeding, and taller grasses for cover while resting. The males will establish and defend territories forcefully, marking their areas by the use of six different scent glands found about the body. A female will hide her newborn in thick grass for the first 3 or 4 days of life, from then on, over a period of about a month, the calf will begin to spend more and more time accompanying its mother. The young grow rapidly and attain full adult height at around 3 months. When alarmed the Oribi will emit a loud shrill whistle and will commence a 'stotting' performance, springing into the air with legs held rigid. Occasionally they will inflict considerable damage to cultivated crops, particularly during their night time feeding.

Klipspringer

(Oreotragus oreotragus)

A small, strongly built antelope, with a wedge shaped head and a thick coat of olive-yellow and grey hair. The muzzle is washed with brown and the chin and underparts are white. The large rounded ears are white-lined with prominent black markings. They have dark preorbital scent glands which are very pronounced. The legs are sturdy, terminating in black hooves which are specially adapted for rocky ground, giving the animal the appearance of 'standing on tiptoe'. The tail is very short and the horns are upright, measuring from 6 -15cm in length, occurring in the females of some populations as well as the males.

An animal of steep, rocky hill sides and screes as well as isolated kopjes and high mountains, having been recorded as high as 4,000m on Mount Kilimanjaro. They live in pairs or in small family parties and can often be seen standing atop a rock or boulder keeping a sharp lookout for predators. They are extremely agile, being capable of racing over boulder-strewn terrain at high speed and with apparent ease. They feed on leaves, shoots and berries, taking fruits when available and very occasionally grass. The young are hidden during their first month of life, being visited by the female for suckling three of four times a day. At about one month old they will begin to accompany their mother during her daily foraging.

Bushbuck

(Tragelaphus scriptus)

One of the most elegant of Africa's antelopes, with rounded hindquarters slightly higher than the shoulders. The colour of the coat varies greatly from yellowish-chestnut through reddish-brown to dark brown. The underparts of the male are black. They have a dorsal mane of longer hair running from the shoulder to the tail. The head is lighter in colour with a dark band extending along the muzzle and a white cheek patch. The body has white vertical stripes and spots, mainly on the hindquarters and the back. The tail is bushy, white underneath, with a black tip. The horns are almost straight, with a single spiral, varying in length from 30-57cm and only occur in the male.

An animal of forest edges and dense thickets, usually living singly or in pairs, but occasionally in small family groups. They are extremely secretive, hiding away during daylight hours in dense cover, feeding mainly during the night. Their main food consists of leaves and shoots, but they will dig for roots and tubers and plunder vegetable gardens from time to time. They will also associate with troops of baboons and monkeys, feeding on the fallen fruit shaken from the trees by the primates as they feed. When alarmed by the approach of a predator, the bushbuck's usual response is to freeze, in the hope of being overlooked.

Sitatunga
(Tragelaphus spekei)

An antelope with a shaggy medium length coat of drab grey/brown fur, often faintly marked with vertical stripes along the back and on the hindquarters. Some faint spotting also occurs on the flanks. The head has white patches on the cheeks and on the muzzle below the eyes. There are two white patches on the front of the neck, one on the throat and the other lower down towards the chest. The horns, which are only found in the male, are long, with spiral twists and measure up to 90cm in length. The hooves are specially adapted to support their weight in wet habitats, being long and splayed at the tips. The animal has a hunched appearance with hindquarters higher than forequarters. The female is smaller than the male and usually has a coat more chestnut in colour.

An aquatic antelope of marshes and swamps. Very secretive and shy, usually staying concealed in reeds and dense aquatic vegetation, only coming to the edge of cover in the evening. They feed mainly at dawn and dusk, as well as through the night, when they venture into surrounding grassland and wooded areas. They spend much of their time partially submerged and are very good swimmers. At the approach of danger they will often immerse themselves completely, all but for the tip of the nose. They often create well-trodden platforms of reeds and vegetation, on which to rest, by and action of trampling and turning. They also maintain a network of paths through the reed beds. Local hunters often make use of these well-defined pathways along which they place wire snares.

Bongo
(Tragelaphus euryceros)

A very striking antelope with a bright chestnut upper coat and dark almost black underside. The body from shoulder to rump is conspicuously marked with yellow-white vertical stripes, usually 12-14 in number. There is a crescent shaped stripe across the base of the neck. The ears are outlined with white hair and on the cheeks there are 2 or 3 white patches. There is also a white stripe on the bridge of the muzzle in front of the eyes. The legs have a broken pattern of irregular black, white and chestnut patches. The horns are large, ranging from 60-100cm in length, have a single spiral and vary in colour from light grey to black. They are less well developed in the female. The white tail is of medium length, terminating in a tuft of black hairs.

An antelope of the densest mountain forests. Being very secretive and mainly nocturnal in habits makes this species one of the most difficult of the large mammals to see. They feed usually in dense cover, on leaves, shoots and the flowers of trees and bushes, occasionally grasses and herbs as well as roots which they unearth with their horns. They will sometimes stand on hind legs to reach higher foliage, using their long tongue to grasp bunches of leaves. They readily use saltlicks and require a constant supply of water throughout the year. The Aberdare Mountains of Kenya remains one of the best areas to see bongo. During the dry season they will move higher into the mountains, (2,500m or higher), usually dispersing to lower elevations during the wet season.

Lesser Kudu
(Tragelaphus imberbis)

An antelope of slender build and medium size. The coat is grey/brown in colour and the sides of the body, from shoulders to rump, are marked with a series of light vertical stripes. The males carry large horns with 2-3 spirals, 60-90cm in length. There are white patches on the cheeks, across the muzzle below the eyes and on the throat and lower neck. The long legs are tawny brown with patches of black and white. A line of short hair extends from the shoulders down the centre of the back to the tail, which is tawny/grey above, white below and black tipped. Females tend to be redder than males, while generally; the males become darker and greyer with age.

An inhabitant of semi-desert regions of thorn bush country, seldom venturing into open areas. They feed by browsing bushes and trees for leaves, shoots, seedpods and fruits, occasionally taking fresh green grass. They are mainly active in the early morning, late afternoon and evening, during much of the day they will rest, either standing or lying, in dense thickets, where the broken pattern of the coat renders them almost invisible. When alarmed they will utter a loud bark and, when fleeing from predators, they are capable of leaping bushes and thickets up to 2m in height. Although they may visit waterholes for drinking when water is available, they are capable of surviving during long periods of dry weather, by obtaining their entire liquid requirement from their food.

Greater Kudu
(Tragelaphus strepsiceros)

A very large elegant antelope, the males having magnificent horns with two and a half to three spirals and measuring up to 180cm in length. The smooth coat is bluish-grey to fawn with the sides of the body boldly marked with white vertical stripes, varying in number from 6-10. The head has a dark muzzle with white upper lip and chin and a conspicuous white stripe running from eye to eye across the bridge of the muzzle. A growth of longer hair extends down the centre of the back from the neck to the tail. The males have long hair growing along the throat and down the neck to the chest. The tail is of medium length, grey above, white below and with a black tip. The female is of smaller build, very occasionally having horns.

Greater Kudu inhabit thickets and areas of bush and scrub, often in hilly country and usually close to water, as they prefer to drink frequently if water is available, they can, however, survive in dry areas obtaining sufficient moisture from their food. They are usually found in small family herds of 4 or 5, but herds of 30 or more have been recorded. They avoid the heat of the day, browsing mainly in the early morning, late afternoon and into the night, on leaves, shoots and occasionally grasses. Females will isolate themselves to give birth, keeping the newborn hidden for 4-5 weeks, from then on the young will begin to accompany its mother more and more. The young grow quickly and by about 6 months are fairly self-reliant.

Eland
(Taurotragus oryx)

The largest African antelope, cattle-like in appearance. They have a hump on the shoulders and a dewlap at the base of the neck which generally becomes more pronounced in older males. General coloration is tawny-fawn to grey, the sides of the body being faintly marked with light vertical stripes, bolder on the shoulder than at the rear. Males have a crest of hair on the forehead and a mane on the nape. Horns are present in both sexes. They have several tight twists and range in length from 60-100cm, generally thinner but longer in the female, sloping backwards following the profile line of the forehead. The tail is long, terminating in a tuft of black hair.

An antelope of open plains and lightly wooded areas, thick forests being avoided. Gregarious by nature, herd sizes can vary from a few individuals to 500 or more. They feed on a variety of vegetation, taking large quantities of fresh grass following the rains, and browsing trees and bushes for leaves, shoots, fruits and seedpods during the dry season. They are active at all times of the day and night, but in extremely hot weather they will seek shade during the midday period. A newborn calf is able to walk almost immediately following its birth but will remain hidden for a period of around 2 weeks, before joining a nursery group along with its mother and the rest of the herd. They do not generally allow a very close approach, moving away when vehicles are still several hundred yards distant.

Beisa Oryx
(Oryx gazella beisa)

A large elegant and very distinctive antelope, with a short coat of grey-fawn, a black horizontal stripe running across the lower flank and black bands around the forelegs just above the knee joints. The facial markings are very conspicuous; a broad black stripe runs down the side of the face through the eye, from the base of the extremely long, thin horns to the lower cheek. The forehead has a black patch as does the upper muzzle. The hair on the lower muzzle is white, contrasting strongly with the black nostrils. A black line extends under the chin and around the upper throat from ear to ear. A thin black stripe extends down the centre of the neck from the throat to the chest and from the back of the neck along the spine to the root of the tail. The tail is long and horse-like, consisting of black hair. The parallel horns, which are carried by both sexes, are almost straight with a slight backward slant and can grow to 120cm in length. Another race of oryx, the Fringe-eared (*Oryx gazella callotis*) occurs in some regions and can be distinguished by a browner coat, slightly heavier build and tufts of long black hair on the points of the ears.

A true desert species of dry arid regions with sparse bush cover and open areas of savannah. They feed mainly on grasses but will also browse trees and bushes. When water is available they will drink daily but they are capable of surviving for long periods without drinking. They are active throughout the day but generally seek shade during the midday period. They are to be found in herds numbering from 6-40 or more. Females seek isolation from the main herd in order to give birth, returning 2-3 weeks later along with the newborn. When under threat from predators they will usually flee, but will sometimes present a spirited defence, lowering the head they often inflict serious and sometimes fatal injuries upon their attacker with their spear-like horns.

Roan Antelope

(Hippotragus equinus)

A large antelope with sloping shoulders and powerful neck and forequarters. The coat coloration varies from dark rufous to reddish-fawn contrasting with the black and white head and face markings. The ears are long and narrow with tufts of long hair at the tips. The under parts are white. A well-defined mane of dark hair extends from the upper neck to the shoulders; a similar growth of hair is present on the underside of the neck extending down the centre of the throat. The legs are rufous, the forelegs having irregular black patches. The horns are heavily ringed and curve backwards in a sickle shape; the length varies from 55-100cm and they are less well formed in the female.

An antelope of open and lightly wooded regions, living in small herds of about 20 animals, but they will gather together in larger herds when food and water are scarce, herds of 150 have been recorded. A dominant bull leads each herd. They feed mainly on grasses, occasionally browsing leaves and shoots from trees and bushes. They are very dependent on water and rarely venture far from a readily available source; they will usually visit water twice a day, taking large quantities. They are active throughout the day, usually finding cover and shade during the hottest period around midday. Females calve away from the herd and hide the newborn in dense vegetation for some weeks, only returning to suckle the infant twice a day.

Sable Antelope

(Hippotragus niger)

A large and magnificent antelope with powerful forequarters. The male has a glossy black coat, white underparts and a striking head of black and white markings. White hair covers the chin and the tip of the muzzle, from where broad white bands extend up the sides of the face terminating on the forehead. The crown of the head and the outside of the ears are light chestnut, the inside of the ears are white. They have a pronounced mane of stiff hairs from the neck to the shoulders and a long black tail. Females and young are often paler and more chestnut in colour than the males. The horns are very long, measuring up to 154cm in length, sweep backwards in an arc and are heavily ridged, they are less well developed in the female.

An inhabitant of light woodland, bush and grasslands. They are found in herds of 10-20 animals on average but will occasionally form larger herds, particularly during the dry seasons when suitable grazing is much reduced. The herds, of mainly females and young, are usually headed by a dominant bull and fights with neighbouring males are quite frequent, the combatants dropping to their knees and engaging horns in bouts of head wrestling. Fatalities are known but they are very rare. They are primarily grazers taking grasses and herbs but occasionally they browse trees and bushes for leaves and shoots. They are heavily dependent on water and although they only drink on average every other day, they rarely wander too far from a dependable source. They are active mainly in the early morning and late afternoon and evening.

Common Waterbuck
(Kobus ellipsiprymnus)

A large antelope with a shaggy coat of grizzled grey with an occasional brown tinge, sometimes the back and lower legs are darker, becoming almost black. The white ears are large, with black tips. Facial markings are limited to a white stripe extending from the eyebrow along the sides of the muzzle to just below the eye and a white patch around the nasal area and the lips. They have a white collar extending across the throat almost from ear to ear. On the rump is a pronounced white crescent shape, which distinguishes it from the sub-species Defassa Waterbuck (*Kobus e. defassa*), which has a circular white patch on the buttocks. The tail is of medium length having a dark tip. The horns, present only in the male, are heavily ringed and curve backwards, upwards and forwards towards the tips.

Waterbuck inhabit woodlands and clearings usually close to water, where they feed mainly on grasses and herbs. They will also occasionally feed on the foliage of trees and bushes, particularly during periods of extreme drought. They are dependent on water and will drink every day or so. Mainly active during the early morning, late afternoon and early evening. They are usually found in small groups consisting of a bull with several females and young numbering on average 5-10 animals in all. Herds of bachelor males may be encountered of 6-40 in number; males are at least 4 years old before they are able to establish themselves as master bulls. When pursued by predators waterbuck will flee and attempt to hide themselves in bush cover or long grass, but there have been many reports of them taking refuge in water, submerging completely all but for the nostrils.

Defassa Waterbuck
(Kobus ellipsiprymnus defassa)

A sub-species of Common Waterbuck.

A large antelope with a long, coarse shaggy coat, the Defassa Waterbuck is a sub-species of the Common Waterbuck and is very similar in appearance. The main visual difference being the pattern on the rump, which in Defassa is a solid white patch radiating from the base of the tail and covering the buttocks, while in the Common Waterbuck the rump markings take the form of white semi-circular stripes. For other identification details see Common Waterbuck. In areas where the distribution of the two overlaps, inter-breeding has been recorded resulting in intermediate rump patterns.

The habitat preference of Defassa Waterbuck is very similar to that of the Common Waterbuck, woodlands and clearing in the vicinity of water, where they feed on grasses and browse leaves and shoots from trees and bushes. The Defassa has a greater and wider distribution throughout Africa than that of the Common and seems to prefer areas with a pattern of greater rainfall. Both have coats impregnated with oil which is secreted from sweat glands, which may serve as waterproofing as well as for individual recognition. They form small family herds of 5-10 animals as well as bachelor herds of up to 40.

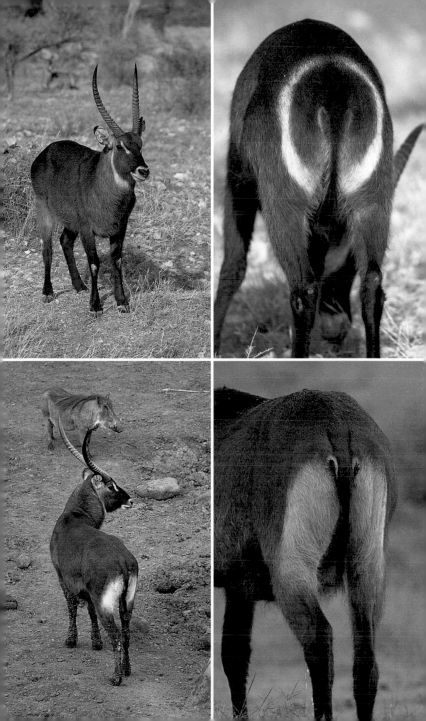

Wildebeest

(Connochaetes taurinus)

A large antelope with forequarters higher than hindquarters giving the appearance of a pronounced 'slope' from front to rear. Greyish in colour with a long mane of black hair on the neck and shoulders and a long beard of hair on the neck and throat, the coloration of the beard varies greatly from almost pure white to black. The neck, shoulders and, to a lesser extent, the flanks show dark vertical stripes. The head is large and broad with a completely black face. The horns are present in both sexes, measuring between 40-73cm in length and from a flat base curve outwards, downward then upward, not dissimilar in shape to those of the Cape Buffalo. The black bushy-tipped tail is extremely long almost touching the ground.

An extremely common antelope of open grassland and lightly wooded regions where it gathers in enormous herds during its annual migration in a continual search for fresh grazing. This circular, seasonal migration from the southern Serengeti to the Masai Mara and back covers a distance in excess of 800km. and at times columns of animals stretch for 40km. They eat mainly grass and are water dependent drinking twice a day if possible. They are active throughout the day usually attempting to rest or seek shade during the hot midday period. The females synchronise their calving with 80 per cent of young being born during a three-week period usually towards the beginning of the rainy season (Feb-March). To avoid predation the females and newborn need to remain mobile and to this end the calves are on their feet within 3-7 minutes of birth. This synchronised calving produces an abundance of food for predators, but over a short period, thereby ensuring the survival of the majority.

Uganda Kob

(Kobus kob)

A graceful antelope of medium size with a short coat of light cinnamon to brown. The underparts are white and the forelegs have a black stripe on the front above and below the knee joints. A light, almost white, area of hair encircles the eyes and a white patch appears on the underside of the throat and upper neck. The insides of the ears are white and the tail is of medium length terminating in a tuft of black hair. The lyre-shaped horns are only present in the male, they are deeply ringed and curve backward, outward before arcing upward to form an 'S' in profile. They occasionally reach 70cm in length.

An animal of open grassy savannah and lightly wooded areas in the west of the region. They generally live in herds of 20-40 animals. They feed on grasses and herbs, as well as occasionally grazing on aquatic vegetation; they are rarely found far from water. They are active throughout the day even on occasions grazing during the hottest midday period. Males are generally 3-4 years old before successfully securing and holding a territory, the females moving at will from one territory to another in search of the strongest males with which to breed.

Mountain Reedbuck
(Redunca fulvorufula)

A small antelope with a shaggy coat of grey-fawn, the head and neck are tinged with rufous-brown; the chest and belly are white. The eyebrows, throat, chin and lips are faintly marked with off-white, as is the short, bushy tail. A gland of dark skin is clearly visible below the ears on the sides of the head; a dark line extends down the centre of the muzzle from the eyes to the nose. Horns are only present in the male and are short, heavily ringed and arc forward. Females are usually larger and often greyer in colour than the males.

An antelope of grassy hill sides and mountains from altitudes of 1,500m upwards, where they feed by grazing grasses and herbage. Over a period of months during the dry season, it is thought that they obtain their entire water requirement from their food. They gather in small herds of 3-8 animals, usually consisting of females and young occupying the territory of a single resident male. Other males tend to form small bachelor groups. They are active in early morning and late afternoon as well as during moonlit nights. Females are able to produce young from 1 year old and on average, will produce a calf every 9-14 months. Females having given birth will leave the young hidden for a period of 2-3 months, visiting only for short periods of suckling.

Bohor Reedbuck
(Redunca redunca)

An antelope of medium size, having a thick coat of uniform reddish-fawn. The underside of the body is whitish-grey. The same white-grey fur appears around the eyes, on the cheeks, lips, chin, and throat and on the insides of the large oval ears. The nose and the centre of the upper lip are black. Occasionally a black stripe is discernible extending down the front of the forelegs. The tail is short with a bushy tip, the white underside being very conspicuous when exposed by the animal when fleeing in alarm. The horns, present only in the male are lyre-shaped, curving forwards and inwards and are heavily ringed particularly towards the base.

An animal of open plains, lush wet grasslands and swampy ground usually in the vicinity of water. They are usually found in pairs or in small family herds of 3-6 animals and feed almost exclusively on grasses. They are active throughout the day, as well as during clear moonlit nights; however, they usually seek the cover of long grass or bushes during the hot midday period, sitting very tight if approached and bolting only at the last moment. Sightings of very young animals are extremely rare, the females keeping them very well hidden for a period of at least two months.

Topi

(Damaliscus lunatus)

A large antelope with a pronounced 'slope', being higher in the forequarters than at the rear. The coat is short and glossy, dark chestnut-brown with bluish-black patches extending from the lower shoulders down the forelegs to just above the knees and from the rump down the back legs terminating just above the hock. The same bluish-black hair extends down the centre of the long narrow face, from the forehead to the tip of the muzzle and on the backs of the ears. The horns, 30-60cm in length, appear in both sexes but are larger in the male. They are heavily ringed and angle backwards, slightly outwards and upwards towards the tips. The tail is of medium length terminating with tufts of long black hair.

An antelope of open grasslands and areas of light scattered bush and scrub, where they feed almost entirely on grasses and herbage. They are found in small groups of around 12 animals, usually consisting of a dominant bull along with a harem of females and young. They can; however, congregate in herds of thousands during the dry season when grazing is scarce. They will readily mingle with Hartebeest, Wildebeest, Zebra and other plains ungulates. Although they will drink regularly when water is available, they are able to survive up to a month without water. They are active both by day and by night. An individual can often be found standing on a termite mound, or similar piece of elevated ground, on the lookout for predators, whilst other members of the herd continue to graze.

Cokes Hartebeest

(Alcelaphus buselaphus)

A large antelope, characterised by its 'sloping' appearance, being higher in the forequarters than in the rear. The coat is of uniform yellow-fawn, lighter on the hindquarters with an almost white rump and underside. The head and face are long and narrow with large pointed ears. The horns are sickle-shaped, curving forwards; outwards then backwards, are deeply ringed and are present in both sexes. The tail is of medium length terminating in a tassel of black hair. The female is similar to the male but usually paler in colour and with smaller, slimmer horns.

One of the most common of Africa's antelopes, inhabiting areas of open grassland and dry savannah, sometimes with lightly scattered trees and bushes. They can be found in herds ranging in number from just a few to many thousands, the larger concentrations occurring during the dry season when available grazing is limited. Old males may be solitary and young males may form into bachelor herds. They are active mainly in the early morning and late afternoon and evening, seeking shelter from the sun during the hot midday period. They feed mainly on grasses and herbage and will drink every day when water is available, however, during prolonged periods of drought they can survive on the moisture obtained from their food. They often associate with other species of plains herbivores.

Impala
(Aepyceros melampus)

A very graceful medium sized antelope with a long neck, a smooth short coat of rufous-brown, being paler on the lower flanks and with white underparts. The males carry magnificent, wide-set, lyre-shaped horns that curve backwards; sideways then upwards, they are heavily ringed and can grow to over 90cm in length. The upper lip, chin, throat and eyebrows are white. The inner ears are white tipped with black. The nose is black and forms a characteristic 'Y' shape. A vertical black line extends down the hindquarters from the root of the tail. Just above the heel of the hind legs there is a tuft of long black hair. The tail is of medium length with a black stripe on the upper side. The female is smaller than the male and lacks horns.

A species of open plains and sparse woodlands, within easy reach of water, they will drink twice a day when water is available. They feed mainly on short grasses which forms up to 95 per cent of their food intake, only occasionally browsing from trees and bushes. They are normally encountered in small herds of around 6-20 animals, although herds of 50+ are quite common. The herds usually consist of a single dominant male and females with young. Males are usually 4-6 years old before attaining the strength and stature to hold a territory and secure a harem of females; fights between rival males during the rutting season can be very fierce. During the dry season they often form larger herds, concentrated together on the small areas of remaining grassland. Their sight is not well developed but their hearing and smell are acute. When under threat from predators they are quite fast and capable of leaps of 11m in length and 3m in height.

Grants Gazelle
(Gazella granti)

A large elegant antelope with long legs and powerful build. The short, smooth coat is fawn often with the head and neck paler. The insides of the legs and the underparts are white. The buttocks are white contrasting with a dark patch extending down the rump. The white of the buttocks continues to a point just above the root of the tail and curves out for a short distance on to the rump. In younger animals the point along the lower flank where the fawn coat meets the white underside is often marked with a darker horizontal band. The head is marked with white patches around the eyes, along the sides of the muzzle, around the nasal area and the chin. A black line extends from the eyes down the muzzle to the corners of the mouth. A black band sweeps over the muzzle just above the nasal area. The horns are carried by both sexes, usually smaller in the female, and grow to 80cm in length. They are heavily ringed and lyre-shaped curving backwards, outwards and upwards, the outward divergence is very variable.

An inhabitant of open plains and dry bush country. Males of at least 3 years old establish territories and gather together females forming harems of 10-30 in number, larger herds form during non-rutting seasons. They feed on grasses and leaves and do not normally need to drink, obtaining sufficient liquid from their food, this allows them to exploit feeding opportunities in drier regions which water dependent herbivores are unable to inhabit. There is some evidence of seasonal migration in search of grazing. They graze mainly during the early morning and late afternoon but remain active throughout the day. Females will leave the herd to calve, moving to areas offering cover, in which the newborn can hide for the first 4-6 weeks of life.

Thomsons Gazelle
(Gazella thomsoni)

Medium-small in size this delicate gazelle is sandy-rufous in colour, darker along the back and paler on the head, neck, lower flanks and rump. The chest, belly and insides of the legs are pure white. A very conspicuous thick black band extends horizontally from the top of the forelegs across the flanks to the thighs. The buttocks are white bordered by a thin black stripe. The forehead and centre of the muzzle are dark rufous-brown; broad bands of white hair extend from the base of the ears through the eyes to the tip of the muzzle. A black stripe extends from the eyes down the cheeks to the corners of the mouth. The lips, chin and throat are white. The horns are deeply ringed and quite long, up to 40cm or more, they are only slightly curved and are much reduced in the female. They have a short black tail.

A common antelope of open plains and grasslands, named after the explorer Joseph Thomson who first saw the species in Kenya in 1883. They live in harem herds of one dominant male with, on average, 6-60 females, but during certain periods of the year, usually the dry season, they gather into herds of many thousands, mixing with other ungulates. They feed almost exclusively on grasses, only occasionally browsing from trees and bushes. They will drink daily when water is readily available but can survive for long periods without. They are most active during the early morning and late afternoon and evening. Newborn calves remain hidden between periods of suckling and in open country their coloration and the ability to 'freeze' makes them extremely difficult to detect. The young grow rapidly being weaned within two months.

Gerenuk
(Litocranius walleri)

A large, slender built gazelle, almost unmistakable having an extremely long neck and long delicate legs. The upper body colour along the centre saddle of the back is reddish-buff, becoming lighter on the flanks, rump, legs, neck and head. The underside is white and clearly defined. A narrow vertical white stripe is present either side of the root of the tail. The tail itself is short and tipped with a tuft of black hair. The head is small and narrow; the large dark eyes are ringed with patches of white hair in which are set dark preorbital scent glands. The ears are large, the insides being white edged with prominent black markings. The horns are restricted to the males only and are short but substantial, measuring up to 44cm in length curving backwards, outwards and turning forwards and upwards towards the tips, they are heavily ringed. Females are slighter in build than males and show a dark patch on the crown of the head.

Living singly, in pairs or small groups consisting of a dominant male with several females and young, the Gerenuk inhabits areas of dry bush and scrub. They feed exclusively on the foliage of trees and bushes. They often reach higher leaves by standing erect on their back legs, this action coupled with the elongated neck allows them to browse leaves and shoots that are out of the reach of most other animals, reaching heights in excess of 2m. They do not need to drink, obtaining their entire liquid requirement from their food matter. They are active in the early morning and in the late afternoon and evening, resting in shade if possible during the hot midday period.

Cape Buffalo

(Syncerus caffer)

An enormous bovid of strong, solid build with short legs and cattle-like appearance. The sparse coat is short and blackish in colour; young animals have a thicker browner coat. The stout muscular neck supports a large head with a wide muzzle and large ears on the sides of the head, beneath massive horns which spread outwards and downwards from a thick broad base before arcing upwards and inwards. The horn size and shape is variable and dependent on age, the old mature bulls carrying the prize sets, they are much reduced in the female. The tail is long terminating in a tassel of black hair.

Found over a wide range of habitats from dense forests and woodlands to open plains. They are primarily grazers but in forest habitats will browse leaves and shoots. They are water dependent and need to drink daily if possible. They are gregarious, living in herds of 20-40 animals on average, but sometimes form into herds of several hundred. Old bulls tend to live a solitary existence or form small geriatric herds. They are often attended by flocks of Oxpeckers or Tick Birds who do a service to the animals by removing ticks and blood-sucking insects from the hide. They are active by both day and night, seeking shelter during the hot midday period. They take great delight in wallowing in mud holes. The eyesight is rather poor and the hearing only average but the sense of smell is acute. In the face of danger or uncertainty they will usually lumber away, but they need to be treated with the utmost respect, being responsible for many serious injuries and deaths among local people.

African Elephant

(Loxodonta africana)

Quite unmistakeable, the worlds' largest land mammal. The elephant is so well known that a detailed description seems quite unnecessary, however, there are many interesting facts worth mentioning. The trunk is unique, being not only a nose, but also acting as an additional limb, with an extremely sensitive and flexible tip. An elephant will also use its trunk for drinking, by sucking up large quantities of water before squirting it into the mouth. The large ears act as a very effective cooling system. A network of blood vessels covers the backs of the ears and the constant flapping helps the animal to regulate its body temperature through evaporation. The tusks grow throughout the animal's life, with the rate of growth varying enormously among individuals. An elephant's eyesight is poor but the senses of smell and hearing are very acute. In spite of their massive bulk, soft cushioned undersides to their feet enable almost noiseless movement.

Over recent years the number and distribution of the elephant has been greatly reduced, the main reasons being the expansion of human settlements and the poaching of ivory. They favour areas of wooded savannah and forests. Elephants eat a wide variety of vegetation from grasses and herbage to bushes and trees. In woodland areas considerable damage can be caused, even to mature trees, by the passage of a large herd. They are active throughout the day and night, although shelter is usually sought during the hottest part of the day. Most females and calves live together in herds averaging 10-20 animals, usually led by an old female they are very protective of their young. By contrast old bulls tend to lead a solitary existence.

Grevy's Zebra
(Equus grevyi)

The distinctive markings of the zebra make for easy identification. The Grevy's is the largest member of the zebra family with narrow black stripes, on a background of white, covering the body, head and the entire length of the legs to the hooves. The neck and body stripes are vertical, those on the neck continuing through the stiff hair of the mane, whilst those covering the legs are horizontal. The stripes terminate on the lower body leaving a plain white under-belly. A broad black stripe extends from the base of the mane to the root of the tail. Each animal has a pattern as unique as a fingerprint. They have large rounded ears, black edged and tipped with white. The point of the muzzle around the nose and mouth is black often tinged with brown. The tail is long, rounded and striped at the base, terminating in a tuft of long black hair. Young animals often have the dorsal mane and the rear and upper body stripes brownish.

A zebra of dry, semi-desert regions, where they are normally found in small herds of 6-20 animals, although large herds of several hundred do gather from time to time. Males often gather in bachelor herds, usually reaching full maturity around 6 years old. In northern Kenya, the last stronghold of the species, they often associate with herds of Beisa Oryx. They feed by grazing on grasses and herbage, being mainly active in the early morning and late afternoon. They are less dependent on water than other zebra species but drink daily when water is available and can only survive for a short period without liquid, often digging in river beds and stream bottoms to reach the subterranean water level.

Common Zebra
(Equus quagga)

Africa's version of the horse, the distinctive markings make the zebra easy to identify. Broad blackish stripes, vertical on the neck and shoulders and horizontal on the rump and legs are set against an almost white body colour. The stripes continue down the legs to the hooves, cover the head, face and the stiff hair of the mane, each animal having a pattern as unique as a fingerprint. The ears are large. The tip of the muzzle, around the nose and mouth, is black and sometimes tinged with brown. A broad black stripe follows the line of the spine from the base of the mane to the root of the tail. The stripes of young animals are usually brown rather than black and have a shaggy appearance.

An animal of open plains, grasslands, hills and mountains, where they roam in large herds often numbering thousands, but generally they are found in smaller family groups of 6-20 animals consisting of a dominant stallion of at least 5-7 years old, with a number of mares and foals. They are primarily grazers but will occasionally browse leaves and shoots from a variety of trees and bushes. They are dependent on water and are rarely found far from a permanent source. They are active throughout the day. They are subject to seasonal migrations constantly searching for better grazing, often mixing with Wildebeest herds. At the approach of danger adults may present a collective defence for themselves and other herd members, particularly young.

Black Rhinoceros

(Diceros bicornis)

A relic of prehistoric times the rhinoceros is almost unmistakeable. The Black Rhino is distinguished from the slightly larger White Rhino, by the narrow mouth and prehensile upper lip. The head is large and carries two horns, the larger front horn measuring on average 60cm although individuals with a front horn over twice that length have been recorded. The ears are oval and tipped with tufts of dark hair. The eyes are small and the eyesight poor, but the senses of smell and hearing are very acute. The huge body is covered with a thick hide of grey skin, although due to the rhino's predilection for wallowing in mud, their coloration can appear very variable. The tail is short and tipped with stiff hairs. In spite of their bulk the Black Rhino is very manoeuvrable and capable of a top speed of 50km/h.

The distribution of this species has been much reduced in the past 25 years as a result of increased poaching. They favour areas of dry bushy savannah and lightly wooded regions. In most areas they survive by browsing leaves and shoots from bushes and trees, although the population inhabiting the Ngorongoro Crater grazes regularly due to the lack of suitable browse. They feed mainly in the early morning and late afternoon, seeking shade or a mud wallow during the hottest midday period. Although they are capable of surviving for several days without water, they will drink and wallow daily when possible, often travelling many kilometres to an available source. During periods of drought they will often dig for water in dried up river beds by use of their forelegs. Rhinos are solitary animals although females are usually accompanied by their most recent offspring.

White Rhinoceros

(Cerototherium simium)

The White Rhino is the world's second largest land mammal - the Elephant being the largest. The animal's name has nothing whatever to do with colour, but is a corruption of the Afrikaans word 'Weit' meaning 'wide' and refers to the shape of the mouth, this being the most obvious difference between the two African species. Far bigger and heavier than the Black Rhino the head is large, square-shaped and carries two horns. The front horn is the larger of the two, averaging 60cm in length, the rear horn is shorter and thicker. The ears are large and oval in shape, the eyes are small and the eyesight is rather poor. The huge body is covered with a thick hide of pale grey skin. The tail is short, terminating with stiff hairs.

Several attempts to reintroduce this species into East Africa's National Parks have been undertaken in recent times, but most of the introduced animals have subsequently fallen to poachers' guns and snares. Hopefully, the latest introduction of seventeen animals from South Africa into Kenya's Lake Nakuru National Park will fare better, thereby securing the long-term future of the species in East Africa. They feed by grazing, using the wide mouth and strong lips to crop short grasses. They will feed throughout the day and night, but usually seek shelter from the hot midday sun. They will drink several times a day if water is readily available but during the dry season they can subsist by drinking every 3-4 days. In spite of their bulk they are surprisingly quick and manoeuvrable.

Tree Hyrax

(Dendrohyrax arboreus)

An animal with the superficial appearance of a rodent that is thought, by some, to be more closely related to the Elephant. The body is round; the head is short and pointed with stiff grey whiskers, rounded ears and dark prominent eyes. The coat consists of dense, soft fur and varies in colour from pale grey-brown to dark brown. The belly is yellowish white as is a variable amount of the dorsal area. They have pale eyebrows and whitish edging to the ears and lips. The tail is very short, the legs are short and slender and the feet have specially adapted pads to aid them when climbing.

An inhabitant of rain forests and woodlands over much of the region, up to an altitude of 4,000m. They spend most of the daylight hours hidden away in tree holes, emerging under cover of darkness to feed. They are very agile climbers. They are very vocal and call frequently throughout the night as a means of maintaining their respective territories. The call commences with a series of groans and creeks, rising to a climax of eerie screams and shrieks. They feed on leaves, bark, shoots, fruits and grasses, as well as taking the occasional bird's egg and insect. Although the senses of sight, smell and hearing are acute they are often taken as prey by large owls and nocturnal cats.

Rock Hyrax

(Heterohyrax brucei)

Easily mistaken at first glance for a rodent, this species is thought, by some, to be the closest living relative to the Elephant. Slightly smaller than the Tree Hyrax the body is round and the head short with a blunted snout and stiff grey whiskers. The ears are rounded and the legs and tail are short. The feet have specially adapted paws, the bottoms of which act like suction pads, aiding the animal as it runs among rocks and stones. The coat is dense and varies in colour from light to dark brown, often with the shoulders and legs lighter. They frequently have a patch of pale ochre-brown fur along the centre of the back. The underside is yellowish white. Like all hyrax species they have large incisor teeth.

A species found in the vicinity of rocky outcrops and cliffs throughout East Africa. They live in medium to large colonies, seeking shelter and safety in the holes and cracks between the boulders. They can often be found in the early morning sunbathing and grooming. They feed on a variety of vegetation including leaves, bark, fruits, twigs, grasses and occasionally invertebrates. They are active throughout the day as well as on moonlit nights. The senses of sight, smell and hearing are acute and when danger threatens they issue a loud warning whistle, which sends all members of the colony scurrying for safety among the rocks. They are a favourite prey item of the Verreaux's or Black Eagle.

Aardvark

(Orycteropus afer)

A rather bizarre, thickset, short-legged animal that would be difficult to confuse with any other living mammal in East Africa. They are grey/brown in colour, with a sparse covering of bristly hair. Also known as the Ant Bear, they have an elongated muzzle, with a soft flexible snout and a long sticky tongue. The short legs are extremely powerful and have long claws that enable them to dig with ease. Their long pointed ears help to provide them with excellent hearing; they also have a well-developed sense of smell, but rather poor eyesight. The tail is long, thick and powerful, resembling that of a Kangaroo and in the female, usually terminating in a white tip.

Aardvarks are shy, solitary creatures, being rarely seen, as a result of their purely nocturnal habits. They spend the daylight hours sleeping in deep self-excavated burrows. These burrows may be single hole affairs or a more complicated arrangement of inter-twining tunnels and chambers. They can be found in areas of open savannah and light woodlands, with sandy or soft soils. They can range over large areas in search of food, covering distances up to ten kilometres in a night. They will visit dozens of termite mounds in turn, the long sticky tongue being used to collect ants, termites and other insects, which form the bulk of their diet. They will occasionally feed on soft, wild fruits. Single young, very rarely twins, are born in a burrow and will start to follow the female into the outside world at about two weeks old, they will remain with the female until the arrival of her next offspring.

Crested Porcupine

(Hystrix cristata)

The largest rodent in East Africa, a most distinctive animal making identification easy. The body coloration is blackish/brown and grey. The upper parts of the body, particularly the back and tail, are covered with long, sharp, black and white quills, which afford the animal good protection against attack from most predators. The belief that the quills can be 'shot' by the animal is a myth. A very stout looking creature with a large head and thick neck, from which grows a long, backward facing mane of bristles. The legs and tail, although substantial, are often hidden from view when the animal is in motion, by the spread and fall of the quills. They have long, sturdy claws which aid them greatly in digging burrows and in finding food.

Widespread throughout the region, although their mainly nocturnal habits make them difficult to see. They can be encountered in a wide variety of habitats including forests, scrub and semi-desert regions, singly, in pairs or small groups. They spend the daylight hours sleeping in burrows, but on occasions may be seen sunbathing outside the burrow entrance. They do dig burrows for themselves but will also use holes excavated by Aardvarks as well as making good use of natural caves and crevices amongst piles of boulders. They have poor eyesight but well developed senses of hearing and smell. Their food consists mainly of vegetable matter including roots, tubers, barks and fruits. They will also gnaw bones, possibly as a source of calcium, but with the added benefit of sharpening their teeth. They will also occasionally take carrion. In some areas they are considered quite a pest, damaging and eating cultivated crops.

Striped Ground Squirrel
(Xerus erythropus)

Although larger than the Unstriped Ground Squirrel this species can at first glance look remarkably similar. The upper pelage colour varies from sandy to darkish brown, the bushy tail, which is almost as long as the body is grey/brown. The fur on the underside of the body is whitish grey. The main distinguishing feature, other than the size, is the presence of a white stripe which extends along the sides of the body from the rear of the forelimbs. The feet have long claws which aid the animal in digging.

Usually found in wetter habitats than those occupied by the Unstriped Ground Squirrel, in open woodlands and rocky areas. They often move quickly into areas of forest recently cleared for farming, thereby coming into conflict with farmers by eating cultivated crops. They usually excavate their own burrows but will modify termite mounds and live happily among holes and crevices on rocky hill sides.

Unstriped Ground Squirrel
(Xerus rutilus)

This species is a true ground squirrel, never climbing trees. They have a thick coat of coarse hair. The head is brown with the face and inner edges of the forelegs pale tawny. The upper back is grey/brown. The coarse hair on the underside of the body is pale grey, almost white. The bushy tail, which is almost as long as the body, is a mixture of grey and black. The ears are small and a ring of white fur surrounds the large dark eyes. The feet have very long claws which are used for digging.

A species of dry, semi-desert habitats throughout Kenya, Somalia and North-eastern Tanzania. They live in self-excavated burrows, which can take the form of a single straight tunnel, or develop into a labyrinth of tunnels, chambers and entrance holes. They can be seen throughout the day scurrying about for food, often stopping and standing erect on hind legs to check for danger.

African Hare
(Lepus capensis)

A common animal with a coat of grizzled brown fur. The legs are long and slender, the hind legs, being nearly twice the length of the forelegs, allowing the animal to run and jump at high speed. The legs are covered with pale rufous fur while the fur on the underside of the body is whitish/grey. The ears are very long, with dark edges and tipped with black. They have long white whiskers and large, prominent golden-brown eyes. The tail is short and fluffy, white below and black above.

Widely distributed in open, dry savannah habitats. They usually keep themselves well hidden amongst vegetation during the daytime, becoming more active in the late afternoon, the evening and throughout the night. They have good eyesight and the senses of hearing and smell are very well developed. They feed on a wide variety of vegetation including leaves, twigs, barks, berries, fruits, roots, tubers and grasses. They will often sit upright on their hind legs, particularly in long grass, on the lookout for danger.

Side Striped Jackal

(Canis adustus)

The least common of the three species of jackal to be found in East Africa. It bears the features typical of the family, sleek body, long legs and a bushy tail. The drab coat colour is a mixture of rufous, grey and black. The tail is blackish with a pronounced white tip, which is not present in the other two species, making it a useful field characteristic. The side stripes vary in prominence from animal to animal, but are usually clearly discernible as a whitish line edged with black extending from the shoulder, along the body towards the base of the tail. The muzzle is blunter than in other jackal species and the ears are smaller.

Found in a variety of habitats including woodland, bush, scrub and open grasslands. They have a varied diet which includes rodents, small birds and mammals, invertebrates ranging from large beetles and crickets to termites, as well as carrion and wild fruits. They can be seen during daylight hours but usually rest up in dense cover, becoming more active during the night and just prior to sunrise.

Black-Backed Jackal

(Canis mesomelas)

The commonest and most handsome of the three species of jackal found in East Africa. The body is slender, the legs are long and the head is fox-like with large pointed ears. The head, the lower portion of the body and the legs are pale rufous in colour. Along the hind neck and back runs a saddle of black fur, flecked with a variable amount of white. The tail is bushy, pale rufous and white edged and tipped with black. The underparts are whitish. Young animals are less well marked than adults, being for the most part grey/brown.

Found throughout the region in open savannah, light woodland and areas of scrub and bush. They are active during both the day and the night, but usually seek shade and seclusion during the heat of the day. Although they scavenge from kills made by the large carnivores their main source of food is derived from small birds and mammals, lizards and a variety of insects and fruits. They will also hunt small antelopes, often doing so in small packs.

Common Jackal

(Canis aureus)

The Common Jackal shares the same fox-like features as the Black-backed Jackal, but has a heavier coat which is subject to some variation in colour. Usually the upper side is uniform dull yellow/grey. The chest and underparts are whitish, with the legs and the backs of the ears showing some rufous/yellow. The bushy tail is yellow/grey tipped with black. Young animals appear grey/brown and rather drab. There have been sightings of animals with blackish coats.

Found in northern Tanzania, north and eastern Kenya and Somalia, favouring areas of open grassland, rocky hillsides and patches of bush and scrub. A species that can readily be seen during the day but is more active under cover of darkness. The senses of sight, hearing and smell are very well developed. Like other jackal species they feed on a wide variety of items including, small birds and mammals, particularly rodents, insects and some fruits as well as taking carrion.

Hunting Dog
(Lycaon pictus)

The coat pattern and coloration of hunting dogs shows great individual variation, but is usually that of dark brown/black with irregular blotches and patches of tan, cream and white. They have a long slender body, long legs, large, rounded ears and a bushy, white tipped tail. The head is rather short and broad, with powerful jaws. Young pups are blackish/brown with individual and irregular white patches, most prominent on the legs. The tail is tipped white.

Once common on the open grassland plains of East Africa, their distribution has been drastically reduced in recent years as a result of disease and persecution by man for stock stealing. Hunting as a pack they are extremely successful. They pursue their chosen victim relentlessly, until as a result of fatigue and by sheer weight of numbers they pull it to the ground. They feed mainly on antelope species but are capable of taking prey as large as zebra. They hunt mainly at dusk and dawn, resting up during the heat of the day. They are a nomadic species covering vast distances during their persistent wanderings over territories up to 2,000 sq. km in extent.

Bat-Eared Fox
(Otocyon megalotis)

This delightful little animal has a slightly shaggy uniform coat of greyish/yellow, paler on the flanks and underside. The lower portion of the legs, the tips of the enormous rounded ears, the nasal area of the muzzle and the tip of the large bushy tail are black. The eyes are set in patches of black fur which are joined across the bridge of the muzzle, giving the animal the appearance of wearing a 'highwayman's mask'. The body is rounded at the rear and higher in the hindquarters than at the shoulders.

An inhabitant of open savannahs, sandy areas and light woodlands. They often dig their own burrows, but will readily occupy tunnels and chambers vacated by other small, burrowing mammals. They are active mainly at dawn, dusk and throughout the night, but will often spend a considerable time lying around their den entrances during the hours of daylight. They feed mainly on small mammals, lizards, snakes and a multitude of insects including beetles, scorpions and termites. They mate for life and live in small family parties.

Honey Badger
(Mellivora capensis)

A robust, stocky animal with thick, loose skin, a long body and short, sturdy legs. The honey badger moves with a purposeful lumbering motion. The coat consists of short, coarse hair, the colour of which is evenly divided into two sections. The crown of the head and the upper portion of the body and tail are greyish/white, while the remaining areas are jet black. Young animals are brownish. The head is large with very powerful jaws and small ears. The front paws are equipped with large, robust claws.

Found throughout the region over a wide range of habitats from open grasslands to forests. They are mainly nocturnal but are sometimes encountered at dawn and dusk. They live in burrows which are easily excavated with the large front claws; they will also readily occupy holes originally dug by aardvarks. They feed on a wide variety of foods including small mammals, snakes, invertebrates, roots, tubers, various wild fruits and the pupae and honey of wild bees.

Large-spotted Genet

(Genetta tigrina)

A very lithe and beautiful small carnivore. The body is long and sleek, the legs are short and the paws have sharp, retractile claws. The short coat is greyish/yellow boldly marked with a black dorsal stripe, either side of which extend several rows of large black spots. These spots are occasionally edged with rufous. The short, pointed face has white patches on the upper cheeks and around the nasal area, large, honey-coloured eyes and pointed ears, the insides of which often show as naked pink flesh. The sides of the muzzle are black. The bushy tail is almost as long as the body and is ringed alternately with grey and black bands, terminating in a black tip. Young animals are generally greyer than adults with fainter markings.

Found throughout the region, favouring areas of woodlands, forests and thickets, usually in the vicinity of water. They often frequent safari lodges as well as other human settlements, on occasions causing considerable damage to poultry stocks. Their diet is extremely varied and includes rodents, lizards, snakes, frog, large insects such as grasshoppers and crickets, plus a variety of wild fruits. They are nocturnal creatures, spending the daylight hours in burrows or hollow trees. They are very agile and accomplished climbers, but are equally suited to life on the ground where they seek much of their prey. The senses of sight, smell and hearing are well developed. Litters of kittens usually number 2 or 3 and by 3 months they are hunting for themselves, by 6 months they are completely independent of their parents.

African Civet

(Civettictis civetta)

A short-legged animal of sturdy build with a long bushy tail, which is ringed with alternate bands of grey and black and has a black tip. The general coat colour is grizzled grey, marked with a varied selection of spots and stripes. In motion the head is carried low and the shoulders are lower than the hindquarters. The coat is shaggy and loose, with the semblance of a mane extending from the neck to the root of the tail. A black dorsal stripe extends from the crown of the head to the tail, the throat, chest and lower portion of the face and limbs are black. Two bands of black fur extend from the ears, down the sides of the neck, to the chest. The whole body is covered with a series of irregular black spots, the lower part of the hind limbs sometimes showing horizontal black stripes. Young animals are browner with only faint markings.

Found throughout much of the region over a variety of habitats including open savannahs, woodlands and forests, they avoid desert areas. A nocturnal animal spending the daylight hours sleeping in a burrow, in dense grasses and thickets or other suitable hiding places. Their food is varied and includes small to medium sized mammals, reptiles, amphibians, berries, fruits and carrion. On occasions they will inflict serious damage to poultry stocks and are often hunted and trapped by man as a result. Eyesight is relatively poor, whilst hearing is good and the sense of smell very acute. They scent mark their surroundings with musk secreted from a gland beneath the tail. For many centuries civets were kept in captivity and 'milked' of their musk, which was found to be an effective fixative in the production of flower based perfumes. In more recent years chemical substitutes have been found.

Slender Mongoose *(Herpestes sanguineus)*

An animal with a long, slender body, short legs, long pointed face and a black tipped tail almost as long as the body. The coat is formed of fine hair varying in colour from light grey to darkish brown, often paler on the underside. The coat colour would appear to vary as a result of the type of habitat occupied, being darker in forest and mountain areas and lighter in drier more open locations.

Widespread throughout the region in a variety of habitats including lightly wooded savannah, woodland, dense mountain forests, to an altitude of 2,500-3,000m, rocky hill sides and cultivated farmland and settlements. They can be seen throughout the day. They feed on small birds and mammals, lizards, snakes, invertebrates and occasionally wild fruits. Although they are able to climb trees quite well, they spend the vast majority of their time foraging on the ground.

Banded Mongoose *(Mungos mungo)*

A well built, sturdy mongoose with a broad head and pointed face typical of the family. The hindquarters are rounded and higher than the forequarters. The tail is quite long, about half the length of the body, and tapers to a pointed tip. The coarse coat is grey/brown with a series of dark brown, almost black vertical stripes on the back and hindquarters. The lower portion of the legs and the tip of the tail are black. The ears are small. The feet are equipped with long claws which aid the animal greatly in searching out subterranean food items.

A highly social animal, found throughout the range in areas of open savannah, often in the vicinity of water. They are active throughout the day, usually foraging in large family parties across the plains, in search of food, which consists of a wide variety of invertebrates, lizards, snakes, small rodents and amphibians, as well as occasional roots and fruits. Whilst foraging they are constantly on the look out for danger often raising themselves into an upright position on their hind legs to gain a better view.

Dwarf Mongoose *(Helogale undulata)*

As its name implies, this is the smallest mongoose species found in East Africa. It retains all the main features typical of the group, a broad head and pointed face, small ears, short legs and long claws. The tail is about half the length of the body and tapers to a point. The fine coat can be variable in colour, from reddish brown to grizzled grey, often lighter below and with darker legs and feet. They utter a wide range of whistles, squeaks and other noises which keep the pack in contact at all times.

Found over much of the region, favouring dry grasslands, woodlands and areas of scrub and bush. They are often common around safari lodges and dwellings, where they become quite tame. They live together in family parties usually numbering between 6-15 individuals, occupying termite mounds, natural crevices between boulders, hollow trees and other suitable safe denning locations. They are active throughout the day, foraging as a group but fanning out and feeding individually. They are continually on the look out for danger, an alarm call from any individual instantly alerting the whole pack. They feed mainly on insects, lizards, small birds and mammals and wild fruits.

Aardwolf

(Proteles cristatus)

The Aardwolf has the appearance of a small Hyaena. The most prominent identification feature is the long, thick mane of hair, which extends along the entire length of the back, from the rear of the ears to the tail. The head has a long muzzle and large pointed ears. The legs are long and slender. The tail is long and bushy. The colour of the coat is yellowish brown with yellow/white throat, cheeks and underparts. The body has an irregular pattern of broken vertical black stripes; the stripes on the forelimbs are horizontal. Like the Hyaenas, the Aardwolf has a sloping back, being higher at the shoulders than at the hindquarters.

Found throughout much of Kenya, Tanzania and northern Uganda, favouring areas of open dry plains and bush. They avoid mountainous areas. Their main distribution is, to a great extent, linked to that of Harvester Termites. These termites prosper in areas that are heavily grazed by plains game animals and domestic stock, as a result the increase in human population and consequently that of domestic animals may well benefit the Aardwolf. They are extremely secretive animals, foraging at dusk and throughout the night, during the daytime they usually remain hidden in underground burrows.

Striped Hyaena

(Hyaena hyaena)

Smaller and less powerful than the Spotted Hyaena, the Striped Hyaena has many similar features, a large broad head, long legs, a sloping body from high shoulders to lower hindquarters and the familiar gait. The coat has a shaggy appearance with a long, buff/grey dorsal mane extending from the nape to the tail. The overall body colour is yellowish-grey, with vertical black stripes on the body, horizontal black stripes on the legs and a black throat and muzzle. The tail is long and bushy, appearing as a continuation of the dorsal mane, with a black tip. The ears are large and pointed and juvenile animals lack the shaggy mane but have a black dorsal stripe.

Found in woodland, dry savannah and semi-desert areas from northern Tanzania to the north African coast. They are almost entirely nocturnal, remaining hidden during daylight hours in dense vegetation, in caves and rock crevices, or in subterranean burrows. They can walk considerable distances during a nights foraging, (average 20km), taking carrion, small mammals, invertebrates, lizards and wild fruits. They will also occasionally plunder cultivated crops.

Spotted Hyaena

(Crocuta crocuta)

The commonest large predator in East Africa. A very substantial animal, with well-developed forequarters, a large broad head with rounded ears and extremely powerful jaws. The hindquarters are substantially lower than the forequarters resulting in a rather ungainly gait. The coat is short, with the semblance of a mane covering the lower neck and shoulders, grey/yellow in colour heavily marked with irregular black spots. The underside and chest are lighter and the lower portion of the legs is black. The tail usually has an unkempt appearance. The tail is of medium length with a black tip. The muzzle is dark brown/black.

Common throughout the region in a variety of habitats, with the densest populations occurring on open savannahs where they live in large communities, some 'clans' numbering up to 80 individuals. Females are larger than males and dominate within the clans. They are extremely successful predators and, hunting as a pack, are capable of bringing down large herbivores. They will also regularly scavenge from the kills of lions and other cats. They are active mainly at night, when their eerie, wailing calls can be heard.

Lion

(Panthera leo)

The largest and most powerful of East Africa's cats. The head is very broad with a short muzzle and small, rounded ears, the backs of which are black. The coat, with the exception of the mane, is very short, the ground colour being a sandy yellow often with faint spots, which are particularly noticeable in younger animals. The mane, which is only present on the males, is variable in colour from pale buff to black and covers the neck and shoulders. A full mane may take up to 6 years to develop.

An animal of open savannahs, grassy plains and lightly wooded areas. They are unusual among cats in being very social, living in prides of 30 or more individuals. Lions are inactive for much of the day, often resting for up to 20 hours in the shade of trees and bushes. Their sight and smell are good and their hearing is exceptionally keen. Lions will hunt singly, in pairs or in large prides and, as a rule, the more lions taking part the larger the prey species. Primarily the lionesses who secure around 80 per cent of the prides food requirement undertake the hunting. Lions will also scavenge whenever the opportunity arises. Although capable of running at speeds of up to 60km/h lions have little stamina and give up most chases if they are not successful within 200m. On the plains of the Serengeti in Tanzania, many of the prides seem less territorial than in other areas, often following herds of plains animals on their annual migrations.

Leopard

(Panthera pardus)

A muscular, thickset cat with short, powerful limbs. The head is broad with a muzzle of medium length, strong jaws and long, white whiskers. The ears are small and round, the backs of which are black with a prominent white marking in the centre. The coat is yellowish/tan and covered with black/brown spots, grouped in rosettes on the body but generally solid black on the head and lower legs. In some individuals the close grouping of the spots and rosettes gives an impression of a much darker pelage. The chin, throat and underside are off-white. There can be a great deal of regional variation in coat colour, length and density, in response to differing altitude and climatic conditions. The tail is long, spotted from the root to the centre but terminating with a series of black rings. The female is smaller and lighter than the male.

Although not common the leopard is found over much of East Africa. Being mainly nocturnal they are seldom seen by day, but can be found wherever there is cover and sufficient food, preferring wooded savannahs and rocky outcrops. They are most likely to be encountered during the day resting in deep vegetation or, on occasions, in a tree. Hunting is mainly undertaken at dusk or during the night. They have remarkable vision, exceptional hearing and a good sense of smell. They prey on many mammal species particularly antelopes; they also have a particular liking for baboons. They have tremendous strength and having made a kill, will often carry it high into a tree to evade the attention of other predators. Adult leopards lead a solitary existence, only coming together during periods of mating. Females will give birth to as many as six cubs, which she keeps well hidden for the first six weeks. They will become independent at about 2 years old.

Caracal

(Felis caracal)

A tall, slender cat with a broad, flat head, large eyes and pointed, triangular ears with long tufts of black fur flowing from the tips. The backs of the ears are black; the insides are white edged with black. The coat colour is usually tawny/red, but on occasions dark almost black individuals occur. The chest, underside and insides of the legs are white, with some faint spotting usually discernible on the lower portion of the legs. The tail is relatively short. Males are usually larger than females. They are extremely fast and agile with powerful, well-developed hindquarters, which slope down to the shoulders.

A shy rather retiring animal, rarely seen during the daytime, being almost entirely nocturnal. They inhabit areas of savannah, usually with kopjes or other natural features offering cover in which to establish dens. They will occupy old Aardvark burrows, caves and hollow trees. They are known to feed on a variety of mammals including small antelope, hares, rats and Rock Hyrax as well as birds, which they often take during the night as the birds sleep, or in flight when flushed from ground cover. They can cause considerable damage to goat, sheep and poultry stocks often coming into conflict with local farmers as a result. Their senses of sight and hearing are very keen, while their sense of smell would appear to be only moderate. They lead a solitary existence, holding territories covering several square kilometres.

Cheetah

(Acinonyx jubatus)

The world's fastest land mammal, built for sheer speed. The body is sleek and flexible, with a powerful chest and very long legs. The coat is yellow/buff, randomly marked with small black spots; the chest and underside are almost white. The small, rounded head has small ears, large, deep orange eyes, black spotting on the forehead and cheeks and prominent black stripes extending from the inner corners of the eyes to the mouth. The tail is long, yellow/buff spotted with black for much of its length, but terminating with a series of black rings and a white tip. Each individual animal has a pattern of tail rings as unique as human fingerprints. A mane of coarse fur is often discernible on the lower neck and shoulders, particularly in young animals.

Found on dry, open savannahs and in areas of bush and scrub, where they hunt by sight throughout the day. They will often seek an elevated position, on a fallen tree, termite mound or rocky outcrop, when looking for prey. They will stalk as close as possible before attacking with a final burst of speed of up to 100km/h. This burst of speed can only be maintained for about 500m. Whilst running at full speed the Cheetah will trip its prey and seize it quickly by the throat in a suffocating grip. Having secured a kill they will attempt to drag the carcass into cover to avoid the attention of scavenging hyaenas and Lions. They prey mainly on small to medium sized antelope, particularly Thomson's Gazelles, but will readily take hares and savannah birds. Cheetahs can live a solitary existence as well as in pairs or small family parties.

Serval
(Felis serval)

One of East Africa's most beautiful cats, with very long legs, small head and very large, rounded ears. The coat colour is yellow/buff boldly and irregularly marked with black spots and bars. The chest and underparts are off-white. The tail is short and has alternate black and yellow/buff rings. The backs of the ears are black with a pronounced white spot towards the centre. In some regions servals with completely black coats are quite common, particularly in the Aberdares of central Kenya and the highlands of Ethiopia.

Found throughout much of the region on savannahs and open grasslands as well as in light woodlands, around marshes and along forest edges. They hunt rodents, lizards, snakes and birds in areas of long grass, pin-pointing the whereabouts of prey by sound onto which they pounce with a final leap. Birds flushed from the grass are often caught in mid-flight with lightening reflexes and a leap into the air. They will also occasionally raid poultry stocks in and around human settlements. They are active in the early morning, late afternoon, evening and throughout the night. They live a solitary existence, maintaining territories up to 5 square kilometres in extent and, when not hunting, will rest up in subterranean burrows, natural crevices between boulders and in dense patches of vegetation. The senses of hearing and sight are very acute, while the sense of smell is less well developed.

African Wild Cat
(Felis lybica)

Widely distributed over much of the region, the African Wild Cat is the distant ancestor of the present day domestic cat. The coat is buff-grey with warmer shades on the face, behind the ears and on the belly. There are marked variations to coat colour in differing parts of the range, with coats being generally darker in humid forest habitats and lighter in more dry, open areas. The legs, tail and, to a lesser extent the body, are blotched, barred and striped with black. The relatively long tail has several black rings towards the terminal black tip. Generally African Wild Cats lead a solitary existence except when mating or when females are tending litters. Litter sizes average three kittens, which are born blind and totally helpless. They become mobile after about a month and will stay together as a family for about six months, before the unit breaks up.

African Wild Cats live in almost all habitats that offer some cover, preferring scrub, bush and lush grasslands that hold good densities of prey species, particularly rats and mice, which form the bulk of their diet. They are mainly nocturnal in habits, remaining hidden in thick cover during the day, but they can sometimes be encountered in daylight hours, particularly during overcast weather conditions.

Greater Galago

(Galago crassicaudatus)

Also known as the Greater Bushbaby, this nocturnal primate has a rounded head, large ears, stout limbs and huge forward facing eyes. The coat is thick and fluffy and shows a wide variation in colour from overall grey with a white tip to the tail, to dark brown with a blackish tail tip. The darker animals tend to be found at higher altitudes and in damper habitats, lighter animals usually being found in drier, lower lying regions. The underparts are off-white and the short, pointed face has dark patches along the sides of the muzzle and around the eyes. The thick tail is longer than the combined length of the head and body, and is very bushy. They are expert climbers and have well adapted digits for this purpose.

Found throughout Tanzania, southern Kenya and coastal regions of Somalia, in a variety of habitats including wooded savannahs, bush and scrub and mountain forests to an altitude of 3,500m. They spend the daytime sleeping in hollow trees or dense foliage, becoming active at dusk and throughout the night. They feed on fruits, berries, seeds, insects, tree sap and small birds. Females build nests in hollow trees or dense vegetation in which to give birth. The young remain in the nest for the first 2 weeks of life, after which the females will carry them during their nightly foraging, provided the young have acquired the necessary growth and strength to hang on. They usually ride 'jockey style' on the mothers back. The senses of sight, hearing and smell are extremely good. Small family groups will maintain a territory several hectares in extent, making their presence known by depositing scent from a breast gland and by urinating on branches and tree trunks.

Lesser Galago

(Galago senegalensis)

Also known as the Lesser Bushbaby, this charming little primate is about half the size of the Greater Galago. They have a rounded head, short muzzle, large eyes and substantial pointed ears. The coat is soft and fluffy, grey over much of the body and tail, with a wash of yellow on the flanks and limbs. The underparts are whitish. They have dark eye patches and the insides of the ears are pink. They have a conspicuous light stripe extending from the forehead to the nose. The tail is longer than the combined length of the head and body and is bushy towards the tip.

Distributed over much of the region in dry woodlands, bush and scrub, wooded savannahs and mountain forests to an altitude of 2,000m. They are active throughout the night, spending the daylight hours sleeping in hollow trees, in forked branches or in self-built nest of leaves and twigs. Family parties will often sleep together in a single shelter. They feed on a wide variety of invertebrates, lizards, young birds and eggs as well as fruits, seeds and tree sap. The senses of sight, hearing and smell are very acute. Family territories are maintained by an old dominant male and, to a lesser extent by females, marking branches and trunks by the use of a scent gland on the breast and by the depositing of urine. The young remain in and around the birth nest for the first 10 days of life, often venturing short distances by riding on their mothers back. They grow quickly and attain full adult size by 4 months old.

Olive Baboon
(Papio anubis)

The commonest of East Africa's primates. A heavily built and powerful animal. The head is large with small, close-set, brown eyes beneath a protruding eyebrow ridge. The coat colour is a mixture of olive grey and black, becoming darker on the lower legs and feet. The underparts are off-white/grey. The long, pointed muzzle is black and devoid of fur. The ears are rounded and sometimes hardly discernible among the long fur of the head, particularly in the males, who develop a mane around the head and shoulders. The tail is of medium length, extending upwards for a few centimetres, before curving downwards at a sharp angle, giving a 'broken' appearance. They have extremely formidable canine teeth.

They are distributed throughout northern Tanzania, central and western Kenya and Uganda in a variety of habitats, including woodlands, savannahs and rocky areas. They live together in 'troops' varying in number from just a handful to 150 individuals, although around 35 would appear to be the average troop size. A distinct hierarchy exists among both males and females within each troop, maintained by alliances between members, often reaffirmed by mutual grooming. Females outnumber males within a troop by as much as 3 to 1. They feed throughout the day both on the ground and in trees, taking fruits, leaves, buds, grasses, insects, lizards and occasionally new born antelopes. Baboons can do untold damage to cultivated crops and, in some regions, are considered to be vermin. At night they roost together in trees or on rock ledges to avoid predation by Leopards and, to a lesser extent, other predators. A female will carry a new born beneath her during daily foraging, but as the youngster grows it soon adopts a jockey style position on its mothers back.

Yellow Baboon
(Papio cynocephalus)

Differs from the Olive Baboon in having a slender build and thin legs. The coat is short, yellowish/grey above with white/cream underparts. The long, pointed muzzle and the hands and feet are greyish. The head is round and the ears are small. They lack the mane around the head and shoulders which is such a distinctive feature of the Olive Baboon. The small, amber coloured eyes are close-set. The eyelids are white/pink and play an important role in communication, particularly in displaying aggression. The tail is long and thin, extending upward for a short distance before 'breaking' downwards at a sharp angle.

An animal of savannahs and woodlands in Tanzania and eastern and northern Kenya, where they forage both on the ground and in the trees. They feed on a wide variety of foods including, roots, tubers, seeds, leaves, grasses, fruits and many species of invertebrate. They live in large groups ('troops') each averaging around 30 individuals, dominated by a large male. Relationships are cultivated within the troop by all members, resulting in a well-defined hierarchy. The baboons will often engage in lengthy bouts of mutual grooming which helps to cement these relationships. They are territorial animals with each troop collectively maintaining a range of up to 30 square kilometres, which they defend forcefully against neighbouring troops. Only the highest ranking males will mate with a female during the peak of her cycle, other high ranking males may mate with females at other times.

Patas Monkey
(Erythrocebus patas)

A long-limbed, agile primate, spending the vast majority of the daytime foraging on the ground in open areas. The coat is shaggy, the back and crown are rufous red whilst the underparts and limbs are white, often with a flush of yellow. The facial colour varies from grey/pink to black, with a distinctive black band extending along the line of the eyebrows. The males have brighter, more pronounced markings than the females or young and, in addition, often have a trace of grey on the shoulders. The long, thin tail is about the same length as the head and body, being rufous in colour and is carried high above the back when the animal is on the move.

Found in northern Uganda, west and central Kenya and in isolated pockets of northern Tanzania. They inhabit dry, semi-desert regions, open savannahs, scrub and woodlands. They usually live in troops, often with a single dominant male and a number of females and dependant young, numbering around 25 individuals. Small bachelor groups may also be encountered. They forage and feed in a loose group on seeds, pods, leaves, grasses, fruits, berries and occasionally invertebrates. They can cause considerable damage to cultivated crops, being partial to maize, millet, bananas etc. as a result they are often severely persecuted by farming communities. During the night they sleep singly or in pairs high in the treetops. They have very acute sight and hearing and are constantly on the alert for possible attack by lions or leopards. They will defend their territory against neighbouring troops of Patas, but will tolerate the presence of baboons and vervet monkeys within their territory.

Sykes/Blue Monkey
(Cercopithecus mitis)

A large, robust monkey with a thick coat of blue/black fur. The back, face and hind legs are flecked with silver/grey hairs and occasionally washed with olive, whilst the crown and forelimbs are black. A band of stiff grey hair extends across the line of the eyebrows. The chest and underparts vary from greyish to black. The small ears are black edged with grey. The close-set eyes are amber. The tail is longer than the combined length of the head and body, thickening towards the black tip. There is considerable regional variation in coat and facial coloration. The Blue Monkeys found in the forests of Mount Kenya having a collar of white fur and a dark reddish back.

A monkey of dense, moist forests of coastal and mountain regions, often to an altitude of 3,500m. They are usually encountered in troops of around 10 individuals, feeding among the trees and occasionally on the forest floor. Their main food intake consists of leaves, flowers, berries, fruits, some insects and birds eggs and young. The troops usually consist of several related females and dependant young, with a dominant male. Female offspring will usually remain within the troop on reaching maturity, males, however, are forced to leave and join other troops or establish their own harem. They are active throughout the day, remaining in the shade provided by foliage, and will avoid direct sunlight whenever possible.

Black-Faced Vervet Monkey

(Cercopithecus aethiops)

One of the commonest of East Africa's monkeys. A very agile and slender primate with long limbs. The coat colour is subject to some regional variation, but is usually grey/brown with a wash of olive on the back, a naked jet-black face surrounded by white hair on the cheeks and across the eyebrow line. The chest and underparts are whitish, the lower part of the limbs are greyish with black feet. The eyes are deep, rich brown, the tail, which is about the same length as the head and body, is greyish with a black tip. The small ears are black. Both sexes have brightly coloured genitalia, the male having a powder blue scrotum and a bright red penis. The males are about 20 per cent larger than the females.

A widespread species found in woodlands, forests, savannahs and areas of bush and scrub. They are active throughout the day and are usually encountered in troops varying in number from 6-50+, foraging in the trees and on the ground. The composition of the troops usually shows an even number of males and females, with up to 50 per cent being juveniles. The size of territory maintained by each troop varies greatly, as a consequence of food availability. Their main food intake consists of fruits, berries, seedpods, small invertebrates, lizards and birds' eggs and chicks. They will readily eat cultivated crops and in areas of intense farming have been almost exterminated by the farming community as a result. Vervet monkeys have a well-developed system of both visual and vocal communication.

Black & White Colobus

(Colobus guereza)(Eastern) - (Colobus angolensis) (Western)

This large black and white monkey is represented in East Africa by two distinct species, the Eastern and the Western. In both species the overall body colour is black, the differences between the two shows in their distribution and in the extent of white body fur. The Eastern Colobus has a black face surrounded by short white fur, has long, flowing white fur extending from the shoulders along the length of the body to the rump and a long black tail with a bushy white tip. The Western Colobus has a black face surrounded by long white fur with flowing white fur on the shoulders only and a long thin all white tail. It is worth noting that the extent of white fur on the body in both species is subject to considerable regional variation. Newborn animals are all white with pink faces.

The Eastern Colobus is found in northern Tanzania, central and western Kenya and Uganda. The Western Colobus is found mainly in coastal regions of Kenya and Tanzania and in south-western Uganda. They inhabit dense mountain and coastal forests, acacia woodlands and wooded savannahs. They feed mainly on fresh leaves, fruits, bark, seedpods and some insects. They are active throughout the day but will usually rest up during the hottest, midday period. They spend very little time on the ground, usually making their way through the forests by leaping from tree to tree. They live in troops of 3-12 consisting of a dominant male with several females and offspring.

Lowland Gorilla

(Gorilla gorilla graueri)

A large animal with immense strength. The head is large and the body broad, the arms are considerably longer than the legs. The face is flat with deep-set eyes and large nostrils. All areas of naked skin on the face, hands, feet and upper chest are black. The mainly black coat is short and dense, compared with the longer, shaggy coat of the Mountain Gorilla. The males acquire a 'saddle' of silver hair across the lower portion of the back on reaching maturity, hence the name 'silverback' used when referring to dominant males. The males generally become greyer with age. On average females are only half the size of the males.

An inhabitant of the lowland tropical rain forests of eastern Congo. Although they will climb trees the vast majority of their time is spent on the ground, feeding on a wide variety of vegetation including leaves, fruits, ferns and tubers. They live in small family groups, usually consisting of a dominant male and occasionally subordinate males with several females and their offspring. Groups generally keep well clear of each other, but when they do meet the dominant males will display by calling and chest beating.

Mountain Gorilla

(Gorilla gorilla beringei)

An animal of powerful build and immense strength. The head is large, the body is broad and the arms are considerably longer than the legs. The face is flat, the forehead low, the eyes close together and deep set and the nose flat with large nostrils. The naked areas of skin on the face, hands, feet and upper chest are black. The black coat is longer and thicker than that of the Lowland Gorilla. The males acquire a 'saddle' of silver hair across the lower portion of the back on reaching full maturity, hence the name 'silverback' used when referring to dominant males. Males generally become greyer with age. Male are around twice the size of females.

Found in the high mountainous terrain of south western Uganda and in neighbouring Congo and Rwanda. They live in relatively stable family groups, each group being led by a dominant adult male. Each group usually consists of the lead male with several females and their offspring. Any other adult males within a group will be subordinate and most probably be sons of the dominant silverback. They are active throughout the day and at night each animal will construct a sleeping nest on the ground or in a tree. A fresh nest is constructed each night.

Chimpanzee

(Pan troglodytes)

A robust and powerful primate, the chimpanzee is our closest living relative. Individuals vary greatly in size and colour but are generally 1-1.7m in height, weigh between 40 and 50 kilos and have a shaggy black coat. They have a sturdy body with well-developed shoulders and arms, the legs are rather short. The face is flat with small deep-set eyes, a small nose, a broad, deep upper jaw and a wide, narrow-lipped mouth. The ears are rounded and prominent. The facial coloration varies from pink in juveniles to black in full adults, with only a sparse covering of hair on the cheeks and forehead. They walk on the hind legs and the knuckles of the forelimbs.

Restricted in distribution to the rain forests and woodlands of western Tanzania and Uganda. They generally live in small, loosely knit groups of 2-50 individuals. They are equally at home in the trees or on the ground, where they forage throughout the daytime, feeding on leaves, fruits, nuts, ants, termites and, on occasions, young monkeys, antelopes and birds. They often fashion crude tools from twigs in order to extract larvae and other food items from holes and crevices. During the night they sleep in nests built in the trees from branches and leaves.

REPTILES

African Rock Python *(Python sebae)*

This is the largest of East Africa's snakes, with many records of individuals measuring in excess of 7m. At birth they only measure 60–70cm, reaching sexual maturity at between 2 and 4 years of age. A non-venomous species that kills by constriction, they are usually found in the vicinity of water. They spend most of the daylight hours hidden in dens or lairs. Occasionally they will take prey items as large as a gazelle, but normally smaller animals are preferred. All prey is swallowed whole. In captivity they have been known to live for up to 25 years. They are often killed by local people fearing such a large creature, as well as being taken for meat and for their skin.

Brown House Snake *(Lamprophis fuliginosus)*

A common snake over much of the region, found in grassland areas, scrub and thickets and on areas of rocky ground as well as in the vicinity of human settlements where they benefit the inhabitants by reducing rodent populations. They are usually reddish brown in colour but darker individuals do occur. They have a faint pale stripe extending above and below the eye which is a good identification guide. Measuring up to a metre in length they are mainly nocturnal, hunting small mammals.

Black Mamba *(Dendroaspis polylepis)*

One of the most feared of East Africa's snakes, its venom is one of the most virulent nerve poisons known to exist. Human victims have been known to die within 15 minutes of being bitten. An extremely agile snake, capable of moving at almost 20km/h. They often move with the head and neck held high above the ground. Surprisingly Black Mambas are not black in colour, but range from pale gunmetal grey to brown and olive green. They can grow up to 3.5m in length and usually reside in termite mounds, abandoned porcupine holes and cavities in hollow trees and among rocks. Mainly diurnal in habits they are equally at home on the ground or in trees where they prey on mammals and birds.

Eastern Green Mamba *(Dendroaspis angusticeps)*

Like its close relative the Black Mamba this species is extremely venomous. A snake of forests and thickets where their bright green body colouration provides excellent camouflage. Smaller than the Black Mamba this species rarely attains 2.5m in length. Mainly arboreal in habits the Green Mamba feeds on birds, their nestlings and small mammals including bats. Green Mambas have been found in large concentrations in some areas, up to five being noted in a single tree.

Boomslang

(Dispholidus typus)

One of the most widespread of Africa's tree snakes, being found in most types of wooded habitats. The Boomslang has the largest eyes, in relation to head size, of any snake species. Adults can measure up to 2m in length. Colouration is very variable, both between the sexes and from region to region. Adult females are generally olive or brown, while adult males may range from brown, black, bright green and red to pale blue. Active throughout much of the day this arboreal species drifts slowly through bushes and trees in search of prey such as chameleons, birds, small mammals and frogs. Having initially gripped its prey the Boomslang adopts a chewing motion to work venom into the victim via large rear fangs. Bites to humans are rare but can prove fatal.

Forest Cobra

(Naja melanolenca)

A venomous species associated with forests and woodlands usually close to water. They are very much at home in water being expert swimmers; they will occasionally catch fish as well as reptiles and amphibians. They will also prey on small birds and mammals. There are two colour phases, one has the upper parts dark brown and is usually found in coastal regions and the other phase is black. Both have the underside pale yellow which, in most instances, spreads on to the lower portion of the dark head forming a series of light and dark stripes. This species is not normally aggressive unless persistently interfered with.

Puff Adder

(Bitis arietans)

The Puff Adder is the most widely distributed of East Africa's vipers, being found in savanna and woodland habitats below 3,500m. They can measure up to 2m in length, but it is the girth of up to 30cm of this and other vipers, that makes for easy identification. They have an angular head shape and a heavy broad body the colour of which is a mosaic of buffs, browns, and blacks that affords tremendous camouflage when they are at rest in leaf litter. A very venomous species that feeds on small mammals, birds, amphibians, lizards and other snake species.

Gaboon Viper

(Bitis gabonica)

The largest of Africa's vipers, some individuals growing in excess of 2m and weighing in the region of 8.5kg. An inhabitant of tropical forests the body colouration takes the form of a geometric pattern of browns, buffs and purples and, like other vipers, this pattern results in wonderful camouflage when set against the leaf litter of the forest floor. The large, wide, triangular head is light in colour with a dark line running down the centre. A small pair of horns are visible on the tip of the snout. They feed mainly by ambush, taking mostly small rodents, birds and amphibians.

Rhinoceros Viper

(Bitis nasicornis)

A species found mainly in wet forest habitats and, like the Puff Adder, is a very broad bodied species. As its name implies this species is distinguished by having horns above each nostril. The body colouration is a random pattern of buffs, browns, greens, yellows and blacks that provide excellent camouflage, as they lie motionless by the sides of paths and trails from where they ambush unsuspecting prey species. This mode of hunting makes big vipers quite dangerous to humans, unlike most snakes these species will not move away at your approach. A last second hiss is often all you get by way of warning before you tread on one. Being extremely venomous this is best avoided.

Agama Lizard
(Agama agama)

A dominant male Agama Lizard is one of the most colourful common reptiles in East Africa. The head is bright orange-red and the body colour is vivid blue. Males are very territorial and can usually be found on a prominent rock or tree from where they will engage in bobbing displays to rival males. By contrast to males, females are rather drab, being brownish grey with a variable amount of brighter spots. Agamas are very common over much of East Africa, particularly in rocky areas. They can often be seen scurrying up and down the sheerest rock faces hunting insect prey, which forms the bulk of their diet. They do, however, on occasions take larger prey, including small lizards and small toads.

Striped Skink
(Mabuya striata)

A very common inhabitant of garden rockeries and open areas over much of the region, where they are often to be seen lying flat on a stone absorbing heat through the belly. Unlike mammals that can generate their own body heat, reptiles are dependant on external heat sources, hence their preoccupation with 'sunbathing'. Adult Striped Skinks measure around 20cm in length and are dark brown in colour with a pale buff stripe extending along the upper sides of the body from the rear of the eyes at the base of the tail. The underparts are whitish.

Common House Gecko
(Hemidactylus mabouia)

A very common species that inhabits houses and settlement buildings below 2,000m, hiding for much of the day behind items of furniture and room decorations and under tile and thatch roofs. They emerge at night to catch insects, mainly moths and small flies, attracted to the house lights and present no harm to humans at all, in fact by reducing the number of biting insects they should be considered as welcome guests in any abode. They grow to around 15cm in length and are found throughout tropical and sub-tropical Africa.

Savannah Monitor
(Varanus exanthematicus)

This species can be found in dry semi desert habitats and grassland areas. They have a uniform body colouration of sandy browns overlaid with olive and lack the yellow speckling which is so distinctive on the Nile Monitor. They will feed, for the most part, on a wide variety of insects.

Nile Monitor
(Varanus niloticus)

A large lizard measuring up to 2m in length and found throughout sub Saharan Africa along riverbanks, in marshes, or in other wet habitats. They are olive green in colour speckled with small spots of yellow. They are extremely good climbers and swimmers and will prey on a wide variety of small creatures, including fish, small birds and mammals as well as other reptiles and amphibians. They are very partial to crocodile eggs and will regularly take carrion.

Flap Necked Chameleon *(Chamaeleo delepis)*

Like many chameleons the Flap Necked Chameleon is famous for its ability to change colour in response to environmental factors such as light and climate as well as emotions such as fear and aggression. The mechanism involved in colour change relates to pigment granules that are activated by the chameleon's nervous system. Colouration changes are generally more varied and brighter in males than in females. Like most chameleons the Flap Necked is relatively slow moving, spending most of their time in trees and bushes where they lay in ambush for insects which are grabbed using the long tongue, the tip of which is coated with a viscous secretion. The tongue is as long as the body and when not in use is neatly stored in the floor of the large mouth. Chameleons also have the ability to move their eyes independently of each other, thereby giving all round vision at all times both in search of food and to spot approaching danger. The ability to swivel both eyes forward when hunting also ensures pinpoint accuracy.

Jackson's Chameleon *(Chamaeleo jacksonii)*

Unmistakable among chameleons of the region, having an ornamental armoured head with a forward facing central horn emanating from the nasal area and two further horns growing from the outer forehead. These horns are used by the males in territorial disputes and during the breeding season. The horns are less well developed or even absent in females. As with all chameleons the tail is prehensile and can be coiled around branches and used as an extra limb and they have zygodactylous toes, a special adaptation for an arboreal existence, that grip branches and twigs with a claw action for extra stability. They are generally solitary in habits with each male maintaining a territory. Unlike many chameleons which lay eggs, the Jackson's Chameleon gives birth to live young after a gestation period of between 6 and 9 months. At birth the young are light brown in colour, changing to the more usual adult green at about 4 months old. Adults grow to around 30cm in length and in spite of their rather fearsome looks they are perfectly harmless, although they may bite if molested.

Nile Crocodile

(Crocodilus niloticus)

A species that hardly requires a detailed description, being found in rivers and lakes over much of the region. They can grow to over 6m in length. The Nile Crocodile, being mainly nocturnal, spends much of the day submerged in water between bouts of basking on sand bars and riverbanks. They are highly adapted predators feeding on water dwelling creatures as well as land based mammals which they capture by lying motionless at the edge of water holes, or by floating like a drifting log until they are within striking distance. Females lay hard-shelled eggs in a bank side nest which they guard jealously to protect the eggs from predators. When the young are ready to emerge they utter squeaking noises which stimulates the female to open up the nest and help the young into the water, often by carrying them in her mouth. The young at this stage are about 30cm in length and are able to fend for themselves immediately, feeding in the shallows on insects, tadpoles, frogs and fish, but at all times keeping themselves hidden from possible predators. They grow at a rate of about 30cm a year during the first few years of life, the rate of growth decreases in later years to a matter of a centimetre of two. Not a great deal is known about the longevity of Nile Crocodile in the wild, but it has been suggested that full grown specimens of 6m or so are probably in the region of a hundred years old. Males do not become sexually active until they have grown to around 3m in length.

Leopard Tortoise

(Testudo pardalis)

The Leopard Tortoise, the largest tortoise in Africa, derives its name from the black and yellow carapace, which resembles the pattern of a leopard's coat. They are widely distributed over much of the region south of the Sahara, being encountered mainly in grassland areas. They can grow to weights in excess of 28kg. They are long lived, fifty years having been recorded in captivity, and lay eggs in an excavated hole about 25cm in depth. Having covered the eggs with soil the female then abandons the site, the eggs hatching 12–14 months later, the young being totally independent. They feed on a wide variety of vegetation and will often travel great distances in search of food. They are active throughout the day but generally avoid the hot midday period and during the hot summer months they may even enter a state of dormancy.

AMPHIBIANS

African Bull Frog
(Pyxicephalus adspersus)

The largest of Africa's frogs, with adult males reaching 20cm in length and weighing in the region of 2kg. They can be found in a variety of open habitats in both wet and dry regions. They have a stout, broad body with a large heavy head and a wide gape. Males have green body colour with a deep yellow throat, while females are dull brown with a cream throat. The females are generally about half the size of males. They are extremely well adapted for burrowing and spend up to 10 months of the year buried underground awaiting the arrival of the heavy rains. In dry areas they may remain buried for several years until wet conditions occur. At the onset of the rains an explosion of breeding activity commences with males congregating at suitable sites and constantly attacking each other to secure females. They have two tooth-like projections set into the lower jaw with which they can inflict severe wounds to each other or intruders. Should humans attempt to handle these males they can expect to receive a fearsome bite. Following mating, males often remain in bodies of water containing tadpoles and even construct escape channels from isolated puddles to main bodies of water to aid the survival of the young. They have voracious appetites and will feed avidly on large insects, other frogs, reptiles and small mammals. When threatened they often inflate themselves like balloons in an attempt to intimidate the aggressor.

Sharp Nosed Grass Frog
(Ptychadena oxyrhynchus)

A frog of open savannah and grassland areas as well as being found around human settlements. The body shape is streamlined with a pointed snout and very powerful hind legs, which places this species amongst the most accomplished leapers of all frogs. The sleek body shape facilitates efficient movement through water and through dense vegetation when on land. They feed on a variety of grassland insects. The body colour is olive with irregular dark blotches on the back and flanks. The top of the snout is unmarked, taking the form of a pale triangular patch. A dark line is present along the sides of the snout from the nostril to the eye. The hind legs are marked with faint bands. The body has a series of raised skin ridges, often pale yellow/buff in colour.

Square Marked Toad
(Bufo regularis)

The common toad of the region they can often be heard issuing their monotonous croaks throughout the night. A species found in moist savannah areas and in the vicinity of human settlements. A rather plain looking toad with a greyish brown body colour and irregular square blotches of darker brown. A medium sized toad of around 6–9cm in length.

INSECTS

Dung Beetle
(Scarabaeidae spp)

A widely distributed group of beetles, found in areas frequented by large game animals and, as its name suggests, they spend much of their time searching for animal dung on which they feed. They are round in shape, dark in colour and have short wing covers – their manoeuvrability in flight is rather poor. Dung Beetles are able to eat more than their own body weight in dung every 24 hours, thereby aiding the process of converting manure into substances usable by micro-organisms. At the onset of the breeding season females seek out fresh droppings which they form into a small ball, often rolling it a considerable distance to soft earth where they bury it, having first laid an egg inside. When the egg hatches in its underground tomb the larva will eat the dung ball before pupating. At the onset of the next heavy rains the pupa hatches and makes its way to the surface in search of dung and the whole cycle is repeated.

African Giant Millipede
(Archispirostreptus spp)

Most millipedes, of which there are many species in Africa, are rather docile, moisture-loving creatures which have the ability to curl into a ball if disturbed. The African Giant Millipede is one of the largest millipedes in the world, growing to lengths of 28cm. They can boast as many as 200 pairs of legs, two pairs to each body ring or segment. Millipedes are to be found throughout much of tropical and sub-tropical Africa, usually among moist debris, leaf litter and rotting wood. They are armoured with dorsal plates as a form of defence and many species have the ability to secrete a pungent toxic liquid if attacked. All millipedes are vegetarian, feeding mainly on rotting plant material, but they will occasionally eat living plant matter.

Scorpion
(Scorpionidae)

There are in the region of 800 scorpion species throughout the world, largely found in tropical and sub-tropical climates. As a result of their capacity to inflict venomous stings with the tip of the long curved tail, scorpions have played a sinister role in fables and legends since ancient times. Scorpions have adapted to life in a variety of habitats from harsh deserts to mountains, forests and jungles. Those species found in deserts are usually light in colour while those from mountain and forest areas are generally dark brown or black. Generally nocturnal in habits, scorpions feed mainly on insects and small invertebrates and are capable of surviving for long periods without food. They secure most prey items by waiting patiently in ambush. They possess sensory hairs which can detect the approach of a likely meal which they grab with pinching fingers at the end of finger-like appendages at the front of the body. At the moment of capture the scorpion will arch its long tail over its back ready to paralyse the victim with its sting if necessary. Although formidable creatures well armed for defence, numerous birds, lizards, monkeys and other mammals attack scorpions. Scorpions are also cannibalistic and kill many of their own kind. They are generally to be found under rocks, behind peeling bark and among leaf litter. The venomous sting of the scorpion is administered via a sharp decurved stinger, the venom being injected by muscular contraction. Most scorpion stings cause only localised pain in humans, but some species can inflict very painful stings that can result in temporary paralysis and fever which may last for several days.

Termites
(Macrotermes spp)

Termites are small soft-bodied insects that live in colonies with well-established caste systems. Worker, soldier and reproductive termites typically make up the castes, the reproductive caste usually being represented by a single king and queen. Workers form the bulk of termites in each colony, they are blind with mouthparts well developed for chewing. Surprisingly the soldier termites are also blind and have enlarged mandibles or well developed chemical systems with which to defend the colony. Termites live in nests usually underground and are constructed in such a fashion as to maintain high humidity with ventilation chimneys incorporated to circulate air around the nest. The excavated material from the nest forms into a dome-like conical mound and may reach several metres in height. The mounds can differ greatly according to termite species and ground conditions. Swarming is the method by which new colonies are formed, with the emergence of enormous numbers of winged individuals when climatic conditions are favourable. They are poor fliers and rarely manage to disperse more than a few hundred metres or so. On landing they soon shed their wings, a couple will mate and dig a small nest which sees the development of a new colony, the new queen being able to lay as many as 35,000 eggs a day for many years. In the early stages of a new colony all new nymphs develop into workers and soldiers, only when the colony is well-established do winged termites appear, flying off to continue the cycle. Termites fill an important ecological niche in many areas. They provide a food source for frogs, lizards, birds and mammals, particularly Aardvarks, Pangolins and Aardwolfs. Termite mounds also offer shelter to numerous animal species, the holes excavated by Aardvarks are utilised by Warthogs and Hyaenas as well as by Banded Mongooses and a variety of snake species.

African Land Snail
(Achatina fulica)

A very large snail, with average shell length of around 10cm, but specimens with 20cm shells have been recorded. They are hermaphrodites (i.e. they are both male and female), this does not mean that they can mate with themselves – they still require a partner. However, one single mating is all that is needed for the production of a number of batches of eggs, which can be laid over a period of months. Eggs are laid in batches of 100–400, are spherical and measure on average 5mm in diameter. Under favourable conditions they will hatch within 1–3 months. Newly emerged snails measure only 4mm, but they grow rapidly and reach maturity after 6–9 months, depending on food availability and climatic conditions. They eat all manner of vegetation.

TREES & FLOWERS

Baobab   *(Adansonia digitata)*

Almost unmistakable, with its swollen trunk and thick root-like branches. Some specimens have trunks measuring 9m or more in diameter reaching a height of up to 18m. During the dry season they bear no leaves but at the onset of the rains they develop a dense canopy. They bear white flowers about 15cm wide and develop oblong, woody fruits up to 30cm in length. The structure of the trunk is fibrous and holds a certain amount of water when no surface water is available. At these times Elephants often inflict considerable damage in search of moisture as relief from the drought conditions.

Yellow Barked Acacia/Fever Tree   *(Acacia xanthophloea)*

A reasonably common species easily recognised by its yellow/green bark colour. It is usually to be found along the banks of rivers and streams and in areas of damp, marshy ground. Early explorers to the region associated the tree with their developing 'fever', hence the name. In fact the 'fever' was due to malaria transmitted by mosquitoes that principally inhabit the damp areas favoured by this tree.

Flat Topped Acacia   *(Acacia tortilis)*

There are some 1,200 species of acacia distributed across the tropical and warm temperate regions of the world. The Flat Topped Acacia is a familiar sight in grassland areas of East Africa, it's spreading canopy providing shade for many savannah animals. A native tree found over much of Africa and the Middle East, it produces prolific amounts of fruiting pods that provide much needed fodder for animals in dry areas. A medium sized tree growing to a height of around 15m in suitable areas. It is extremely drought resistant and can survive in dry semi desert areas with low annual rainfall. Under these conditions it may only grow to a height of a metre or so. The flowers are white and grow in small clusters; they have a very aromatic smell. In some regions of Africa the Flat Topped Acacia is the main species collected by local people for firewood and for charcoal production. In some areas of Tanzania this species has been severely reduced by Elephants that strip and eat the bark.

Whistling Acacia   *(Acacia drepanolobium)*

An abundant small bush armed with long white spines and adorned with blackish galls the size of small golf balls. The galls, each of which has several small holes leading to its hollow centre, are inhabited by colonies of aggressive *crematogaster* ants, which form a mutually beneficial partnership with the acacia. The bush offers housing for the ants by way of the galls and the ants provide protection for the acacia by swarming over any browsing animal and inflicting unpleasant bites to the lips and tongue. Despite the presence of the ants and the sharp spines, Giraffes often browse unconcerned at least for a few minutes until the ants begin to bite home, thereby encouraging the individual to move on elsewhere.

Sausage Tree
(Kigelia africana)

A widely distributed tree in wet savannah areas and along water courses at altitudes below 1,850m. A substantial tree growing to a height of about 9m, the flowers are trumpet shaped, dull red in colour, about 12cm in length and possess a rather unpleasant smell. The flowers hang on cord-like strings and bloom during the night, falling to the ground during the early morning. The fruits are large and hang on the tree like long sausages, hence it's popular name. The fruits are not edible but are used for medicinal purposes in some areas. They reach lengths of 60cm and can weigh up to 7kg.

Candelabra Tree
(Euphorbia candelabrum)

A succulent tree common in some areas of the Rift Valley. A large forest of Candelabra Trees can be found in Lake Nakuru National Park. They grow to a height of 15m. The trunk is short and thick and forms a solid base from which spread a multitude of branches that resemble the shape of candelabras.

Flame Tree
(Delonix regia)

Originally discovered in Madagascar in the early part of the 19th century, this beautiful tree has since been cultivated in tropical regions throughout the world. Growing to a height of around 15m and flourishing at altitudes below 1,500m, this tree creates a stunning sight when in full flower. The flowers, which appear before the leaves develop, are rich scarlet red and grow in dense clusters. A deciduous tree that sheds its fern-like leaves at the onset of the dry season, having flowered and developed long brown seedpods.

Date Palm
(Phoenix spp.)

Common throughout much of the region in the hotter drier areas, usually to be found along the banks of streams and rivers. Arab traders first introduced the Date Palm to the region as a source of food. Growing to a height of 20–50m, the slender trunk is crowned with 30–40 pinnate leaves up to 4m in length. There are in the region of 40 different cultivated varieties of Date Palm throughout the tropics, the fruits of which ripen at different times of the year. The leaves are used in the production of baskets and mats.

Doum Palm
(Hyphaene coriacea)

One of the easiest palms to identify, being the only one having branches which divide regularly into two. They often reach heights in excess of 15m. The fruit is orange/brown in colour and about 8cm long. It is not edible by humans but is eaten by elephants that are, to a great extent, responsible for seed dispersal. The leaves of the Doum Palm are used in the weaving of baskets and mats.

Coconut Palm
(Cocos nucifera)

Some mystery still surrounds the original home of this species, but it is assumed by many to have drifted on ocean currents from South America to colonise the African shores. Growing to a height of around 30m, the slender trunk is usually swollen at the base and is crowned with 20–30 pinnate leaves reaching up to 6m in length. Restricted in distribution to coastal regions the Coconut Palm is extremely salt tolerant and can live for up to 100 years, producing 50–80 fruits each year. The fruiting nut provides a valuable source of food and drink in some areas as well as the outer husk fibres providing material for rope making, matting and house thatching.

Jacaranda
(Jacaranda mimosifolia)

An original native of Brazil this tree can now be found in parks, gardens and city centre avenues over much of the region. They grow to a height of 10m or more and have fine fern-like leaves which they shed during the dry season. They flower after the short rains blossoming into a mass of delicate bell-shaped violet blue flowers, which grow in clusters.

Bottlebrush Tree
(Callistemon citrinus)

Originally from Australia these very ornamental trees have been extensively planted in parks and gardens throughout the region. It derives its name from the numerous red flowers arranged around a stem in the shape of a bottlebrush. They produce woody fruits that are disc shaped. They can grow to heights in excess of 7m.

Candle Bush
(Cassia didymobotrya)

A comparatively small shrub reaching a height of around 3–4m at most. It has a rounded shape and bears very handsome erect spikes of yellow flowers giving the effect of a candelabra bearing numerous candles, hence its common name. It is commonly found along roadside verges and woodland edges over much of the region.

Sisal
(Agave sisalana)

A native plant of Mexico imported to East Africa by early settlers and extensively cultivated for the manufacture of twine and rope. Although not cultivated to the same extent today it can still be found in parks and gardens and along roadside verges. It has elongated leaves up to 1.5m in length that have sharp spines at the tips and grow in a circular formation at ground level. The flowering spike, which erupts from the centre of its cluster of leaves, grows to a height of 6m and bears branches of yellow flowers.

Aloe
(Aloe volkensii)

There are in the region of 60 Aloe species to be found in East Africa. *Volkensii* is tall, growing up to 6m in height. It has grey-green leaves forming a rosette at the top from which branch spikes of red flowers. They are found at altitudes up to 2,300m, usually on rocky ground.

Frangipani
(Plumeria spp)

Originating in the West Indies this familiar small tree is often found in parks and gardens throughout the tropics. It has a distinctive shape with regular branching. The flowers are variable in colour including pink, white and yellow and are strongly scented. The petals are arranged in an overlapping fashion, reminiscent of an open fan. It is thought to have been named after the French botanist Charles Plumier who first described it during his travels in the Caribbean in the 17th Century.

Desert Rose
(Adenium obesum)

An indigenous succulent scrub or small tree of dry areas and rocky hillsides throughout much of the region at low altitudes. The trunk and branches have a swollen and stunted appearance and bear very attractive pink flowers about 5cm across. The sap is very toxic and in the past was used by local people to impregnate arrowheads.

Bourgainvillea
(Bourgainvillea spp)

A very attractive and common native shrub of Brazil found throughout East Africa. It is a thorny shrub often forming dense hedges in parks and gardens and is a mass of the most colourful bracts which range from purple to crimson, pink, red, white and yellow.

Pyjama Lily
(Crinum macowanii)

This very attractive plant has long tubular flowers that are pink and white striped, giving rise to its popular name of Pyjama Lily. The leaves are grey-green in colour. It is a reasonably common plant of open grasslands at altitudes up to 2,700m.

Fireball Lily
(Scadoxus multiflorus)

This superb lily appears soon after the first rains in areas of open grassland and savannah, on rocky hillsides and forest edges at altitudes up to 2,200m. The spectacular red flowers are carried on a single stem and as many as 150 individual flowers can be found in one spherical spike which can be 20cm in diameter. Once the flowers have faded and died the thick upright leaves appear.

Sodom's Apple
(Solanum incanum)

There are around 50 species of *solanum* to be found in East Africa; *incanum* is very common along roadside verges and on areas of waste ground. It is quick to colonise recently excavated ground. It is a very tough shrub with fearsome spines on the stems and stalks. It bears flowers that are blue to mauve with yellow centres that measure around 15mm across. The fruits take the form of hard yellow balls which although edible are rather bitter.

Leonotis nepetifolia

There are 9 species of *leonotis* to be found in East Africa, *L. nepetifolia* is very common over most of the region, flourishing along roadside verges. A plant growing to 1.5m with spherical clusters of orange flowers growing at intervals along the plants woody stem. The individual flowers, of which there are many on each cluster, are about 25mm in length.

INDEX

Black - headed Gonolek